MOVING BEYOND BORDERS

LATINOS IN CHICAGO AND THE MIDWEST

Series Editors

Frances R. Aparicio, University of Illinois at Chicago
Pedro Caban, University of Illinois at Urbana-Champaign
Juan Mora, De Paul University
Maria de los Angeles Torres, De Paul University

*A list of books in the series
appears at the end of the book.*

MOVING BEYOND BORDERS

 Julian Samora and the
Establishment of Latino Studies

EDITED BY
ALBERTO LÓPEZ PULIDO
BARBARA DRISCOLL DE ALVARADO
CARMEN SAMORA

UNIVERSITY OF ILLINOIS PRESS
Urbana and Chicago

Library of Congress Cataloging-in-Publication Data
Moving beyond borders : Julian Samora and the establishment
of Latino studies / edited by Alberto López Pulido,
Barbara Driscoll de Alvarado, Carmen Samora.
p.   cm. — (Latinos in Chicago and the Midwest)
Includes bibliographical references and index.
ISBN 978-0-252-03463-3 (cloth : alk. paper)
ISBN 978-0-252-07656-5 (pbk. : alk. paper)
1. Hispanic Americans—Study and teaching.
2. Hispanic Americans—History—Study and teaching.
3. Samora, Julian, 1920–1996.
4. Samora, Julian, 1920-1996—Influence.
I. Pulido, Alberto L.
II. Driscoll de Alvarado, Barbara.
III. Samora, Carmen.
E184.S75M69   2009
371.829'68073—dc22   2009009432

Para Los Valientes: Betty and Julian. May your example lead us to discomfort, deliver us from power, and teach us to organize.

—Alberto López Pulido

With the hope that this tome captures the spirit and dedication of Doña Betty and Don Julian, and that their example inspires all those who seek to mentor.

—Barbara Driscoll de Alvarado

To Amy Digeno, Jamie Berlin, Zoë Samora, Moses Samora, Alicia Samora, and Magdalena Samora. May the light of your grandparents burn brightly in your hearts.

—Carmen R. Samora

EL CORRIDO DE JULIAN SAMORA

Señores, voy a cantarles
Un corrido verdadero
Lo que pasó en Albuquerque:
Murió Julian Samora,
Era un hombre verdadero.

Pagoso Springs, Colorado,
Mil novecientos veinte,
El dia primero de marzo,
Fecha que tengo presente,
Nació Julian Samora;
Según nos dice la gente.

Era en San Luis, Missouri
Donde acabó el doctorado
En Washington University
Año de cincuenta tres
El primero Mexicano
En sociología, ese mes.

Es una historia de lucha
Y de logros permanentes.
Luchó toda su vida
Para su pueblo y su gente,
Para sus estudiantes
Preparándoles la mente.

Siempre apoyo la lucha
De los derechos civiles
De Mexico-Americanos,
En los años setentas,
Formando Concilio Nacional de la Raza
Para ayudar a la gente.
En Michigan State University
Y también en Notre Dame
Estableció el estudio

De Mexico-Americanos,
Escribiendo varios libros,
Estudios y sus hermanos.

Decía Herman y el espírito de Ernesto:
No se sienten tristes, hermanos,
Porque la luz está prendida
Y ha cambiado de manos.
La luz la cargan muy alto
Muchos Mexico-Americanos

Ya con ésta me despido
Aquí en presencia de todos
Recordándoles la vida
Del Doctor Julian Samora
Quien siempre luchó por su pueblo
¡Y les regresó su historia!

 —by Jesus "Chuy" Negrete
  Mexican Cultural Institute—Chicago, Illinois
  April 1996

SAMORISTAS' CREED

1. There is no substitute for a solid education and a well-rounded academic experience.
2. Use the pursuit of education and the power of knowledge to better oneself and one's community.
3. Carry willingly the burden of leadership and responsibility to serve others.
4. Always strive to give back to the community and to those less fortunate.
5. Make sure that future generations consider and appreciate the good work, selfless sacrifices, heroic efforts, and valiant struggles of past generations.
6. Never forget 1 through 5.

—Marcos Ronquillo

CONTENTS

Photographs follow page 64.

FOREWORD

Herman Gallegos

Herman Gallegos was behind, at the side of, or ahead of
everything important that has happened to Chicanos in the
second half of the 20th century.
—JULIAN SAMORA, 1985

For most people in the United States, "giving back" is regarded as something
worth doing—praiseworthy, optional, and usually an act of free will. But
for those of us who are members of racial or ethnic minorities, it is different. We see "giving back" as a duty to advance the common good of the
communities from which we come. Most of us who have had some kind of
success in the larger society feel a special responsibility for helping those
left behind, the materially poor, and the politically marginalized. In the case
of the Mexican American community, few people I know "gave back" so
nobly and on so lasting a scale as Julian Samora.

Though he received important recognition during his lifetime, Julian did
not require lots of nurturing reassurance. He was more concerned with
getting about the job of building just and equitable communities where
everyone has access to the opportunities and resources to realize his or her
individual potential. This book celebrates his life and his dedication to looking squarely at the powerful forces at the root of the imbalances affecting
the lives of Mexican Americans and others of Latin descent in this country.
It also offers an understanding of the cultural forces and relationships that
influenced his choices as a scholar, activist, and mentor, with the aim of
answering the question: Who was this visionary and engaging person, and
how did he become the pioneering and influential leader that he was?

It is some forty years ago that I first met Julian, entirely by chance, in
Washington, D.C. We were there to interview for what were being characterized as possible "high level" appointments in the Peace Corps. I also had
another reason for making the trip, and that was to lobby the secretary of
labor, Willard Wirtz, to end the "Bracero Program," or Public Law 78, a

program for the recruitment of manual laborers from Mexico for employment in the United States in agriculture and railroad maintenance. Midway through my interviews, I met with Sargent Shriver, head of the Peace Corps, at which time I gratefully declined to pursue whatever opportunities he had in mind. He seemed to understand when I explained that my greater commitment was to continue seeking justice and equity here at home. Walking down an empty hallway on my way out, I spotted someone I had not met before, sitting quite relaxed on a bare, gray government desk, his back to the wall, left leg bent and left wrist resting on his knee. As I approached, we nodded and introduced ourselves. His name was Julian Samora. Little did I realize then how much we had in common or that the friendship that began at that moment would last for years to come.

I asked Julian if he planned to join the Corps and he shook his head, laughed, and replied, "Nooooo." I mentioned my pending meeting with Secretary Wirtz regarding Public Law 78. Julian expressed his knowledge of the issue and suggested we meet later to get better acquainted. So, following my meeting with Secretary Wirtz, we got together in Julian's room at the hotel where the Corps was putting us up. I was immediately impressed with Julian's sense of humor. On spotting several mushrooms sprouting from a corner of the hotel rug, he asked, "Just what kind of a 'high level' appointment did they have in mind?" We both laughed. Always the consummate host, Julian opened a half-pint of inexpensive whiskey. Years later, we recalled this first drink together and noted that when we could afford better, we couldn't drink—at least not as much.

During our conversation, I grasped in Julian a strong sense of focus and commitment to the advancement of justice and human dignity. I was also impressed with his accomplishments as a scholar. Like another colleague, the late Dr. Ernesto Galarza, Julian valued the importance of defining and articulating historical events as a way to learn from them, to gain vital insight into the present and perhaps to affect the future.

Thanks to Julian's loving family and colleagues, this book will recall many situations where Julian's contribution made a difference. There are many landmarks to choose from, but two of Julian's achievements that merit particular remembrance had a lasting beneficial impact on Latinos and reflect how his leadership was consistent with his character and spirit.

Years before Cesar Chavez became a household name, Dr. Ernesto Galarza, former farm worker, union organizer, scholar, and activist, was busy exposing the myths and misrepresentations perpetuated by the agribusiness industry to justify the deplorable treatment of farm laborers. In 1952, Galarza began a campaign against the bracero system, a program he viewed as an obstacle to organizing farm workers in the United States. Galarza's probing and exposing of the interactions between growers and the agencies regulating them made him a pariah in the eyes of agribusiness and many powerful politicians. The controversy surrounding his work made it nearly impossible for him to find a publisher for his writings, a critical step to getting the word out on his findings.

Thanks to Julian's intervention and assistance, Galarza's books, now classics in understanding the underpinnings of agribusiness, were published by the University of Notre Dame Press. Public Law 78, passed in 1951, continued the original Bracero Program that had begun in 1942. For the thirteen years Public Law 78 was in effect, Galarza exposed the evils of the hiring system it had put in place and provided the philosophical base and understanding for its eventual repeal. Ironically, Cesar Chavez once said to me disdainfully, "You can't change anything with research." Yet in the end, it was Galarza's research about the structure and social realities of the agricultural industry that ended the Bracero Program and brought knowledge and renewed confidence to Chavez in his own farm worker organizing efforts.

During the mid-1960s, Julian championed other initiatives that led to significant and lasting benefits for Latinos. These included the publication of an important new work about Mexican Americans and the opening up of major philanthropic support for Mexican American and other Latino causes. In 1964, the California-based Rosenberg Foundation, on the strength of Julian's first-rate reputation as a scholar, engaged him to edit a book about Mexican Americans in the United States. The book, *La Raza: Forgotten Americans*, sold more than 50,000 copies in its first printing, and its success encouraged the publication of other works by Mexican American authors.

The process of completing this seminal work produced another unexpected breakthrough. Invited to attend an editorial meeting to discuss the book were a mix of well-known Mexican American intellectuals and activists and a special guest, Dr. Paul Ylvisaker, then vice president for national affairs at the Ford Foundation. The passionate and well-informed discussion that took place, about the root causes of the most pressing needs of our community and strategies for solving them, influenced Ylvisaker to consider a possible Ford Foundation initiative to support Latino causes. Out of this meeting, Dr. Ylvisaker engaged Ernesto Galarza, Julian Samora, and me as consultants to make an assessment of Mexican Americans in the Southwest. In 1966, we submitted a thorough report recommending Ford's involvement. At the foundation's suggestion, we published parts of our report as a book, titled *Mexican-Americans in the Southwest*, and in 1967 the foundation approved a small planning grant to explore the formation of a new, tax-exempt regional structure to address issues we had raised.

With this encouragement from the foundation and leadership from an exploratory committee of Mexican Americans from each of the southwestern states, I took part in organizing a regional structure that became the Southwest Council of La Raza. In 1968, the foundation made a grant of $638,000 to launch the Council of La Raza, forerunner to the National Council of La Raza. Financial support for the Mexican American Legal Defense and Education Fund also followed. I was elected to serve as the council's first executive director.

While overall foundation responsiveness to Latino causes remains inadequate, it is increasing throughout the United States. Organizing the council and opening the door to funding from Ford and other national grant makers would not have been possible without Julian Samora and Ernesto Galarza. They never sought recognition for lending their credibility, time, and advice to this effort, which helped cut a new path to advocacy for our community, not of the fiery kind, but one of calm and reason, always respectful of our own and others' dignity.

In the chapters that follow, we celebrate and honor the life and work of an extraordinary leader, one who "gave back" in full measure and at just the right time to help a community of once "Forgotten Americans" to advance in its struggle for survival, place, and meaning in American society. Through the many causes he championed and the many scholar-activists he mentored and inspired, Julian's legacy lives on.

PREFACE

Vilma Martínez

In 1973 I was selected to serve as the president and general counsel for the Mexican American Legal Defense Fund (MALDEF). I had received superior legal training from Columbia University Law School and experience as a litigator from the NAACP Legal Defense Fund, which aptly prepared me to take on this challenge. Yet I lacked the historical context of the Mexican American experience in the United States needed to fully appreciate the impact of discriminatory policies and practices on our Latino community. My search for the historical context of MALDEF's work led me to Dr. Julian Samora at the University of Notre Dame.

Julian Samora provided me and so many others with the answers to questions that had previously been unanswerable. He became a guide and a mentor in providing the answers to complex issues and challenges facing Mexican Americans. One vivid example takes me back to 1974, when Attorney General William Saxbe was saying that "illegal aliens" constituted a severe national crisis because they were taking jobs away from American citizens. In a speech to the Cameron and Hidalgo County Bar Association in October of that year, the attorney general suggested that the Immigration and Naturalization Service (INS) deport one million "illegal aliens" in an attempt to meet what he described as a severe national crisis:

> Illegal immigrants do not constitute a trickle or a stream. They form a torrent that threatens to grow into a tidal wave unless effective action is taken soon. . . . They hold millions of jobs; they receive social services ranging from schools to welfare; large amounts of money sent out of the country drain funds from our troubled economy; and they mock our system of legal immigration. . . . The Immigration Service has estimated to me that it could open up one million new jobs during the next year—by the simple process of removing illegal aliens holding those jobs.

On behalf of MALDEF, I sent the attorney general a letter (with a copy to President Gerald Ford) informing him that I was gravely concerned because his plans were being conceived with little if any concern for the rights of Mexican Americans. The plan did not solicit input from the community that was most likely to be affected by this plan. In retrospect, Julian Samora, joined by scholars Rudy Acuña, Ernesto Galarza, and Wayne Cornelius, assisted me in better understanding immigration policy and formulating effective arguments against the proposal offered by Attorney General Saxbe. I began to read the books and articles of those scholars, and I learned about Operation Wetback in the 1950s and the repatriation of Mexican Americans during the Depression and their impact on the rights of Mexican American citizens. The scholarship of Dr. Samora and others helped me articulate solid arguments against subsequent efforts such as the Simpson-Mazzoli and Rodino legislative proposals, as well as the Carter and Reagan plans during my tenure at MALDEF.

Without Dr. Samora's guidance, MALDEF would not have been as successful as it was in opposing the efforts of one administration after another to scapegoat "illegal aliens" for economic problems confronting our nation. At the time, there were few Chicano Studies Departments or research centers that I could turn to for guidance and support; this is why my professional relationship with Julian Samora was so invaluable. Dr. Samora was available to talk about these issues. He provided me with a knowledge base that I could continue to draw from in this recurring theme of the U.S.-Mexico border.

This discovery led me to link academic research to litigation. What I did at MALDEF was create a center for public policy and research within MALDEF where we hired a scholar to direct and conduct studies on topics such as voting rights violations among other civil rights topics. We subsequently asked Dr. Samora to become an active member of the MALDEF board, and he quickly became identified as a key person who could advise us on the issues. Julian Samora represented an invaluable resource because he had the knowledge and was willing to assist us in imagining the key issues we were trying to represent at the time. It is fitting that we honor the legacy of Julian Samora.

ACKNOWLEDGMENTS

The genesis of this book went beyond the prescribed academic methodologies. Our goal of understanding the depth and breadth of Julian's life and work involved both highly personal and qualitative research as well as social scientific methodology. We feel that this dynamic intersection of non-academic and academic, private and public, and qualitative and quantitative approaches best captures the impact of Julian's life.

The authors thank the following: Christine Sierra for coining the word "Samorista" at the 2004 National Association of Chicana/Chicano Studies meeting, the Samoristas for their enthusiasm for the project and their many contributions, and Herman Gallegos and Vilma Martínez for generously sharing their expertise.

At the University of New Mexico, we thank Tobías Durán and the Center for Regional Studies for monetary support during the preliminary writing phase, L. M. García y Griego and the Southwest Hispanic Research Institute, and Gabriel Melendez, chair of the American Studies Department, University of New Mexico.

Teresa Delgadillo suggested we approach the University of Illinois Press; Frances Aparicio recommended our project to Joan Catapano of the University of Illinois Press, who supported it from its inception.

At Michigan State University: Dionicio Valdes, chair of the Chicano Studies Department; Israel Cuellar, former director of the Julian Samora Research Institute, Michigan State; Diana Rivera, librarian, and Anita Garza and Danny Layne, staff members, at the Julian Samora Research Institute gave us collegial support.

Gilbert Cárdenas, director of the Institute for Latino Studies at the University of Notre Dame, Caroline Domingo, and Zoë Samora read our prospectus and provided encouragement as we began our process.

Ann Hartness, former head librarian, Margo Gutierrez, interim head librarian, and Christian Kelleher, head archivist at the Nettie Lee Benson Latin American Collection at the University of Texas-Austin, provided access to the Samora papers and shared their expertise.

We thank Edelle Nissila-Stone, the archivist at the Ford Foundation, for her assistance, Roberto Trujillo, head archivist at the Green Library at Stanford University, for permission to use the Seventh Annual Galarza Lecture, and Phil Jones, librarian at Adams State College, for keeping a map drawer of information about Julian Samora just in case a researcher came in asking.

Thanks also to David Avalos, Tony Blasi, Breanne Ertmer, Dawn McIlvain, Mario T. García, Arturo Madrid, Richard Navarro, Michael and Marianne O'Shaughnessy, Arturo Zendejas, and Vanesa Zendejas for editorial help and expertise.

We wish to acknowledge Julian's colleagues, Tom Broden, William V. D'Antonio, Fabio Dasilva, Richard Lamanna, Joe Scott, and Andrew Weigert, our "elders" who generously supported Julian at Notre Dame and provided us with the personal narratives that enabled us to tell the story.

In addition, Kirsten Pai Buick, Frances Moffat, and Margaret McKenzie read several preliminary drafts and gave critical feedback. David Samora and John Samora generously shared their memories of family events, and John took the photograph of Julian we have used for the cover. Geoff Samora, Mary Samora, and Jill Tiedemann offered editorial assistance that enabled us to meet deadlines. Clifford Lucero helped with the endless formatting duties. Rose Diaz, Jane Young, Martha Fiedler, Virginia García, Roberta Chavez, Caroline Orcutt, Bridget Olguín, and Elsie Lazero offered encouragement and good cheer through the long process of birthing this book. Very special thanks to Steve Moffat, who read every word of every draft, encouraging Carmen as she found her voice, and who welcomed Barbara and Alberto when they came to Albuquerque to work.

Mónica Verea Campos and Paz Consuelo Márquez Padilla, in their capacities as directors of the Centro de Investigaciones sobre América del Norte at the Universidad Nacional Autónoma de México (UNAM), graciously extended administrative and personal support to Barbara for research in Latino Studies, particularly for her work on Samora. Further, an institutional agreement between UNAM and the University of Texas graciously provided funding for Barbara to travel to Austin to use Julian's papers at the Benson Library.

The Ethnic Studies faculty at the University of San Diego provided an engaging and supportive environment for Alberto. Of particular help were Michelle Jacob, Jesse Mills, Gail Perez, Belinds Lum, Thomas Reifer, Evelyn

Diaz Cruz, Leonora Simonovis, Roy Brooks, Judy Liu, Michelle Camacho, and Orlando Espin. Invaluable administrative support was received from Esther Aguilar and Marcia García Venegas. Patrick Drinan, while dean of the College of Arts and Sciences, provided great leadership and support. Members of the López, Pulido, and Valdez clans supported us with their prayers and loving support.

The authors would also like to acknowledge the Bonfils family, who supported the scholarship that enabled the young Julian to leave Pagosa Springs and prepare for the wider world, and special thanks to Neal Hermanowicz, MD, who correctly diagnosed Julian's final illness, ending several years of frustration for Julian and the Samora family.

And finally, the process of writing became a spiritual experience as the authors followed Betty and Julian's lead; we hope this book honors their memory.

PART ONE

THE LEGACY OF JULIAN SAMORA
Introduction: Moving Beyond Borders

Alberto López Pulido
Barbara Driscoll de Alvarado
Carmen Samora

When asked why he had chosen the path of education, the prominent scholar Julian Samora answered simply, "I wanted an indoor job." Given the magnitude of his legacy, this answer may seem a little too facile, yet it makes perfect sense when one considers his humble beginnings. Born and raised in the mountain village of Pagosa Springs, Colorado, in the early twentieth century, Julian Samora observed the male Mexican Americans (Mexicanos) of his community labor under harsh and extreme working conditions. Some worked in the woods for the forest services, others were sheepherders who left their families for months at a time, and others worked in the mines and on the railroads. Most employment opportunities open to members of Julian's community required hard physical labor in exchange for low wages. Many jobs were seasonal and there were no guarantees that this backbreaking labor would improve one's life chances toward success. With little more than the self-knowledge that he was not skilled with his hands, did not like sleeping on the ground, and loved to read, Julian Samora chose a career that broke new ground for the Mexican American community. His personal choices and human agency revolutionized higher education in the United States by creating an educational and political space for Mexican American students and Mexican American Studies at a national level. As illustrated above, Samora demonstrated that our actions, based on our personal choices, have the potential to challenge existing structures and transform lives. This is Julian Samora's gift to us, his legacy of leadership and scholar/activism.

It began when Julian was still an undergraduate at Adams State College in Alamosa, Colorado, and was fully realized at the University of Notre Dame in the mid-1960s. His legacy continues into the present through the professors, administrators, community organizers, and cultural workers that were mentored and influenced by the life and career of Julian Samora.

Julian's early life choices put him on the path toward a formal education that opened the door to leadership opportunities for his community and the larger society. To earn a living with the mind and not with the hands was a worthwhile ambition, yet the implications behind that choice were much more profound than simply avoiding manual labor. Such a choice drew on commitments and obligations—*compromisos* made with his community that Julian learned through the example of his mother and grandmother.

His grandmother was a *partera* and *curandera,* and she modeled leadership skills with and through the collective. She had an important role in their small community as she selflessly served others and provided comfort and healing expertise. Just as influential was Julian's mother. She encouraged and supported his ambition of advanced education, and she urged him to attend high school, making sacrifices to do without his full-time salary. His mother took on extra jobs, and Julian worked nights during his high school years. He was raised with his community's *dichos, consejos,* and cautions that guided him throughout his personal and professional development.

In addition, Julian's drive put him on a path that led him beyond his village and region and into new geographies. Formal education provided macro-intellectual vistas for understanding the disparities that existed between Mexican Americans and Anglos; his own lived experience had been one of unrelenting discrimination in his childhood. This emerging intellectual foundation reinforced his conscious choice to make life appreciably better for Mexican Americans in his community. He left Pagosa Springs to attend college, thinking to leave behind the stinging memory of discrimination and the constant humiliation of racism. As he encountered discrimination beyond his village, he found that his family and community had equipped him with a tool kit of lessons of self-worth and resistance that helped define his tenacious intellectual vision to transform the reality of Mexican Americans in the United States. This book is about his legacy of leadership and the establishment of Latino Studies. We show what Dr. Samora achieved in his forty-plus years as a teacher, researcher, scholar, mentor, and national advisor as he shaped Mexican American Studies in higher education.

It is fitting that the title of this book is *Moving Beyond Borders* because it represents a metaphor in the life of Julian Samora and in the lives of his students. Borders can serve to constrain and restrict the fluidity between sites and communities that are divided by borders. By their very nature borders produce limits and demarcate restrictions. As borderland historian Oscar J. Martínez has written in his study of borders, frequent interchange across borders is practically nonexistent and this in turn fosters unfavorable conditions for new and innovative thinking.[1] Groundbreaking knowledge occurs only when someone chooses to challenge set limits and begins to move beyond them both physically and intellectually. A world without constraining borders liberates and permits one to engage communities in new pursuits and vistas. One sees the world in a way one never has before and is free to imagine new possibilities.

By choosing to leave his community, Julian Samora challenged the existing boundaries that kept Mexican Americans locked in poverty and marginalized by overt racism. By breaking these bonds of shame, he challenged the limitations with which he grew up; he challenged himself, his family, and his community to do something different and look outside that defined world, a challenge that took him to cities and universities outside the American Southwest. Not surprisingly, he found common ground with Mexican Americans in all the cities and regions in which he traveled, but not within the universities. Traversing the midwestern cities of Madison, St. Louis, East Lansing, and South Bend, Indiana, where he settled, Julian imagined new opportunities and possibilities for Mexican American and emerging Chicano communities throughout the United States.

Samora's vision was to create a border-crossing national conversation among Mexican Americans from all over the United States. This dialogue was engaged in by students from throughout the country accepted into the Mexican American Graduate Studies Program (MAGSP) that Samora established at the University of Notre Dame in 1971. Even though the prominent view at the time was that Mexican Americans resided mostly in the Southwest, Samora knew that large communities of Mexican Americans existed in all regions of the country. He was tenacious in looking beyond the border of commonly held beliefs, and he recognized that the challenges facing the Mexican American community and other communities of color were similar regardless of where one lived in the United States.

As a result of his vision, Julian Samora gave a national voice to the Mexican American experience in the United States. In acknowledging his own experience as an ethnic scholar, he validated the stories and experiences of countless people, students and community elders alike, regardless of their origin and orientation. Many speak of reading his books and feeling pride in the realization that their *gente* was being heard from. Mexican American students recall the thrill of being taught by a fellow Mexican American and feeling for the first time that their cultural knowledge was important, as were the voices and perspectives of other Mexican Americans from all over the country.

With the creation of the MAGSP at the University of Notre Dame, Julian Samora's actions created a unique pedagogy of space that provided for emerging Mexican American scholars and scholars of Mexican American Studies. As a space identified in the American Midwest, it was a portable and evolving cultural region free from any boundaries. It was a translated and transplanted place for the study of Mexican Americans in the United States, and it became a place of national scope with a national agenda. It became the site where young Chicanas and Chicanos from throughout the United States could find a home in the Midwest at a private Roman Catholic University and examine the issues that impacted their communities. Students from all over the country, Chicano and non-Chicano alike, were attracted to the Mexican American Graduates Studies Program. The community of young scholars, led by Samora, was encouraged to examine Chicano issues outside of the American Southwest. Consider that *Aztlan: A Journal of Chicano Studies* published a special issue on Chicanos in the Midwest in the summer of 1976 titled *Los Desarraigados* (The Uprooted). This special issue introduced the impact of region and history on the Chicano experience and was edited by Samora's student Gilbert Cárdenas. Six of the nine essays that appeared in the special issue were authored by students of the MAGSP at the University of Notre Dame.[2]

Most of Samora's students reproduced the path their mentor had traversed some ten years earlier to find new and unique intellectual insights and perspectives. In a real yet mystical way, becoming a Samorista required one to leave the comfort of familiar surroundings to learn the lessons Samora had to teach. One had to experience the cold weather and the isolation to reflect on and imagine the relevance and significance of one's work. Leaving the familiar forced this emerging cohort of young scholars to compare the personal with the intellectual, to contrast the students' formative personal experiences relating to family and community with all those new experiences in the Midwest. This created an intellectual milieu in which scholars inspected and interrogated themselves in relation to the unfamiliar surroundings, which proved to be a challenge to their core sense of being. New possibilities for understanding and interpreting Mexican Americans on a national scale was the result. The critical outcome was the development of an intellectual character by students who for the first time in their lives were in community with fellow students from other regions of the United States. They now were all part of the Mexican American Graduate Studies Program experience. For Julian knew that each student carried in his or her heart and mind a story and history as a result of his or her unique lived experiences. The outcome was an awakening for numerous students and a re-evaluation and personal interrogation of their perspectives that compared the local Mexican American experience to the national one. The MAGSP was a model of consensus, where people agreed to gather at a new and unfamiliar space to discover their intellectual identities as young Chicano intellectuals with a mission to look back and seek answers to the issues facing their communities. Furthermore, it was a macro approach to Chicano Studies throughout the United States and the world.

The Julian Samora vision was the creation of a Chicano Studies landscape with a national agenda, and this is the reason he is being honored in this book. As a scholar, professor, teacher, administrator with little institutional support, and with the creation of an academic program in Mexican American Studies outside of the Southwest, he was extremely successful in developing and creating an intellectual space in higher education for Mexican American students. This triggered a larger critical national dialogue and conversation within Mexican American Studies.[3] By attracting a significant number of students from throughout the nation, Samora was able to create a national agenda. Outside their familiar environment, formerly marginalized students were able to raise questions about Chicano issues beyond their immediate surroundings and compare, contrast, and incorporate their perspectives in relation to Chicano issues in all the United States. This articulated a national perspective on Chicano issues. Samora created an esprit de corps at an emerging Roman Catholic University in the Midwest. This represents the Samora vision and legacy.

A national conversation on social issues reinforced the Samora-led dialogue on Chicano issues during the late 1960s and early 1970s in the United States. As a result of the unpopular war in Vietnam and civil unrest in the cities of America, for the first time in history a significant number of youth of color were acquiring access to higher education. Philanthropic institutions along with some federal agencies, in response to the dialogue regarding this national crisis, were asking what they could do to "improve" the conditions of youth of color. Prior to this historical watershed in American history, youth of color were not gaining access to higher education in significant numbers. Some who were gaining access were beginning to question the existing curriculum. At worst, this curriculum ignored the contributions of communities of color, and at best it identified and described them in U.S. history as slaves or menial laborers, highlighting their weaknesses and studying them in numerous disciplines through the lenses of dominant frameworks and perspectives.

Julian Samora's pioneering work at the University of Notre Dame made him a key player at the center of this debate, especially for Mexican American and Chicano students. As illustrated in chapter three of this volume, Samora would be solicited by national foundations outside the University of Notre Dame to take up the cause of educating Mexican Americans students, and he responded in the most powerful and affirmative way possible. It was a vision from within the academy that resonated with a national collective movement in search of social justice and civil rights for the marginalized in our society, with a specific focus on Mexican Americans in higher education. With this book we expose a movement in higher education that for so long went unnoticed by many because it occurred in the Midwest, a region not identified historically with Mexican American populations within a private Roman Catholic university.

Part of the Julian Samora vision included training intellectual and community leaders and engaging their responsibility to their community by studying and writing about leadership issues within the Mexican American community. His early childhood and life experiences taught him that the challenges facing all these communities was the lack of indigenous leadership with a vision of identifying and articulating the most pressing issues of the times. Furthermore, he recognized the central role played by the key educational, political, economic, and religious institutions in developing leadership.[4]

This represented part of an emerging dialogue among scholars of Mexican American Studies that from the outset was a pedagogy that exploded all traditional disciplinary borders. Samora saw the need to train intellectual leaders in all academic areas of the social sciences, the humanities, the natural sciences, and the law. Julian's visionary theoretical framework was inductive and interdisciplinary in its approach. The focus was placed on the problems faced by Mexican American populations, then all and any scholarly materials that addressed these issues were sought out. Hence, the challenges of immigration, medical care, leadership, spirituality, and education were always at the forefront of the Samora intellectual agenda. He would seek answers from multiple sources, regardless of discipline, to address the challenges facing the Mexican American community, and he trained his students in this approach. Finally, Julian Samora was the first to train within an academic setting leaders in any significant numbers that would build bridges between Mexican American educational leaders and the larger society. He was central in creating a new type of leadership that used intellectual skills to help build and strengthen urban Mexican American barrios throughout the United States.

Julian Samora's scholarly vision was central in generating original research on the Mexican origin population as a national minority and an integral part of the U.S.-Mexico border region and the Midwest. Early in his career Julian placed more emphasis on identifying those researchers who had done or who were doing research on the Mexican American community, but as his career and life's work unfolded, he placed increasingly more emphasis on original research. He did as much original research as he could, and he made it a hallmark of training and mentoring students.

Moving Beyond Borders represents a living document because it is being lived through the many voices of Samora's students, friends, and colleagues that are collected through the words and stories found in these pages. It is made up of interpretive essays, biographical essays, and personal testimonies.

The book is divided in two sections. Part One, The Legacy of Julian Samora, focuses on Julian Samora the scholar and the man. Chapter one, Grace and Redemption: Julian Samora 1920–1996, is a biography written by Samora's daughter Carmen Samora. Chapter two, A Scholar and Visionary in Mexican American and Latino Studies, covers Samora's career up to 1968 and is written by Barbara Driscoll de Alvarado. Chapter three, Philanthropy, the Creation of a National Minority and the Mexican American Graduate Studies Program at Notre Dame, written by Alberto López Pulido, covers Samora's career from 1968 until his retirement in 1985.

Part Two of the book, Samoristas@57, comprises twenty-three reflective essays by Samora's former students and colleagues, now known as Samoristas.[5] Each section is introduced with a scholarly reflection summarizing the section. Part Two begins with a general introduction written by Carmen Samora, Creating an Intellectual Community, which details the components of Samora's multifaceted mentoring that includes political activism, pedagogy, and research and its impact on the whole person. Community and Political Activism is introduced by Richard A. Navarro with an essay titled Constructive Marginality: *En el otro lado,* followed by seven essays by former students and colleagues. The second section, The Pedagogy of Julian Samora, is introduced by Teresita E. Aguilar. Her essay, Reflections on Education: Post-Samora, leads six essays. The third section, composed of five essays, is introduced by Alberto López Pulido with an essay titled Translating the Whole Person: Julian Samora as Research Mentor, which introduces the integrative process used by Samora to teach his students about research. The final section in Part Two contains personal reflections by five Samoristas who examine the lasting impact of Samora's mentoring. This section is introduced by Miguel A. Carranza, himself a protégé of Samora's, titled Personal Visions: "Coming of Age with Samora."

The appendix contains Mestizaje and the Formation of Chicano, the lecture Samora delivered at the Seventh Annual Galarza Lecture Series at Stanford. It is included in this volume because it is the last public document produced by Julian Samora and is the only example of autobiographical writing Samora is known to have produced. In it he reveals personal information about his own search for *mestizaje*.

The editors of this volume invite you to read this book as a living document, legacy, and testament to Samora's life as produced by his students, Los Samoristas. The many reflections and stories captured in this book are a kaleidoscope of remembrances and personal encounters with Professor Julian Samora. They are representative of countless human moments, spoken words, and silent gestures that shape and breathe life into his legacy. As a result of Samora's life choices and experiences and emerging visions for Mexican American and Chicano communities, many people, both inside and outside academia, were drawn to his ideas and community-building skills.

Our friend, mentor, guide, and father passed in 1996. We are left with his words and strategies that continue to guide our intellectual and personal paths, which we, the editors, wish to share with the general reader, the scholar, the student, and the community. The collective words and stories are a metaphor for perseverance, struggle, and determination in the life of an individual who sought to bring long-lasting societal change through the power of knowledge and education.

Notes

1. Martínez defines such a space as an Alienated Borderland. Oscar J. Martínez, *Border People: Life and Society in the U.S.-Mexico Borderland* (Tucson: University of Arizona Press, 1994), pp. 6–7.

2. *Aztlan: A Journal of Chicano Studies* 7(2) (1976).

3. This dialogue included overt criticism of the emerging perspectives in Mexican American studies, such as a critique of Samora by Romano. See chapter 3.

4. From 1944 to 1949 he was director of the San Luis Institute in southern Colorado. See chapter 2.

5. The anointing of Samora's students into Samoristas occurred at the National Association for Chicana and Chicano Studies Conference in 2004, at a session on the life of Julian Samora chaired by Dr. Christine Sierra, who coined the phrase. Samoristas is used throughout the book to identify former Samora students.

CHAPTER ONE

Grace and Redemption

Julian Samora, 1920–1996

Carmen Samora

> When I was a little kid, growing up in Colorado, in Spanish, *éramos nosotros los Mexicanos,* but in English, we were Spanish American. That was because the dominant society didn't like things Mexican.
> —JULIAN SAMORA

If there is a theme in the life of my father, Julian Samora, it would have to be his lifelong fight for social justice: for himself, for other Mexican Americans in this country, for Mexicans struggling against the brutalization of working in U.S. fields and factories, and for the multitudes of people once labeled "Spanish surnamed" and now identified under the umbrella of "Hispanic/ Latino" in the United States. Their fight was his fight: for basic human and civil rights and resistance against societal discrimination and denigration by the dominant culture. Their collective numbers grew substantially during his career, which spanned four decades, and he helped in remarkable ways to bring their struggles to light. Having himself suffered discrimination as a way of life, Julian was passionately determined to eliminate the discrimination he and other persons like him experienced.

> I think the thing that has gotten me going is discrimination. I tried to be equal to, and as good as, the Anglos. I wanted to make as much money, speak as well, and have all the goodies as the dominant society. But no matter what I did, I was always a "Mexican."

Childhood

Small towns and villages in Colorado could be particularly cruel places for people of Mexican origin, and Pagosa Springs, where Julian was born March 1, 1920, was no exception. Anglos and Mexicans worshiped across the aisle from each other in the small Catholic church in Pagosa Springs. Anglos lined up first to receive communion and only when they were finished could the Mexicans line up for their communion. Mexican Americans were permitted in movie houses and theaters only if they sat in segregated balconies. Custom and convention limited where Mexican Americans could go and what they could do for a living.

Julian's mother, Carmen M. Samora, was born on October 16, 1896, in Park View, New Mexico territory. Julian's father, Fred Harris, was born in Saguache, Colorado, on August 14, 1893. Fred and Carmen never married and apparently had no relationship after Julian was born. Julian was raised by his mother, was given her family name, and grew up without a father. His status as an illegitimate child, as children with unmarried parents were called then, was the cause of shame and embarrassment for the young boy.

Carmen had two older sisters, Antonia (Tía Toñita) and Adelina, and an older brother, Miguel. Their parents, Selza and Manuel Samora, had three other children who died of *viruela* (smallpox). The Samora family moved from New Mexico to Colorado in 1903, perhaps to make a fresh start.

I have photos that show members of the Samora and Harris families together in Pagosa Springs, and old-timers I interviewed told me the two families were close and remained so after Julian's birth. Julian lived with his mother and grandparents, Selza and Manuel, in a wooden house on the Mexican side of Pagosa Springs. The house burned down before I was born, but, as children, we visited the house his aunt lived in, Tía Toñita's house. It had small rooms with linoleum floors and, according to Julian, was typical of the housing of that era. When Julian was three years old, his grandfather died, leaving Carmen and Grandmother Selza to raise the boy by themselves. Selza was a midwife and a *curandera,* a healer. Carmen worked cleaning offices at the bank and rooms at the hotel. Both were helpful and friendly women, very well-regarded in their community. In fact, old neighbors I interviewed spoke fondly of the Samora women. Carmen was remembered as very cheerful and always kind. Selza, with her curing abilities, was the person *la gente* went to with their medical problems and birthing needs. There was an Anglo doctor in town, but he would have been the solution of last resort for the Spanish-speaking town folk.

Fred's parents, Delubina Gallegos and Carlos Eduardo Harris, were both born in Saguache, Colorado. They had eight children, were quite well off, and owned a big ranch outside Pagosa Springs. Julian remembered that when his paternal grandparents visited in the winter they typically stayed a week with his family. They drove into town in a sled pulled by huge draft horses; the sled was loaded with a side of beef, root vegetables, and sacks of flour and beans to help get their grandchild and his mother through the winter. However, Julian remembered many meals of only beans, red chile, and tortillas. Occasionally, Julian spent a week at his paternal grandparents' ranch during the summer. He was much younger than his Harris cousins, and they were instructed to "be nice to Julian." But the cousins had to work on the ranch and there was little time for them to play. Julian, moreover, was somewhat of an outcast within his community because of the circumstances of his birth. In 1920, it was not uncommon to blame the child for the supposed failings of the parents. Although he never said so, I suspect his childhood was a lonely one.

The first groups of Anglos that came to Colorado were outnumbered by the Spanish-speaking who had settled on land grants deeded them by the Spanish, who had taken the land from the indigenous peoples they encountered. For the most part, the newcomers learned Spanish and they shared the customs of the people with whom they lived. Julian's Harris grandfather spoke both languages, but his other relatives spoke only Spanish. In fact, Harris was given a Spanish pronunciation and Julian grew up hearing the name pronounced Jerez. There was a strong oral tradition in his community and there would have been no reason for Julian to see the name in print.

The Promise of Education

After Colorado became a state in 1876, as more and more Anglo settlers moved in, English became the dominant language. English was the language of commerce and of the courts. Through the nineteenth century, most school-teachers were Spanish-speaking and subjects were taught in Spanish. By the turn of the last century, English had replaced Spanish in the schools, although a significant portion of the population still spoke Spanish as a first language. By the 1920s, all Spanish-speaking children in Colorado were made to repeat first grade, ostensibly to develop their English language skills. Julian was no exception. He was made to repeat the first grade without benefit of testing to assess his English acquisition. Julian and his *compañeros* were put in the "Mexican room," where they were separated from the Anglo students. He and a friend, Freddy Martínez, tried to learn one new word a day, and they would run home together practicing their English words. Julian knew that English was *la lengua del éxito,* the language of success, and he wanted to speak it perfectly.

Julian loved school, despite the slow start. Years ago, Tía Toñita gave me a scrapbook. Julian's mother, Carmen, had created the scrapbook as a record of her son's many accomplishments both in elementary and high school; it included all his school report cards, athletic ribbons, pictures, and newspaper articles describing his track and basketball wins. He received many certificates to mark his good behavior, his good spelling, and his achievements in history and English. He was a good student, and the report cards reflect his drive for success, even at a young age. That scrapbook is the material record of Carmen's belief in her son's present and future success. It not only tells the story of the care and love a proud mother had for her son, but it holds the clues to help us understand how Julian was able to rise from such poverty. His mother's faith in his abilities is written all over its pages. One can only imagine Julian, the child and later the teen, bringing home the rewards of his excellence, and then the solemn ritual between elder and child of placing those symbols in the book. Year after year, the evidence of his potential, the positive reinforcement of his abilities, grew so that "he" became his own model of success.

Although Julian enjoyed his school experience, it was not without the bitterness and pain of discrimination. In high school, when he was cast as the lead in the school play, Anglo cast members threatened to quit; the teacher, also an Anglo, appeased them by telling Julian he could not play the lead. Many years later, when I asked him how he felt about that, he said, "Oh, it hurt so much, it's hard to get over that kind of rejection."

Throughout high school, Julian had various jobs to help the family. In the summer, he worked with his uncle cutting and hauling logs for the forest service. He didn't really like working outdoors. He wasn't particularly good with his hands. He couldn't fix the equipment if it broke down. When school was in session, he worked as the evening desk clerk at the hotel where his mother worked days. That job suited him better. He could read all he wanted when it wasn't busy. And the hotel was heated by the water from the hot springs Pagosa was named for, so there was no boiler to keep an eye on and nothing mechanical in his job duties.

When Julian graduated from high school, he knew he wanted an indoor job, but he also knew that indoor jobs required an education, and in order to get an education he would have to leave Pagosa Springs. All the Spanish-speaking men he knew were laborers, working for wages for the Anglo establishment, having long since lost their lands in the U.S. courts. In his little town, Julian did not see Mexicans who were shopkeepers, owners of ranches, or businessmen. He did see many Mexican men who were defeated by alcoholism (including his Uncle Mike), joblessness, and illness. Julian knew there was vitality in his people because he was vital, but he did not yet know how to access it. Julian told me about a male teacher he had in junior high who championed him and encouraged him to go on to high school. Julian said the teacher was a father figure for him, and the idea of becoming a teacher too was born. Once in high school, though, Julian had no one to model the next steps. Few of the Mexican American friends with whom he started high school stayed in school very long. No one in his family had much elementary schooling, much less high school. But he did have the unwavering support of his mother and grandmother. Without their support, a college degree would have seemed like an unreachable goal. It was significant that Julian had their encouragement to graduate from high school.

But in 1938, along with 582 other Colorado students, Julian applied for the Frederick G. Bonfils Foundation scholarship, sponsored by the Bonfils family, which owned the *Denver Post*. Julian's hard work and good fortune placed him among the twenty-nine students selected, and he chose to go to Adams State Teachers College in Alamosa, Colorado. It was just the beginning of his academic journey, a journey defined by hard work and rewarded by good fortune. Attending a Colorado institution was one of the conditions of the scholarship, and Adams State offered a lifetime teaching license and was just over the pass from Pagosa Springs. It seemed like a good choice to be away from home, but not too far away.

Julian flourished in college. It must have been liberating to leave Pagosa Springs and reinvent himself. He was no longer the bastard kid, but a smart, good-looking, energetic young man with a dry sense of humor and a serious purpose. He took advantage of his college experience and joined many clubs as a freshman. His yearbook shows a skinny, dark-skinned, curly-haired youth who ran track, played basketball, and joined the drama club.

The summer before his sophomore year, when he was nineteen years old, his mother was dying of metastatic breast cancer. In those days there was little effective treatment, and Carmen refused to go to Denver for a radical mastectomy. Julian spent that summer caring for his mother. She died in July 1939. The following summer, his grandmother Selza died, and with her death, Julian, now just twenty years old, was doubly left an orphan. He had only Tía Toñita and a few Samora cousins to claim as family.

He had several jobs to augment the scholarship, which paid only for tuition and books. He worked in the college library where he met Betty Archuleta, who would become my mother. She remembered seeing a dashing, well-dressed, and handsome young man who seemed to be everywhere on campus. Mom said she started studying more and spending more time at the library to be sure to catch sight of Julian. One of Julian's favorite stories about himself was how he earned travel money. He set up a business washing shirts. He was so well-dressed because after washing and ironing his classmate's shirts, Julian wore them, then washed and ironed them again and returned them to the owners. He earned a nickel a shirt.

In his freshman year, Julian joined the newly formed El Parnaso Club, which was designed to promote friendship and understanding among the peoples of the Western hemisphere. The keynote speaker at the first annual conference was Dr. George I. Sánchez, and Julian gave the invocation. Dr. Sánchez, who subsequently became a pioneering scholar on the education of Mexican Americans, had received his PhD in Education from the University of California at Berkeley in 1934. Julian struck up a relationship with Dr. Sánchez and the two men remained colleagues and friends until Dr. Sánchez's death in 1972. Already in his first year of college, Julian was making the connections that would serve him throughout his long career.

A further look at his annuals shows that by his senior year he was president of most of the clubs he belonged to. Julian used college effectively as a training ground to learn to work among the ranks of the collective and then take leadership positions. Enjoying his success and popularity in college, he ran for student body president his senior year and lost when his roommate cast the deciding vote against him. His roommate told him, "Well Julian, I couldn't vote for a Mexican." He then ran for a more prestigious position and was elected president of student/faculty government. In that capacity, he oversaw the running of the college, as the governing body determined the yearly budget and made decisions about campus life.

Motivated by his pain and remembering the kindness of his long-ago teacher, Julian decided he could be an effective agent for change if he became a teacher. He told me he saw so many of his friends drop out of school and become swallowed up by low-paying jobs. He wanted something else for himself, and he wanted something different for his people.

Extended Family

Julian graduated in May 1942, with a degree in history and political science. On November 27, 1942, Thanksgiving Day, Betty and Julian were married. Betty provided Julian with an extended family, became his most ardent cheerleader, and raised their five children. She created an atmosphere of hospitality wherever they lived, from the humble Quonset hut that served as graduate student housing at the University of Wisconsin to the palatial house on Paseo de la Reforma in Mexico City, provided by the Ford Foundation when Julian worked there as a consultant on population in 1966. Julian's choice for a helpmate and life partner was brilliant. He was an intense person and an admitted workaholic, not much given to socializing. It was her vivaciousness and capacity for fun that set the tone of their social world. But Betty brought more than her liveliness to their union. She believed in him and fully supported his vision of social activism.

Raised in Monte Vista, Colorado, she too, had experienced discrimination firsthand. She was constantly packing and unpacking their household. That meant leaving the house they had just vacated so clean you could figuratively "eat off the floor." Usually the house they moved to required the same kind of scrubbing before they could occupy it. When I was old enough to help with these chores, I asked my mother why she bothered leaving the place so clean; the owners would never see us again. She explained to me that we had dignity and self-respect and no one would ever have an excuse to call us "dirty Mexicans."

Julian's poor vision prevented him from serving in the war as a soldier, so he was able to begin teaching right after college graduation. His first teaching position was at Huerfano High School in Walsenburg, Colorado, for the school term 1942–43, where he taught history and geography and was the boys' basketball coach. That spring, he traveled to Fort Collins, Colorado, near the Wyoming border, to interview for a graduate fellowship. He took the train from the southern part of the state and arrived in Fort Collins in the evening. Looking for a place to stay the night, he was turned away from lodging by signs that read "No Dogs, Indians or Mexicans Allowed." He was finally admitted to a fifth-rate hotel. The next morning, as he was leaving the flea-infested hotel, the owner asked him what part of India he hailed from.

Julian received the fellowship enabling him to attend Colorado State College of Agriculture and Mechanic Arts. He taught only one year in the high school. After his acceptance to graduate school, his teaching career continued at the college level.

Although she was pregnant with their first child, Betty served as the co-investigator for the research that led to Julian's master's thesis, titled "The Acculturation of the Spanish Speaking People of Fort Collins, Colorado in Selected Cultural Areas." They both joined the Spanish Activities Committee at Holy Family Church, and Julian served as secretary to Fr. John Fullana, the parish priest. The Rev. David Cisneros, of the Spanish Presbyterian Church, had been a school friend of Julian's in Pagosa Springs, and he introduced both Betty and Julian to his parishioners and appointed them co-directors of the recreation program for Spanish-speaking youth. They lived for a year in the Spanish-speaking section of Fort Collins. In that way, they came to know both the Catholic and Protestant Spanish-speaking community they wished to study.

On October 11, 1943, the pregnant Betty suffered severe abdominal pain. She was taken to the hospital and underwent an emergency appendectomy. The doctor advised Julian that he could not save both mother and child; whom should he save? Julian had to choose, and he chose Betty. Fortunately,

Betty's situation improved and Julian Robert was born that day, six weeks premature, but healthy.

In the fall of 1944, Julian was appointed the associate director of the San Luis Institute, a branch of Adams State College. The institute was Julian's brainchild. Julian had noticed a high dropout rate among the GIs who enrolled at Adams State. They had been to war and were finding it difficult to attend classes with eighteen-year-olds. The institute served its purpose; the older students attended their first two years in San Luis and then transferred to Adams State for their remaining two years. Eventually the institute evolved into a community college and trade school. In addition to his duties as associate director, Julian coached the men's basketball team.

Mose Trujillo, married to Betty's sister Ida, was one of those returning GIs. He credits Julian for encouraging everyone in the family to complete college. Julian was only a year or two older than Mose and Al Medina, who had married Ruth, Betty's youngest sister. But because Julian was their teacher they thought of him as being much older than they were. This perception gave Julian the authority to insist that they all finish school. The three Archuleta sisters completed college and all the men did postgraduate work, quite a feat for that ethnic group in that time period. Mose had a growing family and complained to Julian about the difficulties of going to school on the GI Bill. Julian replied, "Try going to school without it."

In July of 2001, I traveled to San Luis. I found the building that had been the San Luis Institute, and it now serves as county offices and a museum. Prominently displayed in one of the cases in the museum is a group photo of the San Luis Institute teachers. My father's is one of the smiling faces.

According to Aunt Ruth, those were wonderful years; the sisters and their husbands lived close to one another, their babies were born just months apart from each other, and they made many good friends. My uncles and aunts all have stories about this time period. None of them had two nickels to rub together, so there were times when they all shared the same house or worked at the same summer jobs, and, of course, they took care of each other's kids. They gleaned the fields for potatoes; they went to Saturday night dances and put the kids to sleep in a back room set aside in the dance hall for that purpose; they bought one steak and split it six ways; they made dandelion wine; they enjoyed picnics in the mountains.

The Responsibilities of Leadership

Still in their twenties, Julian and Betty already deeply felt the burden of leadership. The Mexicanos needed leaders. But being a leader in the Mexican community meant learning about and understanding the Anglo culture in order to bridge the two cultures. The challenge for the Mexicano leader was to learn about the Anglo world without giving up his Mexican culture, in other words, to become bicultural.

There was an unending torrent of bigotry leveled at Mexicans and Mexican Americans during this time. Some was subtle and some was quite overt. I visited with Mr. Al Salazar, whose wife Connie had been one of Betty's closest friends in college. He gave me some insight into the life my parents led as a young couple and the more or less constant assault to their dignity they all endured. What made my parents different is that they fought back by changing the institutions. After the war, when the two couples were living in Alamosa, Al and Julian joined the Knights of Columbus, the service organization connected with the Catholic Church. Betty and Connie wanted to join the Rosary Society, a club for educated women, Anglo women, that read and discussed books, did good works, and so forth. The priest suggested the two women join the Altar Society, whose membership was composed of Mexican American women who washed and ironed the priest's vestments and altar cloths. I can just imagine those two college-educated women, with their own laundry considerations, telling the priest they would much prefer to discuss books. Mr. Salazar told me that at my father's urgings, the priest combined the two societies and opened them up to all women, and Betty and Connie became members of the Altar and Rosary Society.

While Julian was still in graduate school and before he felt fully trained, Latino community leaders approached him for guidance in a political matter. They had been approached to support an Anglo candidate, but in the last election they had been promised a health clinic that had not materialized. Julian's scholarship had included research for the need for a medical delivery system in the San Luis Valley. Julian provided the local leaders with convincing data, and they were able to successfully negotiate with the *políticos*. Many people told me Julian was responsible for bringing the long-sought and much-needed clinic to reality, and, while it was a community effort, Julian was proud of his contribution. It showed him that research, good research, could help bring about community-led changes.

But he very much felt the burden of leadership and worried that he was not prepared and would never be able to carry the weighty needs of the Mexican American people. I know this motivated him to work very hard, and it was a burden that never quite left him, no matter how prepared he was. I have a strong image of my parents as young ambitious people with a heightened sense of responsibility. They launched themselves fearlessly into their life of service with only their hopes and dreams and commitment to serve *La Raza;* there were few role models, fewer examples, and no proven path. They were pioneers on the frontier and they were in uncharted territory. They relied on their traditions and mores to guide their separate and united commitments to serve those in need and to strike back hard at the discrimination that dogged their lives.

In May 1947, Julian earned an MS in Sociology from Colorado State College of Agriculture and Mechanic Arts, now Colorado State University. Also in May of that year, their second son, David Dennis, was born. A year later in the fall of 1948, Julian and Betty and their small family moved to Madison, Wisconsin, where Julian started work on a PhD. They lived in a Quonset hut, which was hot in the humid midwestern fall and bitterly cold in the winter. Julian's fellowship was not renewed, and after a year he ran out of money. They moved back to Alamosa and Julian taught again at Adams State and applied for money for another try at graduate school. He was awarded a Hermans Fellowship for the 1949–50 school year and started classes at Washington University in St. Louis, Missouri. The next year, Julian won a John Hay Whitney Fellowship, and in May 1953 he earned his PhD from Washington University. He was the first Mexican American to earn a PhD in sociology and anthropology. Betty gave birth to me, their only daughter, in August of 1951. Francis Geoffrey, the next to last child, was born in Alamosa in August 1953 following Julian's graduation.

With his training completed and four of their five children born, Betty and Julian moved back once again to Alamosa, where Julian rejoined the faculty at Adams State for the 1953–54 school year. Because of his large family and his natural cautiousness, Julian never quit Adams State; rather he took leaves of absence so he would always have a position to return to if their plans did not quite work out.

While at Adams State, they met a young woman, Margaret McKenzie, who was newly hired to teach modern languages at the college. Margaret came to town "trailing clouds of glory."[1] Her family home was in Beverly Hills, California, her master's was from Harvard, and her PhD was from the University of Chicago. Both Anglos and Mexicanos in the small town were intimidated by her pedigree. Margaret, Betty, and Julian formed a friendship that lasted until my parents' deaths and which continues with their children and grandchildren. Margaret was a newcomer, and Betty and Julian risked their standing in their own community by befriending an Anglo woman so far removed from their social class.

Margaret tells a story about one of their evenings together. After going to a movie in Manassas, the three of them decided to get something to eat. It was too late to cook a meal at home, so Margaret suggested they eat at the El Monte, the hotel in Monte Vista on the way back to Alamosa. What Margaret did not know, and that Betty and Julian did know, was that it was closed to Mexicans. They had never set foot in the El Monte. Because they did not want to embarrass Margaret, they followed her into the hotel with trepidation. They were served without incident. In telling me the story, Margaret thought perhaps they had been served because the hotel dining room was empty and their presence did not cause a stir. After the meal, Betty and Julian confessed their worry and then expressed relief that all had gone well. Margaret remembered thinking at the time how dignified Betty and Julian had been and how punishing the customs of those times were. In the mid-1960s, Julian was invited to give a lecture in Monte Vista; included in the invitation was a night at the El Monte. He gave the lecture, but he stayed with friends.

In 1954, Julian spent a year as a visiting professor at the University of New Mexico. He applied for a permanent position but was turned down, and he was disappointed that he did not get the job and worried about where his professional life would take him. How different would his career have been had he been hired by the University of New Mexico? It may be that his extraordinary accomplishments were ultimately made possible precisely because he was working outside the boundaries of the Hispanic Southwest.

Lyle Saunders, a colleague with whom he'd been corresponding since 1948, recommended Julian to the University of Colorado School of Medicine in 1955, and Julian became an assistant professor of Preventive Medicine and Public Health. Noticing that Anglo doctors did not understand or connect with their Mexican and Mexican American patients, Julian undertook a study on the practices of delivering medical care to Mexican Americans in Colorado. That study, and the resulting papers and presentations of his ideas in his classes, represents the foundation of the field of medical anthropology, which Julian helped to establish. Julian took his observations back to the classroom, and through his lectures the medical students and doctors developed new methods to deliver health care to their Spanish-speaking patients.

Julian's work attracted the attention of the noted sociologist Charles Loomis, who was on the faculty at Michigan State University. Loomis was doing research on the populations along the U.S.-Mexico border and was interested in hiring a Mexican American to join his research team. Julian, attracted as much by Loomis's personality as by his ability to get research money, joined Loomis at MSU during the 1957 and 1958 academic years. Julian finally resigned his position on the faculty at Adams State, severing a more than fifteen-year relationship with his alma mater. He was ready to embrace the Midwest as the site of his mature academic life.

The Midwest Connection

In the fall of 1957 we moved to East Lansing, Michigan. While at Michigan State, Julian was on the dissertation committee of a young man named Bill D'Antonio, and the two became friends and colleagues and our two families socialized. Julian and Bill volunteered with the St. Vincent De Paul Society. It was Julian's custom in every community in which he lived to join St. Vincent De Paul or the Knights of Columbus to get to know the community of working-class Mexican Americans and learn about their needs and to help out. Bill D'Antonio, also a Catholic, went with Julian to a meeting for recruits new to the society. He remembered they were to pass out chits that evening to families in need of groceries. One of the new volunteers asked Julian how they could be sure a family really needed the groceries and was not cheating the system. Bill remembers that Julian gave the young man a long, slow look and told him that he should really look at the people he would meet that night and judge for himself if anyone was making a game of it. Julian became a national figure in his academic field and helped found nationally significant organizations, but his concerns grew out of his personal and local experiences.

Betty returned to Denver in April 1958 to await the birth of her last child.[2] Betty was accompanied by her three youngest, leaving their eldest with Julian until the end of the term. John Mark was born May 20, 1958. I found a series of letters my parents wrote each other during that separation. Mom inquired about naming the baby Harris, and Dad wrote back that his father deserved no such honor.

In 1959 Julian and Bill D'Antonio went to a conference at Notre Dame. They found themselves heavily courted by the chair of the sociology/anthropology department, John Kane. Fr. Theodore Hesburgh, then president of Notre Dame, had serious plans to expand the social sciences and was looking for sociologists who were practicing Catholics. Michigan State, an institution dependent on state funds, found its funds frozen by a recession. Loomis was unable to match the offer made by Notre Dame and found himself saying good-bye to two of his bright stars. It was in South Bend that Julian's career really began to have definition. Building on his research with Charles Loomis, Julian's work at Notre Dame took a more national focus.

For a few more years we continued to travel together as a family. I remember my father telling us he wanted to raise citizens of the world. We had spent the summer of 1959 in Truchas, New Mexico, where Julian was doing research with Loomis, before driving across the country to find South Bend, Indiana. We went to Bogotá, Colombia, in 1963, where Julian was teach-

ing at the National University. In the summer of 1964, we lived in Venice
Beach when Julian was hired by the English department at UCLA to teach
two courses on teaching English as a second language to U.S. citizens. These
courses were part of an exploratory effort that would result in bilingual
education for children in both elementary and secondary schools. In 1966,
we lived in Mexico City for fifteen months when Julian was a program officer in population control for the Ford Foundation.

In 1966 Julian met Herman Gallegos and Ernesto Galarza. Dr. Galarza, the
elder of the three, forwent a career in the academy to advocate for Mexican
and Mexican American laborers. Dr. Galarza is credited with exposing the
abuses that led to the termination, in 1964, of the Bracero Program.[3] Dr.
Gallegos had been forming pioneering relationships between foundations
and Latinos and had a relationship with the Ford Foundation. All three were
deeply concerned with the issue of leadership and how to promote social
justice for Mexican Americans. The Ford Foundation had invested heavily
in issues related to African Americans and was interested in learning more
about Latinos. The three scholars received a grant from the Ford Foundation and began conducting the research and planning the organization that
would become the National Council of La Raza.

I think 1966 was the turning point for Julian and our family. Julian's national agenda combined with his academic schedule was so time-consuming
that the family took a back seat. The only family vacation I remember going
on where Dad was not working occurred when I was five years old and our
youngest brother, John, was not yet born. Once we moved to South Bend,
the trips to visit relatives became infrequent, and Dad's attention was away
from home.

During this period he was on the board of, or was a consultant to, the following: the U.S. Commission on Civil Rights; the U.S. Public Health Service;
the Rosenberg Foundation; the National Endowment for the Humanities; the
National Institute of Mental Health; the Weatherhead Foundation; the U.S.
Human Resources Corporation; Harcourt Brace Jovanovich, Inc.; the Bureau
of Census; the U.S. Department of Labor; the National Science Foundation;
the W. K. Kellogg Foundation; the Colorado Anti-Discrimination Commission; the National Upward Bound Program; the President's Commission on
Rural Poverty; the President's Commission on Income Maintenance Program;
the Indiana Civil Rights Commission; the Mexican-American Legal Defense
& Educational Fund; the National Assessment of Educational Progress; the
National Advisory Committee to the Bureau of the Census; the National Advisory Committee to Immigration and Citizenship Conference; the National
Advisory Committee to U.S.-Mexico Border Research Program; the National

Advisory Committee to Harvard Encyclopedia of American Ethnic Groups; the Committee on Opportunities in Science; the American Association for the Advancement of Science; the Council on Foundations; the University of Notre Dame Press; and the Allocations Committee for United Way.

There is no question how important the work was, how groundbreaking the research was, how vital that the new information reach the policy makers. However successful Julian was in his scholarly pursuits, he was not successful in making time for his family after 1966. Perhaps he was never able to shed the feelings of responsibility for carrying the whole of the Chicano people. And now the load was much heavier, and Betty was cut out from sharing in much of it simply due to the sheer magnitude of Julian's activities. His work was now of a national scope and he was traveling three or four times a month to meetings. What had once been a local and shared commitment between them was irrevocably changed. Betty's role became more home-centered as she was left with the responsibility of raising the five children, while Julian kept to a hellish schedule of travel, research, and teaching.

Yet it was Betty's continued support that made possible what Julian considered his greatest legacy. By 1971, Julian's brilliant vision to educate the next generation of scholars, educators, policy makers, and lawyers was coming to fruition, made possible by grants from the Ford Foundation and later the Graduate and Professional Opportunity Program from the U.S. Department of Education. In all, fifty-seven students were accepted into the Mexican American Graduate Studies Program, and almost all received advanced degrees in sociology, government, law, history, psychology, or economics. Julian considered this program his greatest contribution and he put his soul and heart into it. All his creative skills went into this plan to train leaders.

And it was Betty's vocation of hospitality, her readiness to share a hot bowl of beans and a warm homemade tortilla with students homesick for their cultural roots that nourished the program. Julian's Mexican American Graduate Studies Program was in full operation, and Betty embraced her role of wise friend as she listened and helped the students and their spouses come to terms with the demands of graduate school and the Midwest.

To stimulate the students and provide mentoring and role models for them, Julian invited many prominent people to speak at Notre Dame. Cesar Chavez; author Paul Horgan; three Chicano archbishops; two Hispanic governors of New Mexico, Jerry Apodaca and Toney Anaya; author Rudy Anaya; Vilma Martínez, chief counsel and president of the Mexican American Legal Defense and Education Fund; filmmakers Moctezuma Esparza and Jesus Treviño. They all came to South Bend, and most dined in our home.

Julian relied on Betty to provide the warmth and welcome to these visitors, which she did.

When the three Chicano archbishops came to Notre Dame, Mom asked me to help cook the meal. I was thrilled to be included; I was in college and not at home very much. Mom told me the guests would arrive at 6:00 p.m. and dinner would follow drinks. In my naïveté, I had no idea how long drinks could take. The meal was simple: beans, tortillas, and red chile, so it held while the guests regaled one another with stories. I remember that Archbishop Flores from San Antonio was especially complimentary about my meal and my efforts as Betty-in-training.

Betty also had her own career. She taught migrant preschool children. She formed a Catholic women's support group in 1966 that still meets once a week. She took on an orphanage in Mérida in the Yucatán, organizing regular donations of goods and money. With us in tow, she picketed the A&P for selling non-union California lettuce, and subsequently we picketed grocery stores for selling non-union grapes. She made bread every week. She made tortillas almost every day. She canned the produce from the garden. She read voraciously, and she was a vivacious dinner companion.

Family Loss and Grief

Late one night in early April 1975, Julian took a call from his son David. David was calling from Arizona where he had been visiting with his oldest brother. Bob had gone missing the day before, and David called with the news that his body had been found. Bob had committed suicide. Julian sat up all night. He waited until morning before telling Betty the horrible news.

They dealt privately with their grief and told very few people how Bob had died. Our family strength was rent and the family started to unravel. These days, going to a therapist to help with grief issues is accepted treatment for families of all ethnicities. But it was not an option for my parents. Their history was of helping others, being role models to others. When they needed help, they could not ask for themselves. Our family was viewed from the outside as a strong family, a view my parents encouraged. It was important to them to demonstrate that this particular Mexican American family embraced successfully both ethnic and American values. How could a family with that image ask for help?

Three years later, in 1978, Betty was diagnosed with ovarian cancer. While she was ill, Julian agreed to cut back on his travel. In September, Betty went to Denver for treatment and I was sent for to care for her. We gathered as a family for Thanksgiving at my brother David's home in Santa Fe. Mom and I went home to South Bend in time for Christmas. My brother Geoff and his wife Mary live in South Bend, and we did our best to care for her, but mostly we stood by helplessly as she died. Betty and Julian had lived in South Bend for twenty years when she became ill. Their community of friends generously lent support to Betty and to us as she weakened. Betty died the last day of spring, June 20, 1979. Her funeral was particularly memorable. Betty had left instructions that her funeral be joyful. Her coffin was draped with a *serape* with colorful butterflies woven into the design. We sang the songs she had requested, and that night her family and her family of students and friends danced in celebration of her memory.

After Betty's death Julian was grief-stricken. For the first time in his life, his drive seemed drained from him. Geoff, Mary, and I ate dinner with him frequently, but Dad spent a lot of time alone in his empty house. Little by little, his work with his students began to sustain him. I was in graduate school at Notre Dame and I took three semesters of Julian's graduate seminar along with the coursework for my degree. I became friends with that particular cohort of students and began to experience from the perspective of a student the work Julian was doing, the *familia* he and Betty had created. I learned a different side of my father as I listened to him counsel students during seminar. I experienced for myself the creative ideas that flowed from him to his students. The distant father was a demanding yet welcoming and warm teacher.

On July 3, 1983, Julian married Marcella (Sami) Ellett. After only a few months of marriage, Julian had a heart attack in January 1984. He had recently learned that Notre Dame was not going to continue the Mexican American Graduate Studies Program. Anthony Blasi and Bernard Donahoe, in their book *A History of Sociological Research and Teaching at Catholic Notre Dame University, Indiana,* suggest the program was phased out by changes occurring in the department of sociology. Julian had never had full support from the administration at Notre Dame, nor, at the time of his retirement, did he have full support for his work from his department. His pioneering work, while meeting important sociological and ethnic needs, was not understood by his own department. The administration failed to realize the growing importance of Latinos, and by discontinuing the program missed a critical opportunity of leadership. Julian administered more than a million dollars in grants during his career at Notre Dame. Fifty students received advanced degrees through his Mexican American Graduate Studies Program. He mentored countless others. He served as chairman of his department. He revived the Notre Dame Press, and many Latino authors were able to publish their work through Notre Dame. Julian Samora's programs, scholarly reputation, and national leadership enhanced Notre Dame's reputation as a leader in civil rights issues. Julian Samora retired from Notre Dame in 1985.

At the time of his retirement, his students organized an unprecedented three-day symposium that recognized Julian's work and showcased their own research. Many at the University of Notre Dame, including its president, Fr. Theodore Hesburgh, commented that they had never seen such a reunion of scholars pay tribute to their teacher and mentor. At one point in the ceremonies, Julian invited all his students to gather around him. It was moving to see Aunt Ruth and Uncle Al, who had been among his earliest students, join the much younger group, completing the picture of a full forty-year teaching career.

In 1989, the first major university research center named for a Latino, the Julian Samora Research Institute, was founded. Julian was quoted as saying, "As I told the gathering, it's about time a major university established a research center; that it bears my name is very emotional to me." But rather than being at Notre Dame, the institute was established at Michigan State University. Other honors followed. In 1990, the Mexican government awarded La Orden del Águila Azteca (The Aztec Eagle Award) to Julian Samora, the labor and civil rights leader Cesar Chavez, and the distinguished University of Texas folklorist Américo Paredes. It is the highest award presented to non-Mexican citizens and recognizes distinguished service provided to the people of Mexico and those of Mexican descent in the United States. These are the highlights among many awards and accolades bestowed on Julian after his retirement.

The summer before he retired, Julian and Sami had visited Spain. While there, they visited the archives in Seville. Julian was looking for his familial ties: Samora, Archuleta, Medina, Trujillo, and "Jerez." He assumed his father's name had been Americanized, as often happens to Spanish surnames. But he was unable to find any trace of paternal ancestors. The next year, Julian received a letter from a Lloyd B. Harris, who had read an account of Julian's retirement symposium in his Kansas City newspaper. Mr. Harris confirmed that he was Julian's uncle and he was Fred Harris's brother. Lloyd had knowledge of the Harris family tree and wrote Julian that his grandfather (Julian's paternal great-grandfather) Edward Russell Harris had been born in Massachusetts about 1830 and had come to the Colorado territory from Boston. He was listed in the 1880 U.S. census as a carpenter. In Colorado, he married Juana Jacques of New Mexico, a woman who claimed to be of French descent. Julian was just as amused as his children to learn that the "Father of Chicano Studies" was of Irish and French as well as Mexican extraction.

What sort of man was Julian outside of his university environment? He had friendly relationships with two of his neighbors, Lew Soens and Andy Weigert, both colleagues of Julian's. He liked to play handball. Sometimes Julian would get off a plane in South Bend and go directly to the handball courts for a game with David and Geoff and Andy Weigert before going home to unpack. He bought a chainsaw jointly with Lew so they could cut trees to feed their fireplaces all winter. Andy joined in the tree cutting and would lend his truck to the endeavor. They would be joined by Julian's youngest son, John, who was taught to keep the chainsaw sharpened (a pain in the ass, as he said). Sometimes Geoff joined them. It took all weekend to cut and stack, but it provided Julian a deep satisfaction when, on a cold winter day, he would bring in a big stack of dry oak logs to feed the crackling fire. In his will, Julian left his share of the chainsaw to Lew. His home in South Bend included an acre of property. On it, he grew New Mexico chiles, made wine (usually it turned to vinegar) from the grapes in the arbor, and planted a huge kitchen garden every spring even after Betty died and his kids had moved away.

The Challenge of Illness

In 1989 Julian began to display health symptoms that were puzzling to his doctors and frustrating for him and for us. For several years it was misdiagnosed as Parkinson's disease. His behavior was erratic and hostile. He began to fall, his speech was affected, and he had difficulty holding on to things with his hands. He resented paying for the expensive medications that had no effect. My attitude was one of exasperation. I resented that he would not take his meds and accept that he had Parkinson's. Sami and Geoff took him to the Mayo Clinic, and Geoff took him to consultations with doctors in Indianapolis. Geoff was with him for a humiliating experience when Julian was left naked on a gurney waiting for a doctor who had stepped away. Julian, who had fought all his life for dignity and justice, turned to his son and said, "So this is what it comes to."

All the while he tried to work. Julian received a grant from the Rockefeller Foundation, and he and Sami spent a month in Bellagio, Italy, where he continued his research for a book titled *Mestizaje*. The book was never completed, for whatever was wrong with him interfered with his capacity to do research. His body was failing him and no one could provide him with a reasonable diagnosis. It was devastating for him, a man who had exercised so much control over his life and his feelings, to gradually lose control of his body and succumb to a disease that as yet had no name.

Julian, Sami, Geoff, and Mary all struggled with the effects of the un-known illness and Julian's resulting ill temper. Sami grew frustrated with the unexplained changes in her husband, and she and Dad divorced in 1993. Since his retirement, Dad had been in the habit of coming to Albuquerque, where I live, for the winter months. He would go to the University of New Mexico library and do some research, visit with staff and students, and try to keep up with the changes in his field. After the divorce, Geoff tried to convince Dad to live with him, but he refused. It became very clear to us that Julian could not live alone. Geoff and I called each other regularly to exchange news and offer support. Then in September of 1994, after a series of conversations, I agreed that Dad should come to Albuquerque permanently. I was not looking forward to having Dad in my house. After he became ill, his visits had become difficult and disruptive.

In the fall of 1994, we visited a neurologist, Dr. Neal Hermanowicz, who carefully examined Dad, addressing him respectfully as Dr. Samora. By this time the illness had progressed to the point where Dad could not walk un-assisted, had difficulty swallowing his food, and frequently fell backwards. Dr. Hermanowicz asked a few questions and then gave us a diagnosis. The doctor said, "Dr. Samora, I know what is wrong with you. You are right. You do not have Parkinson's." Dr. Hermanowicz explained that he had spent his post doc at the University of Michigan and had studied more than fifty patients that had had progressive supra nuclear palsy, a terminal neurological disorder. "What you have," he told Dad sadly, "goes quicker to death. There are no medications you can take. I will talk to Carmen about how to make you more comfortable. The end can be difficult." Dad looked up at him and said through his tears, "Thank you, Doctor. It is better to know." Not knowing what was wrong with him had eaten into my father's keen mind and stable emotions. There was immense relief for my father in finally having the correct diagnosis.

In the car on the drive home from the hospital, I squeezed his hand. He smiled and said, "What next?" What did come next I could never have predicted. He seemed to accept the reality that he had completed all the work he was going to complete. For the remaining eighteen months of his life, the all-consuming drive to succeed ebbed. It was replaced with sweet-ness, a cheerful openness to the love of his family. David came down from his home in Santa Fe nearly every weekend to spell me and to visit with his father. John and Geoff and the grandchildren, including Bob's daughter Amy, came to visit frequently. Colleagues and former students visited from across the country and the visits cheered him immensely.

The disease attacked his brain stem and he became unable to hold a book to read; he could not hold a pencil to write; he could not feed himself; he could barely talk. But the growing failure of his body did not victimize him. Dad and I spent some good time together. I liked to read to him. We talked a lot about his youth, about his years with Mom. He told me he knew he never could have achieved what he had without Betty's creative input and support. Dad became jolly and good-natured. The O.J. Simpson trial was the current event and Dad watched every day. When my husband Steve, a lawyer, came home from work, Dad would greet him with shouts of "He's innocent, he's innocent." And then Dad would laugh mischievously. He was a champion for my daughter Alicia; they were good company together. He did not sleep well, and, in the early months of his illness, he often woke Alicia, who was only too happy to get up hours before dawn and build a fire with Grandpa. Dad was always a great grandpa. He gave himself over to his grandchildren completely even before the illness.

Most revealing to me, Dad never complained. He was in constant discomfort or pain, he was often completely helpless, but his abiding cheeriness made caring for him a beautiful and intimate experience.

A year or two earlier, I had found a home health aide to help with Dad's care when he visited me. I tried to leave work at lunchtime to check on him, but inevitably, he needed full-time care. Elsie and I worked out a schedule to cover Dad's care needs. Elsie Lazero and my father developed a deep friendship, the likes of which I doubt he had ever experienced before. Elsie accepted him, respected him, enjoyed his stories, and absolutely brooked no nonsense from him. They had endless arguments about Elsie's claim of being pure Navajo. This played into Dad's final research project, the one on *mestizaje*, which explored the mix of peoples that make up Mexican Americans. Dad kept insisting that she and he were from the same biological mix. The day before he died, Elsie was in the kitchen brewing a foul-smelling Navajo herbal tonic as a remedy for Dad. Aunt Ruth came over and put on a pan of her own New Mexico herbal remedy. When I looked in the pans, those two were brewing the exact same herbs.

The night before he died, I was awakened by the sounds of his struggling to breathe. I went to his room to offer whatever comfort I could. David was asleep on the floor, having stayed up late reading to Dad. I read to him for a bit and wanted to keep him company. As I gave him sips of water, he took my hand and struggled to say, "I am not in pain."

Julian died later that morning. Elsie led us in the Lord's Prayer. She then washed and prepared his body. We dressed him in his suit because, as Elsie said, "He needs to look nice to meet Betty." I thought at the time that Mom would appreciate Elsie's gesture. Mom was always dismayed that Dad would leave for school and the office dressed in jeans and work boots.

There were three memorial services for my father, one at Notre Dame, one at the Julian Samora Research Institute at Michigan State, and one at the University of New Mexico. I quote from the remarks Geoff made at Michigan State.

> When Julian and Betty bought a car with air conditioning to provide comfort in the hot, humid Indiana summers, neither would drive the car off the lot, as they were embarrassed to own such luxury. I drove them home and my mother stated that she was ashamed to have indulged herself when so many people suffer greater pain than being hot and humid on a summer's day. I remember telling my parents that they deserved the comfort of an air-conditioned car, but the lesson was clear—in this family one is expected to suffer for the greater good.
>
> Although Julian did not play catch with me as a child, he later taught me to play handball, a game I still play today. Although he traveled much more than my mother would have liked, he always had time for me when, as a Notre Dame student, I stopped without an appointment at his eleventh-floor office.
>
> Julian reached a balance in the last years of his life. He became a devoted *abuelito* to his grandchildren and learned to express his feelings verbally. He was open with his love for his family and friends, and he died knowing that his life's work helped lay the foundation for future generations to experience justice and equality.
>
> As Julian's work for *La Causa* progressed, he left to our mother the task of raising the family. Our mother taught us love, our father devotion. Our mother taught us compassion, our father perseverance. Our mother taught us to relax, our father patience. Our mother taught us harmony, our father discipline. Our mother taught us to give back to the community, our father taught us to search for truth and justice.
>
> Julian, it has been said, was a non-emotional man. It has been said he combined Spanish dignity and pride with Native Indian stoicism. I want to set the record straight. His hurt and anger from the complete neglect from his father and the crushing "you're not good enough" attitude of a neglectful society fired his drive to make things right—and not just for himself, but for all his people. Given the demand of such a grand task, academic endeavors, research, writing, mentoring, etc., etc., his own family ironically came to feel as he had felt, hurt and angry at his absence. But we learned also that sacrifice is necessary to progress.
>
> If I may suggest something to you, I hope you will heed it. Pioneers are few and far between. Personal balance is needed in the lives of all those who struggle for justice, for what is more just than for a parent to enjoy the pleasure of his family's time?

Grace is granted to children who care for their parents. Grace is granted even to the child who is reluctant and unsure, as I had been. And grace is granted to the parent who allows his children to care for him as he reveals his loving nature to them. It is never too late for redemption. For the eighteen months that my father lived with my family in Albuquerque, he modeled a graceful dying. He allowed my brothers and me to talk about his death with him, to plan for our futures as *huérfanos*. We were able to bring up past hurts with each other and gain a clean slate. It was as if his suffering was enabling us to heal the family wounds. My father's final gift to me was the gift of his love.

Julian Samora died February 2, 1996, in Albuquerque, New Mexico, on the 148th anniversary of the Treaty of Guadalupe Hidalgo.

Notes

1. From *Intimations of Immortality* by William Wordsworth.

2. Fortunately for my brothers and me, our mother insisted that all of her children be born in Colorado.

3. The Bracero Program was a guest worker program begun during the Second World War to provide U.S. agriculture and other industries with labor from Mexico. It brought in close to five million Mexican workers and ran from 1942 to 1964.

CHAPTER TWO

A Scholar and Visionary in Mexican American and Latino Studies

Barbara Driscoll de Alvarado

Julian Samora's retirement from Notre Dame in 1985 provided perhaps the first opportunity to view and review his career. Many colleagues and former students, many of whom were graduates of the Mexican American Graduate Studies Program (MAGSP), gathered at Notre Dame to publicly speak about their professional and personal relationships with Dr. Samora and to bear witness to the already manifest Samora legacy. Former students spoke to the extraordinary influence that Dr. Samora wrought in the development of their career choices and priorities, and colleagues acknowledged the significance of his work for the academy. While the presentations varied greatly, all recognized the philosophy that Don[1] Julian brought to his life and career, most obviously exemplified by the Mexican American Graduate Studies Program.

My historian's curiosity motivated me to study Dr. Samora's early career, but my knowledge of him did not prepare me for my discoveries. As mentor and director of MAGSP, Don Julian encouraged students in many disciplines and at all levels to include original historical research about Mexican Americans whenever possible. In the course of examining Don Julian's early career, however, I came to understand that Dr. Samora's relationship with the study of the past transcended the discipline of history in the academy and even his own role in Mexican American Studies. Coming to terms with entrenched legacies of discrimination and social injustices directed toward Mexican Americans defined his life's work and inspired his mentoring, research, and teaching.[2] In other words, studying the past was a personal as well as professional passion for Don Julian.

This chapter outlines Dr. Samora's undergraduate and graduate education, describes his first academic positions and details the parameters of his career after completing his graduate education. Dr. Samora was no overnight sensation. By the time Julian had achieved national stature in the late 1960s with the publication of *Los Mojados: The Wetback Story*, he had already dedicated twenty-five years of work to the academy. His early life and career remain relatively unknown, yet even a cursory review demonstrates a lifelong commitment to teaching and researching Mexican American Studies and a determination to address social injustices of the past.

Don Julian's Formative Years

I learned that Dr. Samora earned his bachelor's degree with a major in history at Adams State College in Alamosa, Colorado, graduating in 1942. He taught history and physical education for a short time at Huerfano High School in Walsenburg, Colorado, but he returned to Adams State as a faculty member in 1944 at the invitation of the institution's founding president, Ira Richardson, and maintained his professional affiliation there until 1956.[3] From 1944 to 1949, in his capacity as an Adams State faculty member, Samora worked mostly as an administrator at the San Luis Institute of Arts & Crafts, an Adams State extension school in San Luis, Colorado. The San Luis Institute was founded in 1943 "to provide instruction in traditional Hispanic crafts, such as weaving and woodcarving," and served as a bridge between local Spanish-speaking populations and Adams State. The San Luis

Institute eventually adopted a high school diploma program to accommodate returning veterans; Julian valued the importance of Adams State
College and its San Luis extension for the then isolated Spanish-speaking
communities of Colorado's San Luis Valley.[4] Adams State College trained
many Mexican Americans to be teachers and other professionals for local
communities throughout southern Colorado.

Julian also used his position as administrator/teacher at the San Luis Institute to bring state public health services to the small community. Founded
in 1851, San Luis is the oldest town in Colorado and to this day remains
a small and relatively poor community of a few hundred families, mostly
Mexican Americans. Samora convinced the Colorado State Division of Public Health to send visiting nurses armed with vaccinations for the town and
other points in Costilla County. Further, Julian founded the Costilla County
Health Association to pressure the state's Board of Medical Examiners to
issue a license for a physician to practice in Costilla County, which at the
time had no physician.[5] The initiatives he demonstrated at the San Luis Institute provided a solid basis for appreciating the dilemmas of leadership in
bicultural communities, a research problem he studied later in his career.

In 1944, Samora applied to the master's program in sociology at Colorado State University, then known as the Agricultural and Mechanical
College at Fort Collins, using his teaching experience at Huerfano High
School and participation in the Inter-American Workshop at the University
of Denver in 1943 to support his application, although his admission was
conditioned on a successful semester of courses in sociology.[6] By early 1946,
Samora had already finished a substantial portion of the work required for
the master's degree from the Agricultural and Mechanical College while
continuing to work at San Luis Institute; President Richardson agreed
that Samora could use the summer of 1946 to finish degree requirements,
including writing his thesis.[7]

In 1947, Julian was awarded a master's degree in sociology by the Agricultural and Mechanical College. His unpublished master's thesis, "The
Acculturation of the Spanish Speaking People of Fort Collins, Colorado,"
presents an original multidimensional community study on acculturation
he conducted in 1944 on the Spanish-speaking population of Fort Collins,
Colorado. Samora posited the research through exploring the question, in
his words, "To what extent have the Spanish-speaking people of Fort Collins
deviated from their original culture patterns and accepted the culture patterns of the English-speaking people in the culture areas of language, food
patterns, family patterns, and mythology and scientific knowledge."[8] Based
on structured interviews with 27 of the 165 Spanish-speaking families living

in Fort Collins identified by Samora through school and parish records, the thesis analyzes the raw data, develops tables and graphs, and ends with a conclusion. Samora framed his study within the general parameters of the culture scheme developed by Clark Wissler[9] and chose specific elements to measure acculturation. The thesis study measured across three age cohorts, the use of English- and Spanish-language usage, family patterns, food consumption patterns, and mythology and scientific knowledge. Dr. Samora described how he built validity and reliability into the study:

> Since the scientific methodology employed in this study is the descriptive method, certain precautions were taken to insure validity and reliability of data. The methods employed were these:
>
> 1. The writer and his wife lived in the Spanish-speaking section of Fort Collins for one year, becoming well acquainted with most of the people and becoming members of the group.
> 2. The writer became very well acquainted with the resident Catholic Priest, serving more or less as his secretary, writing letters and translating for him.
> 3. The writer was a schoolmate and good friend of the Spanish Presbyterian Minister. These relationships enabled him to get the backing of both the Catholic and Protestant church.
> 4. The writer and his wife were active in the Spanish Activities Committee and also served as directors of the recreation program for the Spanish-speaking youth while in Fort Collins.
> 5. The writer checked twenty per cent of the schedules chosen at random, with Father John Fullana and Reverend David Cisneros: also with Mrs. Whiteford and Mrs. Foreman of the Spanish Activities Committee. In the opinion of the writer, the four people named know the people under study, have worked with them, and were well qualified to check the schedules for possible errors.[10]

The themes that Julian selected to analyze in his master's thesis suggest several research questions that guided later work, such as the delivery of medical services, immigration status, and belief systems. For Julian, the challenge as a graduate student was to devise research methods that resulted in concrete knowledge about the Spanish-speaking community. As a pragmatist, Julian already knew that his research had to be considered valid by the academy.

Samora knew he needed a doctorate to prosper in higher education. In the fall of 1947, Samora left for Madison, Wisconsin, to begin doctoral work at the University of Wisconsin, where he worked as a teaching assistant for the academic year 1947–48. That year was a disappointment. Samora discovered that although the University of Wisconsin was prestigious, the research priorities of the doctoral program in the social sciences did not fit his research interests and certainly did not include Colorado's Mexican American population. He returned to Adams State.

Julian returned to his position at Adams State for the academic year 1949–50, although Richardson wanted him to remain at the main campus in Alamosa to teach courses in the social science department rather than return to the San Luis Institute. Further, the trustees awarded him tenure in July, so he enjoyed more job security and flexibility.[11] In the spring of 1950, Samora was notified that he had been awarded the Hermans Fellowship to pursue a doctorate at Washington University in St. Louis.[12] Again, Adams State gave Samora a leave of absence; President Richardson enjoyed support from the college's faculty, and he actively supported Julian's efforts to pursue graduate work even though Julian had not been physically in Alamosa as much as the college would have wanted.

His disappointment in Wisconsin showed Samora that he had to focus his choice of a doctoral program; therefore, as soon as he returned to Colorado he identified academic researchers who were studying the Spanish-speaking community. He learned that doctoral students from Washington University in St. Louis under the direction of James B. Watson[13] were conducting serious primary research in the Spanish-speaking communities of Colorado. Don Julian approached the researchers to propose that he pursue his doctorate at Washington University, and he subsequently moved to St. Louis with his family to do class work for the doctorate in sociology, knowing that this time his dissertation would have the necessary support. It would address the needs of the Spanish-speaking community of Colorado.

Indeed, Don Julian did return to Colorado in 1952 to resume his teaching duties at Adams State in Alamosa as a tenured professor,[14] and he conducted his doctoral fieldwork in Del Norte, where Watson and his students had already completed a number of studies. The small town of Del Norte, Colorado, was first settled by Spanish-speaking families in 1859 although the town was not incorporated until 1872. By that time, the local population included many Anglos attracted by gold prospecting in the nearby San Juan Mountains,[15] and Julian characterized the research problem as follows:

> In the historical development of Mountain Town, certain patterns of adjustment between the two parts of the population have occurred which can be described as dominant-subordinate relationships. The Anglo part of the population occupies the dominant position and the Spanish part of the population occupies the subordinate. The culture, in practically every aspect of behavior, reinforces these positions. One need only consider the educational system or the economic system or the political system to see how forcefully this is so. In spite of the

numerical superiority of the Spanish people of Mountain Town, they occupy
the subordinate position in the general culture and even in those areas where
numbers count, namely politics.[16]

For his dissertation, Julian returned to problems he observed while he
worked at the San Luis Institute. He understood firsthand the limitations and
potential of minority leadership in a small bicultural town such as San Luis,
and in his dissertation he sought to understand it in a nearby small town
to generate original research pertinent to Mexican American communities.
However, Julian must have appreciated the politics of academic investigations; his dissertation advisor at Washington University, faculty member
Stuart A. Queen,[17] was no less than a former president of the American
Sociological Association. Moreover, Queen's approach to research must
have appealed to Julian. Queen's long trajectory in social work and community studies work eventually brought him to a position in Washington
University's Department of Sociology.

Julian used a theoretical framework derived from George C. Homans,[18]
generally considered to be the founder of social exchange theory, to study
leaders and leadership in Del Norte, and specifically how Mexican American
leaders emerged and related to their community as well as to the Anglo.
Julian and his family lived in Del Norte for several months on two occasions to study the Spanish-speaking population, Anglo civic and business
leaders, and organizations in the Spanish-speaking community. Betty, his
wife, was particularly instrumental in generating information about women
and church groups.

Samora concluded that:

> The dominant system, therefore, very effectively siphons off the only possible
> inter-ethnic leadership, without fully accepting it, and the subordinate group
> feels that there is no leadership. . . . They do render favors and provide counsel,
> but only on an individual basis.[19]

It should be noted that Samora's dissertation bibliography contained only
one citation authored by a Mexican American, namely George Sánchez.
Of forty-two items listed in the bibliography, only ten treated Mexican
Americans specifically. Only one entry studied Mexican American leadership; Sánchez wrote a two-page article published in 1950 by the Southwest
Council on the Education of Spanish-Speaking People about "The Default
of Leadership."[20] Julian's dissertation was the first academic research conducted on the question of leadership in the Spanish-speaking community
and its relationship to the Anglo-dominated system.

Julian's Washington University circle yielded two articles. First, in 1954,

Samora co-authored an article with James B. Watson titled "Subordinate Leadership in a Bi-cultural Community: An Analysis" in the prestigious *American Journal of Sociology*. Based on research done by Watson, Samora, and other Washington University students, the article is still widely recognized as a major contribution and has since been reprinted at least twice in later compilations for students of sociology and Mexican American Studies.[21] Although the original data included in the dissertation was much broader, this article derives from four main suppositions. In Samora's words,

> The Hypothesis Of Leader Deficiency
>
> It is the contention of this paper that four principal conditions account for the inadequacy of Spanish leadership in Mountain Town and probably to some extent among the Spanish of the larger Southwest.
>
> 1. Traditional forms (patterns) of leadership, which functioned well enough in pre-Anglo-Spanish culture, have been unadaptable and possibly a handicap to the development of adequate patterns of group leadership in the contact situation.
> 2. Increasingly, the status goals of the Spanish group as a whole lies in the direction of Anglo culture; for the achievement of such goals, hence, leaders relatively well adapted to the Anglo system are increasingly indicated.
> 3. General ambivalence and suspicion are accorded individuals of Spanish background who are "successful" since the terms of success are now largely Anglo terms (viz. 2., above), and it is widely assumed that success is bought by cooperation with the outgroup and betrayal of one's own.
> 4. Although caste-like enough to give sharp definition to the two groups, Anglo structure is relatively open to competent Spanish and thus permits the siphoning off of potential Spanish leadership, individuals relatively well adapted to the Anglo system.
>
> The net result of these conditions is that, in the lack of adaptable traditional types, the only potential leaders who might be qualified to provide the kind of leadership indicated today are by virtue of their very qualifications absorbed into the larger body politic and are disqualified in the minds of their own fellows.[22]

Julian's interest and research in leadership led him to conclude that "deficient leadership" in the Spanish-speaking community originated in the dominant-subordinate system in which *barrios* were imbedded.

Samora's work at Adams State and particularly at the San Luis Institute, as well as his experiences in the community (including research for both the master's and PhD), provided him the viewpoint to observe the nature and limitations of leadership in the Spanish-speaking population and the evolution of relations between the majority and the minority. Samora also perceived the potential that more effective leaders and leadership would have in the community; this is a theme he pursued until his retirement thirty years later.

Dr. Samora's First Years as a Doctorate in the Academy: 1954 to 1962

By the mid-1950s Don Julian moved with more confidence, ease, and energy into the academic community in the United States beyond Colorado. His decade of teaching, research, organizing, and administrative experience accrued through his years at Adams State College had garnered him a reputation throughout the Southwest. As our examination of his career unfolds, it will be apparent that Julian's vision as an academic, his recognition that the Spanish-speaking population of Colorado and New Mexico had been severely underserved by the institutions of higher learning, and his efforts to facilitate Spanish-speaking civic organizations combined to make him an agent of change within and beyond the academy. During his years at Adams State and San Luis, he formed a number of professional relationships and collaborations that over time would produce important research, promote the study of Mexican Americans, and open opportunities for him.

The prestigious journal *Sociology and Social Research* published the second article emerging from his Washington University circle. Samora co-authored an article with William N. Deane to explore elements of sociolinguistics as applied to Mexican Americans and other ethnic groups in the United States. A colleague Samora met in the doctoral program at Washington University, William Deane took Samora's place at Adams State for the two years Samora was in St. Louis. Deane finally left Adams State in 1954 for the state of Washington, but in 1955 he and Samora published an article in *Sociology and Social Research*, then edited by immigration scholar Emory Bogardus.[23] Titled "Language Usage as a Possible Index of Acculturation," the authors proposed that "language usage, in a culture-center situation, is an excellent measure of acculturation." Although relatively short and actually more of a methodological note, the essay asserted first that patterns of language usage reflect personal psychological orientation of individuals and their perception of their place in their environment. The authors then proceeded to analyze several possible levels of conscious and subconscious language usage among ethnic minorities, using data generated by instruments prepared in the interviewee's preferred language. This approach to studying the relationship between language usage and acculturation was presented in the context of other countries, without specific references to individuals or groups in the United States. However, Dr. Samora drew on research he did for both his master's and doctoral theses, and his work as administrator in San Luis reinforced his conclusions.

Although his professional activities of that period always centered on Mexican Americans of the Southwest, Julian explored various opportunities and academic approaches until he found the approach to Mexican American Studies that enabled him to direct his efforts most effectively. He was eager to explore whatever promising field of inquiry that would be conducive to generating knowledge about Mexican Americans. While Dr. Samora was active early in his career in rural sociology, sociolinguistics, and Latin American Studies, I will concentrate on the new field of medical sociology and the rapidly evolving disciplines of U.S.-Mexican Border Studies, since they led most directly to Mexican American Studies and his tenure at Notre Dame.

Medical Sociology

From the moment he graduated from Adams State in 1942, Julian enthusiastically searched for researchers and publications relevant to the Spanish-speaking population, particularly the community in Colorado. His position as professor at Adams State bestowed him with enough prestige in the community to promote networking, discuss problems, and encourage leadership, and his correspondence shows that he took every opportunity he could to make that research accessible and available to the community. In the mid-1950s, Julian became involved in the Colorado Latin American Conference and was the organizer for the 1954 annual conference. The conference always attracted professional and activist members of the Spanish-speaking community, and the annual conferences provided a statewide venue to discuss a plethora of issues facing Mexican Americans in Colorado. Julian's organizing skills were evident in the annual conference held in Walsenburg on April 23–25, 1954, as he invited experts from Colorado, but also Tomás Weaver from New York.[24] His correspondence in the 1950s shows a committed young academic working in an isolated environment but trying to collect serious research about the Spanish-speaking community of Colorado to make it accessible to students and other academics.

One professional inquiry that Samora initiated in the 1940s blossomed into an important professional collaboration and friendship. Julian contacted Lyle Saunders, a regionally recognized sociologist working as a research associate at the School of Inter-American Affairs at the University of New Mexico in Albuquerque, who was publishing at that time about the Spanish-speaking community of New Mexico and Colorado. Although Saunders is not widely recognized today, his research and advocacy was pivotal in Colorado and New Mexico in the 1940s and 1950s for generating academic work about Mexican Americans. The Samora-Saunders collaboration led to a long, productive intellectual relationship that spanned several decades and places; the correspondence they exchanged over twenty years reflects mutual admiration, shared interests, and a lively personal rapport.

In fact, as early as 1944 Saunders mailed Samora published materials about the Spanish-speaking formally requested by Samora. By 1949 Samora and he were on a first-name basis. Saunders was enthusiastic about Julian's pursuing a doctorate and urged him to do his dissertation on the "Texas Study" he was doing with George Sánchez, and he encouraged him and Sánchez to sign onto the multiyear multidisciplinary study.[25]

It is interesting to note that in July of 1949 Saunders was already looking for ways to study undocumented immigration from Mexico. Saunders wrote Samora that Sánchez and he were "thinking tentatively about an intensive study of the wetback situation,"[26] a topic that Julian would address many years later in *Los Mojados*.

Early in 1952, Saunders moved to Denver to become perhaps the first sociologist to work at a medical school. His contribution to the University of Colorado School of Medicine in Denver made him a pioneering social scientist. In 1954, Saunders wrote in *Cultural Difference and Medical Care*[27] that cultural differences played a critical role in the delivery of medical services. Indeed, Saunders tried to convince Samora that he should design his doctoral research to be compatible with his own project on the cultural dimension of the delivery of medical services and the Russell Sage Foundation's interest in community leadership, because funding would be almost guaranteed. Samora quickly responded that he would be interested.[28] In April and May of 1952, Julian and Lyle exchanged ideas about using the failure of a health cooperative in San Luis where Julian had been interested in local community leadership and the delivery of services; the model for the San Luis health cooperative was based partly on the success of the Taos County Health Cooperative in New Mexico. If a health cooperative had worked in New Mexico, Lyle and Julian wondered why it did not in Costilla County. Julian received support from Washington University through approval from Watson, who thought it an interesting case, and so by the summer Julian was doing research in Del Norte, Costilla County, in collaboration with Saunders. Lyle paid Julian for life histories, an analysis of the problems of the Costilla County Health Cooperative, and details of "healing ways," or local folk medicine. Saunders thought that widespread distrust of the American mainstream medical profession may have caused the failure of the health cooperative.[29] This research was conducted at the same time as that for his dissertation and probably overlapped, but Samora does not acknowledge either Saunders or the Russell Sage Foundation.

Saunders also had contact with Benjamin Paul, then professor of anthropology at Harvard University and considered to be the founder of medical anthropology, to do an article on the Costilla County Health Cooperative for a book he was editing. Although Julian actually wrote most of the article, he treated Saunders as a co-author and they shared the honorarium. By the end of November of 1953, Julian had a good first draft (Lyle's words),[30] and by March of 1954, Paul was pleased with the article.[31] Titled "A Medical Care Program in a Colorado Community," the article was published in a seminal anthology of medical sociology-anthropology, *Health, Culture and Community,* edited by Benjamin Paul.[32] It focused on the delivery of medical services in the cultural context of a Spanish-speaking community in southern Colorado. The study assessed problems and obstacles encountered in establishing a cooperative health care program in 1946 in a Mexican American community in Colorado. Samora and Saunders used the brief life of the association's board of directors to explore the problems of meeting the medical needs of the local Mexican American community and to suggest guidelines and recommendations for successful implementation of future programs. The article recognized the cultural isolation and the identity of Mexican Americans, described the relations between Anglos and Mexican Americans, and indicated that although Anglo medicine had been introduced as early as 1887, it supplemented rather than replaced traditional folk medicine. Further, the researchers identified variables related to the delivery of medical services that were significant in the particular case they studied. For example, individuals who were instrumental in developing and chartering the organization were Anglos and others from outside the community and often associated with large bureaucracies. Moreover, Samora and Saunders opined that such an organization was not compatible with local Mexican American culture, and often openly antagonistic. Traditional regional folk healing had been direct and personal and partially dependent on a longstanding relationship with a practitioner, whereas the new health care organization bureaucratically and impersonally delegated tasks and procedures related to health care. This particular analysis fell within medical sociology, but can also be considered applied sociology within the general framework of rural sociology.

Julian and Lyle accepted an invitation from the president of Fisk University in Nashville to participate in the Eleventh Annual Institute of Race Relations the summer of 1954 and speak about the Spanish-speaking minority in the Southwest. They exchanged much correspondence in preparation for the session, "Social and Cultural Integration in the Southwest," and settled on a general introduction for Lyle and a specific study on leadership for Julian. Lyle was looking forward to flying his plane to Nashville. Julian later complained that Fisk was not prompt in paying their expenses and honorarium.[33]

Simultaneously, Julian and Lyle actively explored several additional proposals to address medical service delivery problems in Costilla County. One leaned in the direction of development of a three-year study of an experimental project of interest to the Colorado State Department of Health; although it was ultimately rejected, the proposal was submitted to the Commonwealth Fund by the department. Another moved toward designing a project together with the Colorado League of Nursing to study the attitudes of medical personnel.[34] Their mutual interest was generated by academic research but also by a desire to improve the delivery of medical services in Costilla County.

The degree of confidence and trust that Julian and Lyle developed by the mid-1950s was evident in an invitation in November 1954 from Lyle for Julian to accept a position at the medical school in Denver. Saunders had already spoken with the Russell Sage Foundation about a research project that would finance a position for Julian for two years. Julian responded that he was flattered but felt inadequate. Saunders reassured Julian and seemed to make every effort to optimize the working conditions for him, maximize the salary, and make the research interesting.[35]

Samora collected data in clinics about the cultural context of the delivery of medical services. Based on his work at the medical school in Denver, in 1960 Samora published the article "The Social Scientist as Researcher and Teacher in the Medical School," in which he discussed the multidimensional role played by social scientists in the world of medicine. Based on his experience, Samora argued that the function of the "medical school social scientist" was twofold: that of teacher-interpreter to the medical profession and the larger academic world, and that of exploring the social and cultural implications of the practice of medicine through primary research. Physicians had never been trained to fully understand the social complexities of the profession until the 1960s. Samora immediately recognized the potential of a medical sociological paradigm for bridging the gap between physicians and patients, especially in terms of cultural implications. More concretely, Samora suggested special research areas in the still new discipline of medical sociology as a point of departure for further academic investigation and as a vehicle to challenge his colleagues in the social sciences, in the process outlining new research agendas. He proposed researching the implications of traditional folk medicine for modern clinical medicine, exploring the correlation between the patient's socioeconomic status and the medical care he or she receives, and probing the complex relationship between ethnicity and the delivery of health services. Viewed many years after its publication, the recommendations seem obvious and subdued, but Samora was among the first scholars to suggest the importance of examining these issues.

The new and burgeoning field of medical sociology permitted Samora to systematically examine many issues of immediate concern to Mexican Americans' well-being in the 1950s. Local public services, attitudes of the medical profession, and availability of health care were paramount to rural Spanish-speaking communities at the time. Julian later published another article in 1961, "Medical Vocabulary Knowledge," co-authored with Lyle and R. F. Larson in *Journal of Health and Human Behavior.*[36]

U.S.-Mexico Border Studies

Ironically, U.S.-Mexico Border Studies at Michigan State University, thousands of miles distant from the U.S.-Mexico border, opened the path for Dr. Samora to join the Notre Dame community. By the time Samora received his doctorate in 1953, colleagues interested in the Southwest had already recognized Julian as an academic with a future, and he attracted the attention of researchers interested in the Southwest. One of them was Charles Loomis of MSU. A national academic figure, Loomis invited Julian in January 1955 to teach a course in the summer school at Michigan State University, as an introduction to his border studies network. This large interdisciplinary group of researchers was based in Michigan, but it included participants from all over the Southwest and realized several innovative multifaceted research projects about the border region. Julian happily accepted the invitation to teach a course and said he would "certainly be interested in working on the committee concerned with the U.S.-Mexican border project."[37] Loomis's Border Studies Project, financed by the Carnegie Foundation, addressed research questions about the binational U.S.-Mexico border that would lead to what we know today as U.S.-Mexico Border Studies. Not only did they study isolated phenomenon but researchers initiated studies about binational and cross-cultural aspects of the border region that illustrated what Loomis coined "linkages." Loomis integrated his recognition that the U.S.-Mexico border was not merely a geopolitical line but a vibrant and dynamic binational region that presented many opportunities to understand a tangible multidimensional encounter of two societies. However, according to Loomis's own recollections, he felt that U.S-Mexican Border Studies had not incorporated one key aspect, the Mexican-origin population. In fact, a long academic tradition attested to research interest in the region, but almost no attention had been paid to the most important ethnic group in the region, Mexican Americans.

Loomis must have been pleased with Julian's collaboration at MSU because on November 14, 1955, he offered Samora a full-time permanent position as a faculty member in the Sociology and Anthropology Department. Julian nonetheless countered that although he was "overwhelmed" with the offer, he thought his eleven years of college teaching experience would justify a position of associate professor, that is, with tenure. Samora must have accepted the position since Loomis wrote not a week later that he was happy at the prospect of his becoming part of the MSU community.[38] The correspondence does not specify the date Samora would join the Sociology and Anthropology Department, and Julian delayed moving to Michigan.

Samora received financial support through the border studies network and submitted reports to Loomis through 1956 describing his activities. In April, Samora toured the border region and touched base with many members of the Loomis research group, from border health officials in Calexico, to Julius Rivera in Sonoyta, Sonora; Frank Nall in Ciudad Juarez–El Paso; Paul Walter in Albuquerque, etc. In Sonoyta, Julian vaccinated thirty-nine of forty prostitutes as a vehicle to collect socioeconomic data about them. Julian remarks that binational differences between two sides of the border vary greatly, that Ciudad Juarez and El Paso are much more similar than are Mexicali and Calexico.[39]

Loomis's campaign to physically bring Julian to MSU continued through 1956. A growing interest in "change and acculturation" in Spanish-speaking people from Mexico was a hallmark of Loomis's research priorities.[40] At least as early as April of 1956, Loomis was looking to finance a study by Samora and Lyle Saunders of the "wetback and alambrista" phenomenon.[41] We should note that the Samora papers show that while Saunders was not greatly impressed by Loomis, he was supportive of his invitation to Julian to join the MSU faculty.

Indeed, joining the MSU border studies network formed professional associations that brought Samora to the University of Notre Dame. William D'Antonio, also a collaborator in Loomis's border studies group and an assistant professor at MSU, was brought to Notre Dame's Sociology Department at the same time. Saunders thought Notre Dame would be a fine option for Julian; in Lyle's words, "It would be good to get out from under Michigan State."[42] Lyle provided a letter of recommendation for Notre Dame, Julian had his interview at Notre Dame on April, 20, 1959, and by the end of the month he had already been offered a position. Julian accepted, beginning his twenty-five-year tenure at Notre Dame in 1959.

Soon after beginning their positions at Notre Dame, D'Antonio and Samora used data generated by the MSU border studies network to co-author an article, published in *Social Forum* in October 1962. Titled "Occupational

Stratification in Four Southwest Communities: A Study of Ethnic Differential Employment in Hospitals," the perspective and content of the articles foreshadowed his work in the sociology of Mexican immigration to and within the United States, the historical significance and contribution of Mexican labor to the creation of wealth in the United States, the increasing urbanization of the Mexican American population, and the promotion of Chicano Studies.

Data for the analysis was extracted from the Anglo-Latino Relations in Hospitals and Communities Project, and the context of the research and discussion readily provided an opportunity to fit many disparate threads of research together into a broader, more inclusive statement. The study proposed to examine the employment patterns in hospital settings. The authors then developed a comparative study of Mexican American employment in hospitals in four Southwestern cities—San Diego, El Paso, Tucson, and Las Cruces—and Italian Americans in New Haven, Connecticut. The authors examined professional, semiskilled, and unskilled categories, as well as administrative and voluntary positions on the Boards of Directors as a basis for comparison and evaluating their relative position with the hospital and the community. However, Julian's appreciation of the importance of hospital settings originated with his forays into medical sociology and his collaboration with Lyle Saunders.

Most importantly, the article discussed its findings and conclusions in terms of the unique relationship of the Mexican-origin community to the American Southwest. Samora and D'Antonio drew upon the unique historical legacy of Mexican Americans in the Southwest, the distinctive character of Mexican immigration to the United States, and the contribution of Mexican American and Mexican immigrant labor to regional industrial development, e.g., railroads, mining, and lumbering. The authors also analyzed the successive generations of Mexican Americans, distinguishing between descendants of the first Spanish settlers of the region, the Mexican American culture of the Southwest, and recently arrived Mexican immigrants. Further, Samora and D'Antonio pointed to the increasing urbanization of the Mexican-origin community already noticeable in the 1950s, but about which few observers had commented in 1962. Finally, Samora and D'Antonio firmly decried the paucity of academic research addressing issues relevant to the Mexican American community.

Samora's professional interests and research after the 1962 *Social Forum* article became even more focused on efforts to research the Mexican American population and to make the dominant Anglo society aware of the national importance of the Mexican-origin community. At the same time,

Samora sought a vehicle at Notre Dame to empower Mexican Americans through education.

By that time, Julian had also completed a report contracted by the U.S. Civil Rights Commission on the Spanish-speaking population that would provide background information to assist the commission in executing its statutory obligation to determine the nature and extent of civil rights transgressions. Dr. Samora deliberately submitted to the Civil Rights Commission a more inclusive document on the national Spanish-speaking population than was stipulated in the contract, a report that reflected the needs of the population as much as it addressed the requirements of the commission. Based on the 1960 census data and secondary literature available at the time, the project yielded a report with a much broader perspective than the commission had originally anticipated, and indeed may represent one of the first attempts to describe and analyze the richness and diversity of Spanish-speaking people in a national context. "The Spanish Speaking People in the United States" addresses many dimensions of the groups' dynamics—group labeling, the unique historical background of the Spanish-speaking people, legal and undocumented migrations, relationships with the dominant Anglo community, vestiges of traditional folk culture, a broad demographic description and analysis, as well as an examination of inequality of opportunity. Moreover, the discussion included consideration of Puerto Ricans and other Spanish-speaking groups as well as Mexican Americans. Samora also included a separate section on the impact of migrant labor on Spanish-speaking peoples. Finally, Samora concluded the report with a number of recommendations, among which are the establishment of a national agency to advocate for Spanish-speaking peoples and oversee the various research priorities that would address the needs of the Spanish-speaking people. Although the early years of Samora's career were grounded in Colorado, by 1960 his vision had come to consider the Spanish-speaking population as a national minority group. Samora's 1960 civil rights report may well be one of the first studies to consider Spanish-speaking people as an important national minority whose points of commonality sometimes transcend group boundaries.

The University of Notre Dame

From 1963 to 1965, Julian was nominated for chair of the Department of Sociology and Anthropology at Notre Dame. Around that time, Julian worked with the Rosenberg Foundation in San Francisco to plan a conference about the needs and problems of Mexican Americans, which would result in the publication of an edited volume about the community.[43] *La Raza: Forgotten Americans,* edited by Julian and financed by the Rosenberg Foundation, was published in 1966 by the University of Notre Dame Press and inaugurated what became one of the most important publications series on Mexican Americans. Samora included authors already recognized for their work on Mexican Americans—Lawrence Glick, Herman Gallegos, George I. Sánchez, Lyle Saunders, and others—to assess spirituality, history, farm workers, and other concerns. While some of the data is now dated, the approach and analysis found in the essays is still valid. Julian's work as editor of *La Raza: Forgotten Americans,* one of the first compilations of original academic essays about Mexican Americans, marked a new phase in his career, as an academic entrepreneur and a visionary of what today we call Mexican American Studies.

The publication of *La Raza* marked the point in his career when Julian became a nationally recognized scholar in Mexican American Studies, although the term did not yet exist. He continued to include what he had learned in medical sociology, U.S.-Mexican Border Studies, and other fields, but after 1966 he openly focused on developing Mexican American Studies as a field of inquiry, keeping in mind that his work in the academy could and already had affected policy. Even though a conservative university such as Notre Dame was not always open to new disciplines, the stability and visibility of his position bestowed on him a prestige he parlayed into proposals, research, and funding. By the late 1960s, the threads of his career integrated to form one goal—Mexican American Studies.

Notes

I am happy to have the opportunity to thank both the Universidad Nacional Autónoma de México of Mexico City and the University of Texas at Austin for financing a two-week stay at the Nettie Lee Benson Library where I had access to Dr. Samora's papers.

1. A title of respect and admiration for a person from the Latino community and usually ascribed to community elders.

2. Barbara A. Driscoll de Alvarado, 1993. *La Frontera and Its People: The Early Development of Border and Mexican-American Studies,* Working Paper #17 (East Lansing: Julian Samora Research Institute, 1993, hereafter cited as Driscoll de Alvarado 1993).

3. Julian Samora Papers, Nettie Lee Benson Library, University of Texas at Austin, Adams State Correspondence, hereafter cited as Samora Papers. Ira Richardson to Julian Samora, July 5, 1944, and August 1, 1944. Julian sent his resignation to Adams

State president Fred Plachy, March 31, 1956. Although the San Luis Institute closed in the late 1950s, the building contains a museum that recognizes the accomplishments of the institution.

4. http://www2.adams.edu./about/asc_history.pdf.

5. Samora Papers, Folder Colorado State Division of Public Health, Correspondence 1946–1953. Most letters are correspondence between Samora and various public health nurses regarding the delivery and administration of immunizations, but one letter documents Samora's activities as the chairman of the Costilla County Health Association to pressure for a physician.

6. Samora Papers, Folder Colorado State University. Data taken from a copy of Samora's application to CSU. Another letter indicates that Samora's tuition was covered by a grant from CSU and the Institute of International Education.

7. Samora Papers, Folder Adams State College, Ira Richardson to Julian Samora, April 16, 1946.

8. Samora Papers, Julian Samora, "The Acculturation of the Spanish Speaking People of Fort Collins, Colorado in Selected Culture Areas" (unpublished master's thesis, Department of History, Agriculture and Sociology, Agricultural and Mechanical College, Fort Collins, Colorado, August 1947, p. 16. Copy available at Colorado State University Library. Hereafter cited as Samora, master's thesis).

9. Samora cites Clark Wissler, *Man and Culture* (New York: Thomas Y. Crowell, 1923).

10. Samora, master's thesis, pp. 30 and 32.

11. Samora Papers, Folder Adams State College, Ira Richardson to Julian Samora, January 1, 1949. Richardson to Julian Samora, June 10, 1949.

12. Julian Samora to Ira Richardson, no date, but appears to be the spring of 1950.

13. In the 1950s, Watson was a quickly rising young anthropologist who was already considered a leading scholar of cultural change. In 1972, he co-edited the widely used tome *Crossing Cultural Boundaries*.

14. Samora Papers, Folder Adams State College, E. Bean, acting president, Adams State College, to Julian Samora, June 30, 1952.

15. For additional information about Del Norte, please consult the website of the Del Norte Chamber of Commerce, http://www.delnortechamber.org/.

16. Julian Samora, "Minority Leadership in a Bi-Cultural Community" (PhD thesis, Washington University, 1953, hereafter cited as Samora, PhD thesis). Also, James Watson and Julian Samora, 1954, "Subordinate Leadership in a Bi-cultural Community: An Analysis," *American Journal of Sociology* 19(4): 413–21. Electronic publication at http://www.jstor.org. Reprinted in George H. Conklin, *Sociology: An Introduction* (Bobbs-Merrill Reprints in Social Science); and F. Chris García, *La Causa Política: A Chicano Politics Reader* (Notre Dame, Ind.: University of Notre Dame Press, 1974), p. 12. Hereafter cited as Watson, Samora.

17. Please see the website of the American Sociological Association for information about former president Stuart Queen.

18. Samora used Homans' approach to leadership in his widely cited study titled *The Human Group,* published in 1950.

19. Samora, PhD thesis, p. 100.

20. George I. Sánchez, "The Default of Leadership" (Albuquerque, N.M.: Summarized Proceedings of the Southwest Council on the Education of the Spanish-Speaking People, 1950).

21. Watson, Samora.

22. Watson, Samora, p. 417.

23. Samora Papers, Folder Correspondence with Wm. N. Deane, 1950–1963, William Deane to Julian Samora, October 11, 1953.

24. Samora Papers, Folder Colorado Latin American Conference, Correspondence, 1952–1957.

25. Saunders was contracted by George I. Sánchez to gather the data for the *Emphasis Study of the Spanish-Speaking People of Texas,* the multiyear, socioeconomic study that aimed to fill substantial gaps in the data then available about the expanding Spanish-speaking population of Texas. Sánchez and Saunders hoped to educate public officials, bureaucrats, and other powerful and influential Texans, as well as the general public. Please see Box 32, folders 4–10 of the George I. Sánchez Papers, Benson Latin American Collection, University Libraries, The University of Texas at Austin.

26. Samora Papers, Folder Lyle Saunders, 1944–1953, Lyle Saunders (while he was working from the University of Texas) to Julian Samora in Colorado, July 7, 1949.

27. Published by Russell Sage Foundation, 1954.

28. Samora Papers, Folder Lyle Saunders, 1944–1953, Lyle Saunders at School of Medicine, CU, Denver, to Julian Samora in Del Norte, Colorado, March 22, 1952. Julian Samora to Lyle Saunders, March 25, 1952.

29. Samora Papers, Folder Lyle Saunders, 1944–1953, Samora to Lyle Saunders, September 8, 1952. Lyle Saunders to Julian Samora, September 18, 1952.

30. Samora Papers, Folder Lyle Saunders, 1944–1953, Lyle Saunders to Julian Samora, November 30, 1953.

31. Samora Papers, Folder Lyle Saunders, 1944–1953, Lyle Saunders to Julian Samora, March 18, 1954.

32. J. Samora and L. Saunders, "A Medical Care Program in a Colorado Community," in *Health, Culture, and Community,* ed. Benjamin Paul (New York: Russell Sage Foundation, 1955). The book is still in use.

33. Correspondence for the Fisk University visit can be found in Samora Papers, Folder Lyle Saunders, 1954–1955.

34. See Samora Papers, Folder Lyle Saunders, 1954–1955.

35. Communication between Lyle and Julian that led to the appointment to the medical school is included in the Samora Papers, Folder Lyle Saunders, 1954–1955. The agreed salary for Julian was $6,000 a year.

36. J. Samora, L. Saunders, and R. F. Larson, 1961. "Medical Vocabulary Knowledge," *Journal of Health and Human Behavior,* vol. 2.

37. Samora Papers, Folder Charles P. Loomis, 1955–1956, Charles P. Loomis to Julian Samora, January 17, 1955, and Julian Samora to Charles P. Loomis, January 20, 1955.

38. Samora Papers, Folder Charles P. Loomis, 1955–1956, Charles P. Loomis to Julian Samora, November 14, 1955. Julian Samora to Charles P. Loomis, November 23, 1955. Charles P. Loomis to Julian Samora, November 30, 1955.

39. Samora Papers, Folder Charles P. Loomis, 1955–1956, Julian Samora in Denver to Charles P. Loomis in East Lansing, April 24, 1956.

40. Samora Papers, Folder Charles P. Loomis, 1955–1956, Charles P. Loomis to Julian Samora, December 6, 1956.

41. Samora Papers, Folder Charles P. Loomis, 1955–1956, Charles P. Loomis to Julian Samora, April 9, 1956.

42. Samora Papers, Folder Lyle Saunders, 1957–1959, Lyle Saunders to Julian Samora, March 31, 1959. Lyle later in the year writes to Julian that MSU should be learning its lesson, since many are leaving the university.

43. Driscoll de Alvarado 1993, p. 56.

CHAPTER THREE

Philanthropy, the Creation of a National Minority and the Mexican American Graduate Studies Program at Notre Dame

Alberto López Pulido

> The Spanish-speaking people of this country have never yet been able to mount a sustained, concerted national drive for an improvement of their status.
>
> —JULIAN SAMORA

With this quote we read one of the most important themes in the first comprehensive study of Mexican Americans. These are the words of Julian Samora written more than forty years ago in his edited volume *La Raza: Forgotten Americans*. Contrary to recent assertions by Telles and Ortiz that *The Mexican American People* was the first critical study on Mexican Americans in the history of the United States, Samora's *La Raza*, published in 1966, is the first of its kind to provide an all-inclusive introduction, presentation, and assessment of educational, religious, political, migratory, and demographic issues for Mexican Americans in the southwestern United States.[1] Concentrating on this "minority population" located in California, Texas, New Mexico, Arizona, and Colorado, *La Raza* provides a comparative perspective of Mexican Americans in the early 1960s that utilized a multispatial analysis of numerous Mexican American communities within major cities in the Southwest. Julian Samora was clear in intellectually coalescing the "Mexican American minority" that up to that point were understood as disparate local and regional communities without a comprehensive national identity or vision. In this pioneering study, Samora was quick to identify Mexican Americans as the "largest ethnic group in the Southwest and among the largest minorities in the United States."[2] Despite being exploited and living on the fringes of society, "misunderstood by public and private agencies, and largely ignored by federal government and programs," the Mexican American population "managed to survive with dignity, composure and pride."[3] For Samora, it was imperative that they establish broad structures, strong organizations, leadership, and resources to pursue a national agenda. He was clear that the future of the Mexican American population would require careful research and analysis of historical, demographic, im/migration, leadership, educational, agricultural, labor, politics, and language issues to completely understand and empower these "Forgotten Americans."

In the early 1950s, Herman Gallegos, along with Cesar Chavez and Saul Alinsky's Industrial Areas Foundation, was successful in organizing the Community Service Organization in East San Jose, California, an area then called Sal Si Puedes. In 1958 Gallegos graduated from the University of California Berkeley and moved to San Bernardino County in California to work for a Rosenberg Foundation–supported project. It was then that Gallegos met Ruth Chance, executive director of the Rosenberg Foundation. Two years later, Gallegos would move to San Francisco and would meet frequently with Chance to discuss possible grant making with Mexican American nonprofit organizations. In 1964, Dr. Chance came to Gallegos with a request for him to identify a scholar who could organize a symposium on Mexican American issues. Mr. Gallegos immediately recommended Julian Samora because of his impressive reputation. Like Gallegos, Samora had been a John Hay Whitney Foundation Opportunity Fellow in the mid-1950s and was well-recognized and respected as a professor of sociology at the University of Notre Dame.[4] This symposium project was to honor the late Charles de Young Elkus, who served as the architect and pioneer of the Rosenberg Foundation for twenty-five years. The idea was for the foundation to undertake a memorial that would contribute to the future of one of the social movements Elkus had experienced great interest in during his tenure with Rosenberg. At the top of his list were the American Indian and Mexican American communities.

As the first comprehensive analysis on Mexican Americans in the United States, the symposium's deliberations would be transcribed into the *La Raza* publication. Along with Herman Gallegos, Ernesto Galarza would be invited to this historic gathering and would meet Julian Samora for the first time. It would mark the beginning of a long professional relationship and, as a result of Samora's influence, the publication of Galarza's important works on Mexican immigration and the Bracero Program through the University of Notre Dame Press.[5] In addition, Ruth Chance would invite Paul Ylvisaker, vice president for national affairs for the Ford Foundation, to attend this historic symposium on Mexican Americans. During his tenure with Ford, Ylvisaker was responsible for developing the greatest private philanthropic initiative to transform public policy, known as the Grey Area Program. Managing the program that would become the blueprint for the federal War on Poverty program during the Kennedy and Johnson administrations, Ylvisaker supervised more than $200 million in grants to assist the urban underclass of U.S. cities.[6] Consequently, taken in by the topics and impressed with the high level of intellectual engagement at the symposium, Ylvisaker invited Samora, Galarza, and Gallegos to serve as consultants to the Ford Foundation.[7]

The same year *La Raza* was published, Ernesto Galarza, Herman Gallegos, and Julian Samora were appointed by the Ford Foundation to serve as consultants and make recommendations regarding foundation projects relating to organizational, economic, and social issues regarding Mexican American communities in the United States.[8] The Samora, Galarza, and Gallegos consultant team submitted a report that contained a detailed presentation and analysis of the evolution of Mexican American communities and their related problems. The vision of these three consultants was to directly address problems of poverty, unemployment, political participation, the border, education, language, housing, urban renewal, and agricultural labor. They emphasized the longstanding tradition within Mexican American communities to establish and seek out organizational efforts, such as, for example, the *mutualista* tradition (mutual aid societies).

Their comprehensive report was published three years later under the title of *Mexican Americans in the Southwest.*[9] It examined Mexican American issues from a macro perspective and drew comparisons between various Mexican American communities throughout the Southwest. This represented a methodology that had begun with the research from the symposium and subsequent publication of *La Raza: Forgotten Americans.* This consultant work set in motion the foundational work for an emerging civil rights agenda for Mexican American urban communities, as issues of racial and ethnic inequality were emphasized with an eye toward social change. With guidance from the consultant team and other Mexican American leaders, the Ford Foundation responded to this report by encouraging the consultants to develop their specific program objectives and programs to empower Mexican American communities.

Southwest Council of La Raza

At the September 1967 meeting of the Board of Trustees, the foundation agreed to support Mexican American organizational activities, which resulted in the establishment of a Mexican American committee made up of Rev. Miguel F. Barragan, Henry Santiestevan, Bernardo Valdez, and Alex Mecure. This committee was to serve as a major "spokesman and enabler for Mexican Americans in the five southwestern states" and was the precursor to the National Council of La Raza that began initially as the Southwest Council of La Raza.[10]

It is critical to underscore the significance of this historical development that had been in process for two years. First, the plight of Mexican Americans became a national issue. Second, it began a conversation on Mexican American issues in which Mexican American issues in different U.S. cities were compared in search of patterns, similarities, and differences. Third and most importantly, it brought forth a scholarly and intellectual construction of an emerging ethnic minority group that scholars, community leaders, and lawmakers had to contend with. In sum, the social and political idea of Mexican Americans as a prominent minority group on a national scale was born.

In June 1968, the Southwest Council of La Raza received a one-year, $630,000 grant from the Ford Foundation to establish a regional council of Mexican Americans and support local action groups. The Ford monies were used for operating expenses of the Southwest Council of La Raza and to set up and fund local boards in San Francisco, Los Angeles, and San Antonio. The major function of the Southwest Council of La Raza would be to give "greater coherence to Mexican American activities, to deepen a sense of issues and priorities, and to develop leadership capabilities to both the regional and local levels." The council sought to link Mexican American leaders and provide a forum for analysis of issues, enabling Mexican American communities to move jointly on issues affecting Mexican Americans as a whole.[11]

A board was established within San Francisco, Los Angeles, and San Antonio that provided technical assistance to community groups, provided leadership development programs, and made small grants to aid the activities of local groups. This board would work to enhance the efforts of Mexican

American communities to obtain available government funds. Voter education and registration campaigns and involvement in model city decision making would also be major programmatic activities with which neighborhood groups would need board assistance in an attempt to help Mexican Americans "receive a fuller share of government funds and positions" with a special focus on the "poorer and less educated Mexican Americans."[12]

The Ford Foundation envisioned a council that would bring together the many disparate themes of Mexican Americans by offering a strong voice and program, strengthening leadership capabilities, and promoting neighborhood and city programs that would improve the economic position of the poorer Mexican Americans and as a result deepen their political participation. A major emphasis of the council was to create, foster, and support leadership within the rank-and-file in Mexican American communities through the Southwest. Recognizing that Mexican Americans as a whole have "not entered into full participation in the social, civic, political and economic life" of the United States, the Southwest Council of La Raza was imagined as an organization that would "rise on the tide of spontaneous and autonomous efforts of the barrios to help themselves."[13] An important objective to emerge from this perspective is to encourage and engage in continuing research and investigation of issues that confront Mexican American communities.

Julian Samora and the Establishment of Mexican American Studies

As noted in the previous chapter, soon after receiving his doctorate, Julian Samora became intimately involved in U.S.-Mexico border research at Michigan State University through the Border Studies Project directed by Charles Loomis. U.S.-Mexico border issues were important topics in his first two books and his interest would culminate with the publication of *Los Mojados,* one of the most important studies to date on Mexican immigration. The monies to support this project came from a three-year research grant from the Ford Foundation. In addition to receiving money from the Ford Foundation to support the Southwest Council of La Raza community initiatives, Samora was also successful in securing additional dollars for immigration research as a professor of sociology at the University of Notre Dame.

In 1968, Julian Samora was awarded a three-year, $140,000 research grant for research into the problems of the U.S.-Mexico border and an analysis of Mexican American history. As a result of these funds, the first two students of Mexican American Studies and the emerging Mexican American Graduate

Studies Program would be funded. Gilbert Cárdenas and Jorge Bustamante (both of whom have essays in part two of this book) would work closely with Samora and bring forth *Los Mojados* in 1971. More impressive was Samora's selfless effort to use these monies to publish the groundbreaking studies of Ernesto Galarza, as duly noted by Herman Gallegos in the foreword of this book.

In 1971 Ford awarded Julian Samora money that would enable him to add to his impressive feats and contributions to ethnic studies pedagogy, scholarship, and mentoring. The Ford Foundation awarded the University of Notre Dame a grant of $499,545, to be matched by Notre Dame ($454,473), for a five-year program in the field of higher education. This would become the Mexican American Graduate Studies Program, the purpose of which was to produce scholars and scholarly materials in the field of Mexican American Studies. It would transform and shape the discipline and mentoring of Mexican American students in higher education.[14]

These funds to Julian Samora and the University of Notre Dame by the Ford Foundation were granted so they could establish an interdisciplinary graduate program designed to develop the field of Mexican American Studies. Ford had simultaneously awarded money to the University of California Los Angeles and the University of Arizona to develop ethnic studies programs. In 1969 and 1970, Ford awarded thirty grants totaling $3.2 million to "Afro-American Studies programs throughout the nation to encourage the development of this new field along scholarly lines."[15] But these monies were granted at the undergraduate level, and by 1971 the foundation was looking to fund graduate programs and programs that incorporated the experiences of other racial and ethnic groups besides African Americans.

In looking to fund Mexican American Studies, the Ford special project staff went immediately to the southwestern United States, since this was where most Mexican Americans lived. University scholars and administrators from the Southwest wisely guided the Ford Foundation to the Midwest and the achievements of Julian Samora. John Scanlon, program officer for education and research, stated, "You've got to be kidding. Why Notre Dame?" After the initial shock, the program officers for Ford were attracted to the active scholarly output in Mexican American Studies by the University of Notre Dame Press.[16]

Mexican American Graduate Studies Program

By the end of the funding period in 1976, the Mexican American Graduate Studies Program had funded twenty-three students, twelve of them in sociology, four in economics, six in history, and one in government. Eight students were pursuing courses and/or preparing for qualifying examinations and nine students were ABD. Among these, some held positions at such places as the University of Texas, the University of Nebraska, New Mexico State University, Wayne State University, and the Flint campus of the University of Michigan. One student had completed a PhD and was associate professor of sociology at the Colegio de Mexico in Mexico City. Two of the students transferred to other institutions and were ABD at the University of Texas and University of California Berkeley respectively. Two students were terminated with a master's degree and one student dropped out before completing the master's program. Numerous publications had come forward by 1976, researching key areas such as Chicano politics, the Raza Unida Party, Hispanos from New Mexico, a history of Mexican Americans, and the U.S.-Mexico border.[17]

From the beginning, the Ford Foundation was clear that they wanted to support an *interdisciplinary* graduate program in Mexican American Studies. But Ford was disappointed by the lack of development of an interdisciplinary set of graduate social science courses in Mexican American Studies.[18]

There had been no explicit course on Mexican American/Chicano history, no course on labor economics and Mexican Americans, and no specific course on the Chicano movement through the Sociology Department, as had been envisioned in the initial proposal. Furthermore, in the request for grant action, Notre Dame had proposed to add three additional Mexican Americans to its faculty, one in history, a second in economics, and a third in sociology and anthropology. This would free Samora's time and allow him to commit full-time to the Mexican American Studies Graduate Program.[19]

The foundation and university jointly committed approximately $175,000 to this expansion, but by the end of the fourth year, the program had consumed 70 percent of the funds without adding a single Chicano to the faculty. In 1976, Samora remained the only Chicano faculty member in the entire university. Peter D. Bell of the Ford Foundation expressed a specific concern about the difficulties Chicano students not majoring in sociology might face in successfully completing their studies without the explicit guidance of Chicano faculty members.[20]

Bell raised some serious issues regarding leadership, coordination, and institutionalization of the Mexican American Studies Graduate Program and the support of ethnic studies in general at the University of Notre Dame. In an interoffice memorandum to Peter de Janosi and Benjamin Payton dated April 5, 1976, Bell stated that in 1971, the dean of arts and letters and other top administrators at Notre Dame enthusiastically backed the proposed Mexican American Studies program. He continued, "Their initial enthusiasm, however, did not translate itself into the University-level and College-level leadership needed to expand the Mexican American faculty and mount a truly interdisciplinary teaching program."[21] Instead, "as the financial realities of the 1970s asserted themselves and the political pressures of the late 1960s receded, the leadership of the program rested at the level of Samora." Bell stated that within the department, Samora received a great deal of support, but, sadly, "significant support for the program has stopped at the Department's edge."[22]

During his 1976 visit to Notre Dame and the Mexican American Studies Graduate Program, Bell met with Dean Isabel Charles; Associate Dean Robert Burns from the College of Arts and Letters; and Francis Kobayashi, assistant vice president for research and sponsored programs. Bell inquired into the "failures" of the University of Notre Dame to develop the Mexican American Studies program as it had been envisioned. In his memo, Bell reflects, "While showing some pride in the publication series, the administrators were apologetic about the program as a whole." By way of explanation, if not justification, Associate Dean Burns stated that "the Foundation moneys had come too easily to us" and that "our commitment was in fact unclear." Burns continued, "Even today . . . it is unclear whether the program is to make social scientists out of Chicanos or to produce scholars of Mexican American Studies." In response, Bell informed Burns that the two objectives he asserted might be actually "reinforcing," "but Burns seemed to see them as posing a real dilemma."[23]

After Robert Gordon, vice president for advanced studies and research, suggested the need for an "interdepartmental committee to improve communication about the program," Bell concludes his memo by affirming that "neither the department representatives nor the deans had thought much, if at all, about the continuation of the Mexican American studies program beyond our [Ford Foundation] grant period." Associate Dean Burns cited the precedent of an existing black studies program and identified the following reasons for Notre Dame's interest in Chicano studies: (1) the distance of the university from the intense local and regional politics of the Southwest, (2) the growing Chicano population in South Bend and the Midwest, (3) the Catholicism of the university and Chicano communities, and (4) the presence of three Chicanos on the faculty. But he and Dean Charles were vague as to what form this interest should take in the future. Their most immediate concern was to see that the present students be assisted to the completion of their studies.[24]

In the end, Bell was extremely sensitive to Samora's predicament as a visionary scholar and mentor with little administrative support. After his visit he wrote to Samora, "While I was disappointed to learn about some of the problems I appreciate your own dedication to the program, and hope that it is still not too late to make additional gains in this stage of the grant."[25]

By August of 1976, the University of Notre Dame, through the words of Robert Gordon, vice president for advanced studies, laid out a plan to continue the Mexican American Graduate Studies Program through 1980. The "strong affirmation of the University's commitment to its Mexican America Program" came with significant changes: (1) "a commitment on the part of the departments to actively participate in the interdisciplinary program and to actively recruit Mexican American scholars whose expertise in a given discipline will serve both the discipline and Mexican American Studies," (2) "the creation of a University Interdisciplinary Committee" (whose function was unclear). It is important to note that part of the impetus for this document was the nearly $25,000 from the original grant that had not been spent.[26]

Samora's report to the Ford Foundation, written the following year in 1977, informed the foundation that a Mexican American interdisciplinary committee had been established in the fall of 1976.[27] Samora does not describe the committee's work but points everyone to Gordon's letter of August 24, 1976.

Ford responds by thanking Julian for the report and expresses its disappointment that "so little progress seems to have been made during that time in implementing the commitment by the University to establish a truly graduate program in the various ways outlined by Dr. Gordon. It had been our understanding that more steps would have been taken although you would be on leave for one-half of the year. Perhaps you can add something to your report along these lines."[28]

The 1978 report by Samora to Ford relays the same information found in the 1977 report regarding the change to the interdisciplinary committee and refers Ford back to Gordon's letter. Samora concludes his report by thanking Ford for all of its generous support over the years, "which has enabled us to help a minority which throughout their history has had very limited access to graduate training." He notifies Ford that the Office of Education has awarded Notre Dame a grant for $85,000 for continuation of the program (for fellowships, admission, and recruitment) for the following year. This would become known as the Graduate Professional and Opportunities Program (GPOP).

In retrospect, it is interesting that in the initial "Request for Grant Action" memo from Ford that approved funding to Notre Dame, there were reservations about Notre Dame's ability or willingness to support the interdisciplinary model of ethnic studies, and warnings that there was nothing in the proposal to indicate that Notre Dame was prepared to back up its scholarly commitment to Mexican American Studies with an equally firm financial commitment.[29] Consequently, this compelled Ford to give Samora what they described as a "holding answer" in response to their concern. Little did they know how prophetic their vision would become in terms of the lack of administrative support for building a first-rate Mexican American Graduate Studies Program at the University of Notre Dame.[30]

The Graduate and Professional Opportunities Program (GPOP), a federally funded program of the Office of Education, became the next source of support for the Mexican American Graduate Studies Program, despite the lack of institutional support from the Notre Dame administration. As noted, Samora had already laid the groundwork for the next phase of the Mexican American Graduate Studies Program once it became evident to the Ford Foundation that the Notre Dame administration was not going to help build and institutionalize the good works of Julian Samora.

Herein lies the Samora legacy that continues to astound us as we reconstruct his story as a scholar, administrator, recruiter, and mentor of the Mexican American Graduate Studies Program. The interdisciplinary vision the Ford Foundation sought to implement under the direction of Julian Samora, but that was stalled by the Notre Dame administration, was vindicated by Julian Samora with his tireless efforts to secure external dollars to mold and shape young scholars of Mexican American Studies. This can be seen by the fact that under the Ford Foundation, the Samoristas were concentrated in sociology and history. Many of his students recall Samora reflecting on how his recruitment method for getting students into various graduate programs at Notre Dame were due directly to personal acquaintances and empathetic colleagues in other departments.

With GPOP funding from 1978 through 1985, there were thirty students who had gone through the program, and post-baccalaureate fellowships were expanded beyond sociology and history. The students included ten in economics, four in psychology, one in international relations, five in sociology, and ten in law. Not only were Samoristas entering academic positions in various universities throughout the nation, but now there were alumni who found themselves working and serving the community in both the private and public sectors outside of the boundaries of academe. In addition to the personal stories and narratives of a giving and visionary mentor, the documented record consistently shows how selfless Julian Samora was toward his students and how his vision to educate students continued long after his official departure from Notre Dame. Consider that in 1984, Samora submitted his final GPOP application as a full-time professor of sociology and director of the Mexican American Graduate Studies Program, only one year before his retirement. This clearly shows how the MAGSP was not about the person Julian Samora, but rather about his vision of opening the doors to graduate education for Latino students in perpetuity. These are the actions that constitute the Samora legacy.

We can only imagine the bouts of disappointment and discouragement that challenged Julian Samora during his lifelong mission to sensitize a reluctant university administration to support programs for Mexican Americans and Latino student in higher education. His perseverance was shaped by his vision of creating opportunity and social justice for the marginalized and oppressed of our society. Samora's vision of legitimacy for young Mexican American scholars would be challenged not only by decision makers in higher education, but also by his contemporaries and colleagues who were working to frame the discourse and knowledge base of Chicano and Mexican American Studies from the Southwest.

In the fall of 1968, Octavio Ignacio Romano-V, a professor of behavioral sciences in the school of public health at the University of California Berkeley, established the journal *El Grito: A Journal of Contemporary Mexican-American Thought* and published the critical essay "The Anthropology and Sociology of Mexican-Americans: The Distortion of Mexican-American History." Both the journal and essay would mark the beginning of Romano's lifelong efforts to legitimate Chicano Studies within the academy and beyond.

"The Anthropology and Sociology of Mexican-Americans" provided a critique of past social science research and explanations of the history of Mexican Americans, and it introduced a new epistemology for interpreting the history of Mexican Americans. It represents the first signs of a revisionist perspective and history that would serve as a contemporary foundation for the Ethnic Studies intellectual movement that evolved into disciplinary programs embracing this perspective. Like numerous other scholars writing in the late 1960s from universities in the Southwest, Romano and his contemporaries sought to offer a counternarrative to challenge the traditional dominant-centered master narrative that told the history of the victor and ignored the history and stories of the vanquished. Along with *El Grito,* there were numerous other journals with an ethnic-specific focus, such as *Aztlán* and several other journals in Black (African American) Studies and Native American Studies. These offered counter and polyvocal voices to the homogenous landscape of academic scholarship and served as a foundation for Chicano scholars such as Mario Barrera and Rodolfo Acuña, who published in the early 1970s to build and strengthen the Romano perspective. Later, scholars like Alfredo

Mirandé, who was credited for imaging and framing "Chicano Sociology," gave credit to the pioneering work of Octavio Romano.

Among the numerous scholarly works challenged and critiqued by Romano in "The Anthropology and Sociology of Mexican-Americans" was an essay co-authored by Julian Samora on East Chicago that was part of the famous *Mexican American People* research project led by Leo Grebler, Joan Moore, and Ralph Guzman supported by Ford Foundation money. In 1967, Samora, along with his colleague Richard A. Lamanna, had published an essay titled "Mexican-Americans in a Midwest Metropolis: A Study of East Chicago," one of the early community studies of the Mexican American experience in the Midwest. As a sociological community study, this was an important scholarly contribution in Mexican American Studies because it was one of the first to juxtapose Mexican Americans in the Midwest against those in the Southwest. It challenged the reader to imagine a Mexican American *colonia* outside the Southwest that did not depict Mexicans as migrant farm laborers but instead as a concentrated Mexican American settlement that had arrived as recruits to work in manufacturing and heavy industry. Through an examination of family, education, occupation, labor, housing, and politics, this study concluded that these Midwest Mexican Americans were an enduring and settled immigrant community in an urban setting and more financially secure in a heavily industrialized economic sector than their counterparts in the Southwest. This important study would serve as a foundation for future work in this area.

According to Romano, the Samora-Lamanna study, along with the majority of social science research, depicts Mexican Americans as an ahistorical ethnic group that is consequently trapped in their isolated traditional culture. Mexican Americans, states Romano, are depicted in these social science studies as possessing agency (a historical identity) only when they go through what Romano refers to as a "metamorphosis" in their movement toward acculturation and assimilation. Instead, Romano argues for a Mexican American collective identity made up of active agents of history who through labor and confrontation have contributed to the American historical landscape. He accuses and indicts social scientists of rewriting history and bringing forward the image of a "docile, fatalistic, non-goal orientated Mexican-American."[31]

Romano's specific critique of the Samora-Lamanna study is its locating the social problems of Mexican Americans within themselves. As an ethnic community whose "value orientation" presents a barrier to their rapid assimilation, Mexican Americans possess a "note of fatalism and resignation in the attitudes and behavior . . . and an orientation to the present," argue Samora and Lamanna, according to Romano.[32]

Having been at the forefront of establishing the discipline of Mexican American Studies in U.S. higher education, Julian Samora was deeply troubled by Romano's published critique of his scholarship. In April of 1969, a year after the publication of the Romano essay, Samora wrote a letter to his colleague Lyle Saunders at the Ford Foundation. He articulated his concern to Saunders and pointed out that his work was "attacked" by Romano, who accused Samora of rewriting history and perpetuating the belief that Mexican Americans were an ahistorical people.

Some of the Samoristas recall Samora pointing out to them how he would maintain extensive files on fellow academics that praised his work, but also files on academics that were critical of his scholarship, while handing them a photocopy of the Romano essay. This would lead to a conversation with Samora highlighting the virtues of struggle and sacrifices of marginal Mexican Americans as an internal strength to be admired. It was this type of persistence, in Samora's estimation, that endowed one with the power to overcome any obstacle, regardless of its source. Samora would always end optimistically by recognizing that traditional intellectual categories were being challenged and deconstructed through these intellectual battles and that higher education was in a period of transition. He felt this was healthy for higher education as it created an environment of inquiry and critique of traditional paradigms. Samora also reflected how these challenges over intellectual perspectives gave him the opportunity to produce more progressive and critical scholarship, such as his book *Gunpowder Justice,* which provided a revisionist history of the Texas Rangers. Alberto Pulido recalls feeling perplexed and filled with mixed emotions regarding these actions, admiring the courage of his mentor and astonished by his openness to criticism, but concerned that other Chicano contemporaries were openly challenging their own distinguished scholar in an open, published forum.

These intellectual encounters within the historical documents and collective memories of all who knew Julian Samora continually point to a trailblazing minority scholar who bravely chose to maintain his identity in his personal, intellectual, and professional life in a competing world that was filled with chaos and contradiction. The most provocative and ironic dimension of the Romano critique is that several of the authors who built their intellectual perspectives on Romano's work would solidify their careers with the support of Julian Samora, who sat on the editorial board of the University of Notre Dame Press, which published these authors' works. Most important was Mario Barrera's *Race and Class in the Southwest,* which became a standard text for Chicano Studies, and Alfredo Mirandé's book *The Chicano Experience,* which begins with a dedication paying homage to the Octavio Romano perspective.

How do we explain this? How do we articulate and resolve these living contradictions within both the personal and professional life and career of Professor Julian Samora? The response is simple yet profound. It is simple because Julian Samora was a decent human being. It is profound because all his work was captured in his many acts of mentoring, guidance, scholarship, and leadership. Julian Samora consistently had his eye on the prize and his work was always larger than himself. It was micro in origins but macro in scope with a vision to always help those in the present, to validate those from the past, and to empower those in the future. This is the Julian Samora legacy. It comes alive and is affirmed in part two of this book.

Notes

Julian Samora, ed., *La Raza: Forgotten Americans* (Notre Dame, Ind.: University of Notre Dame Press, 1966), p. 206.

1. Edward E. Telles and Vilma Ortiz, *Generations of Exclusion: Mexican Americans, Assimilation, and Race* (New York: Russell Sage Foundation, 2008). Joan Moore, co-editor of *The Mexican American People,* published in 1970, makes the same assertions in the forward of the Telles and Ortiz study.

2. Samora, *La Raza,* p. xi.

3. Ibid., p. viii.

4. Herman Gallegos, e-mail correspondence with Carmen Samora, July 11, 2007.

5. Ernesto Galarza, *Barrio Boy* (Notre Dame, Ind.: University of Notre Dame Press, 1971); E. Galarza, *Merchants of Labor: The Mexican Bracero Story* (Santa Barbara, Calif.: McNally & Loftin, 1964); E. Galarza, *Spiders in the House and Workers in the Field* (Notre Dame, Ind.: University of Notre Dame Press, 1970).

6. http://www.cof.org/Learn/content.cfm?ItemNumber=799.

7. Herman Gallegos, telephone interview with Alberto Pulido, Albuquerque, N.M., June 13, 2005.

8. "Proposal for the Southwest Council of La Raza," Rev. Miguel F. Barragan, Henry Santiestevan, Bernardo Valdez, and Alex Mercure, March 1968, PA680–0564, Ford Foundation Archives.

9. Ernesto Galarza, Herman Gallegos, and Julian Samora, *Mexican Americans in the Southwest* (Santa Barbara, Calif.: McNally & Loftin, 1969).

10. "Proposal for the Southwest Council of La Raza."

11. At present, the National Council of La Raza has expanded its base to advocate for "Hispanics" and to work to reduce poverty and discrimination and improve opportunities for Hispanic Americans with the five strategic priorities of education, assets/investment, economic mobility, health, and media/image/civil rights. http://www.nclr.org.

12. "Proposal for the Southwest Council of La Raza," p. 6.

13. "Proposal for the Southwest Council of La Raza," p. 10.

14. "Request for Grant Action" (RGA) to McGeorge Bundy from Howard Howe II, April 27, 1971, PA710–0372, Ford Foundation Archives.

15. John J. Scanlon, memorandum to James W. Armsey, January 19, 1971. PA710–0372, Ford Foundation Archives.

16. Ibid., p. 1.

17. Additional funding was granted by the Ford Foundation in 1975 to both the University of Notre Dame in the amount of $30,000 and El Colegio de Mexico in the amount of $20,000 for a binational study of the issues of the U.S.-Mexico border. This was a co-project with Julian Samora and Jorge Bustamante that promised to produce a book-length manuscript titled "The Dilemmas of the U.S. Mexico Border. Mexican-American Studies." Julian Samora, 1976. PA071–0372, Ford Foundation Archives.

18. Peter D. Bell, memorandum to Peter de Janosi and Benjamin Payton, April 5, 1976. PA071–0732, Ford Foundation Archives, p. 1.

19. Ibid., p. 2.

20. Ibid., p. 3.

21. Ibid.

22. Ibid.

23. Ibid.

24. Ibid.

25. Peter D. Bell to Julian Samora, March 23, 1976. PA071–0372, Ford Foundation Archives.

26. Robert E. Gordon to Peter E. de Janosi, August 24, 1976. PA071–0372, Ford Foundation Archives.

27. Julian Samora to Marion Coolen, August 19, 1977. PA071–0372, Ford Foundation Archives.

28. Marion Coolen to Julian Samora, November 23, 1977. PA071–0372, Ford Foundation Archives.

29. Peter D. Bell, "Visit to Mexican-American Studies Program University of Notre Dame (PA71–372)," memorandum to Peter de Janosi and Benjamin Payton, April 5, 1976. PA 71–372, Ford Foundation Archives.

30. Also see Anthony J. Blasi and Bernard F. Donahoe, *A History of Sociological Research and Teaching at Catholic Notre Dame University, Indiana* (Lewiston, N.Y.: The Edwin Mellen Press, 2002).

31. Octavio Ignacio Romano-V., "The Anthropology and Sociology of Mexican-Americans: The Distortion of Mexican-American History," *El Grito: A Journal of Contemporary Mexican-American Thought* (1968): 25.

32. Ibid., p. 23. Samora's co-author Richard Lamanna recalls that their research was guided by commonsensical questions as to how Mexican immigrants were integrating into their community. Their work was very much about integration and adaptation to the dominant culture. Richard Lamanna, e-mail to Alberto Pulido, April 16, 2005.

Julian Samora, seated
at his desk, mid-1940s,
Adams State Teacher's
College, Alamosa,
Colorado. Unidentified
photographer. Courtesy
of the Samora Family
Collection.

Julian Samora as a freshman at Adams
State Teacher's College, Alamosa, Colorado,
1938. Unidentified photographer. Courtesy
of the Samora Family Collection.

Carmen M. Samora holding her son, Julian Samora. They are standing in front of Antonia Velarde's home (Carmen's sister) in Pagosa Springs, Colorado, 1922. Unidentified photographer. Courtesy of the Samora Family Collection.

Julian Samora with his children, (L-R) David, Carmen, John, and Geoff. October 1995, Albuquerque, New Mexico. John Samora, photographer.

Lyle Saunders and Julian Samora standing in front of Lyle's plane. Denver, Colorado, circa 1952. Unidentified photographer. Courtesy of the Samora Family Collection.

Julian Samora pictured after receipt of the Aguila Azteca award, Mexico City, November 1990. Marcella Samora, photographer. Courtesy of the Samora Family Collection.

Julian Samora with some of his fifty-seven graduate students at his retirement symposium, Notre Dame, Indiana, April 1985. Marcella Samora, photographer. Courtesy of the Samora Family Collection.

Herman Gallegos, Raul Yzaguirre, and Julian Samora at the twenty-fifth anniversary conference of NCLR in Detroit, Michigan, July 1993. Unidentified photographer. Courtesy of the Samora Family Collection.

Julian Samora studying as a graduate student circa 1940s. Unidentified
photographer. Courtesy of the Samora Family Collection.

Betty and Julian Samora on their wedding day, Thanksgiving Day, 1942, Monte Vista, Colorado. Unidentified photographer. Courtesy of the Samora Family Collection.

Julian Samora at the pyramids in Teotihuacan, Mexico, November 1990. Marcella Samora, photographer. Courtesy of the Samora Family Collection.

Samoristas @ 57

Introduction: Creating an Intellectual Community

Alberto López Pulido
Barbara Driscoll de Alvarado
Carmen Samora

Just after World War II, a young Mexican American professor noticed that returning GIs who entered as freshmen at Adams State Teachers College in Colorado were dropping out as rapidly as they enrolled. The returning students were finding it difficult to attend classes with eighteen-year-olds. Early in his career, the young professor, just a few years from his own college graduation, had realized the importance of preparing the next generation of leaders, scholars, and community activists. Noting that many of the older students were Mexican American like himself, the young professor devised a plan to retain these particular students. These new students were part of the first large group of Mexican Americans entering college, and he did not want to lose them before they had the chance to see what college was all about. He convinced the college administration to start a satellite program in a nearby town to serve the needs of the returning GIs. The young professor was Julian Samora, and he became the associate director of the San Luis Institute of Arts and Crafts in San Luis, Colorado, a branch of Adams State College. The institute served its purpose. The older students attended their first two years in San Luis and then transferred to Adams State in Alamosa for their remaining two years. Samora administered the program for four years, and the program lasted well into the 1950s.[1]

We began this introduction with a story about Samora's mentoring to illustrate the importance it held in Samora's long and distinguished academic career. From the beginning, Dr. Samora was actively engaged in creating opportunities for minority students, particularly Mexican Americans. He was determined to level the playing field in academia. Beginning in 1971, Dr.

Samora was able to offer scholarships to forty-six men and twelve women, most of them Mexican Americans, through the Mexican American Graduate Studies Program (MAGSP).[2] They earned advanced degrees in sociology, law, government, history, economics, and psychology. The program lasted until his retirement in 1985, when the University of Notre Dame dismantled it. That his program had a near 90 percent retention rate is due primarily to the mentoring provided by Dr. Samora and his wife, Betty.

This second part of *Moving Beyond Borders* gives voice to the students and colleagues who experienced Samora's mentoring firsthand. In its four sections—community and political activism, Samora's pedagogical style, research and the integrative process, and closing with personal reflections—twenty-three authors summarize their insights into their growth as they negotiated the narrow confines of academia. Each section is introduced by a scholar who points to aspects of Samora's unique mentoring methodology and epistemology. Samora, as illustrated by the opening story, was first and foremost about educating *La Raza*. Each essay provides ample proof of Samora's commitment to educating the whole person and validating each person's knowledge and experience base. Many of the authors wrote about the simple act of being listened to. This unusual characteristic of Samora's mentoring style afforded the student or colleague the opportunity to be heard, to have a voice. The importance of this quality cannot be overemphasized. Being heard leads to empowerment and self-actualization, both necessary qualities in maturation and growth. As early as 1944, Samora was listening to the needs of his students and taking action, as the story illustrates. While it may be comforting, understanding without the appropriate action ultimately goes nowhere. Samora knew this and embodied a model of action that empowered his students and colleagues to have the confidence to take life-changing actions.

Dr. Samora knew all too well that women and minorities are underrepresented in academia.[3] It has been difficult for them to find appropriate mentors to help guide them through their training.[4] Once in the ranks of junior faculty, they find the pressures and stresses difficult to negotiate without the assistance of more experienced faculty members.[5] Perhaps because of these difficulties, women and minority junior faculty members leave the ranks of academia without receiving tenure in greater numbers than white male faculty members.[6] Samora was intent on training women as well as men, and the essays written by the women speak to his concern for their academic life.

We acknowledge that the number of women Samora mentored are low by today's measures, a little better than 20 percent of the total. Considering that when the MAGSP was started, Notre Dame was still an all-male institution, the fact that women were accepted into the program has its own significance. Nine women, more than 30 percent of the total number of authors, contributed to this volume. Because there has been a paucity of women and minorities in higher education, there have been few of either available to mentor female and minority students.[7] Even though there were no women academic mentors available to the students as a formal part of the MAGSP, women did come forward and provide invaluable modeling to the men and women of MAGSP.[8] Four classic studies show that in both corporate and academic settings, fewer women mentor men than men mentor men or women in the same settings.[9] Both junior women and junior minority faculty members have performance demands on their time; committee meetings, publishing demands, and large teaching loads make it difficult to take on the responsibilities of mentoring.[10] It is they themselves who need mentoring and help to gain entrée into the "complex and often ambiguous professional culture."[11]

As a man of color, Dr. Samora was the only Latino on the Notre Dame faculty for almost twenty years of his twenty-five-year career. The first African American faculty member, Dr. Joe Scott, was hired in 1970, and remained the only black faculty member for a number of years. Notre Dame has admitted students with Spanish surnames for all of its 163-year history, yet it failed to hire Latino faculty members to match the percentage of Latino students.[12] Despite his teaching load, his research projects, his publishing commitments, and his service on national boards and commissions, Dr. Samora provided a much-needed and valuable service by engaging in mentoring relationships with Latino undergraduate and graduate students. Anecdotally, many Mexican American men and women have expressed how affirming it was for them to discover on the first day of class that their Introduction to Sociology class was taught by a Spanish-surnamed teacher. For many of these students, Dr. Samora was their first and only experience having a Mexican American teacher.

Mentoring As Process

Mentoring is more of an art than a science. One common feature in mentoring, whether in academia or business, in an informal arrangement or a highly scripted program, is that mentoring takes time. Mentoring is a relationship, a relationship that cannot be rushed, and it involves a commitment from the two who engage in the relationship.[13]

The commitment Dr. Samora made to mentorship was definitely a lifestyle choice. Nowhere in our reading of the mentoring literature have we encountered a description of the kind of mentoring conducted within *la familia Samora*. Dr. Samora, with the full involvement of his wife, was building community. As a pioneer scholar, mentoring students was a crucial component of his career. His method of mentoring, his lifestyle choice, evolved from his sense of urgency to prepare as many students as possible to enter the professions so they could act as change agents for the next generation. This model of mentoring was based on the close relationships of family and community.

Because of his own humble beginnings, Dr. Samora was keenly aware of the kinds of students he was looking for and the characteristics they would bring that the academy would see as deficits. Many of his students were firsts, as was he: first in the family or community to graduate from high school, first to attend college, first to go to graduate school. Many of his students were away from home for the first time, and away from cultural and regional comforts. Several were immigrants; for many, English was their second language. Samora recognized in each of them a drive similar to his own, and he supported them all.

Early in his career, Samora "articulated . . . a dilemma endemic to minority group leadership,"[14] that Mexican American leaders were co-opted by Anglo culture and thereby rendered ineffective as leaders within their Mexican culture. Samora sought to train leaders who would be fully invested in their own culture and yet fully accepted by academia. Samora wanted to create opportunities for his students to be well-trained, effective leaders in both the academy and in the community. Concerned with the question of leadership since the inception of his career, he was presented with an opportunity to bring change to the academy. He sought recognition from the academy through his solid scholarship, a scholarship that embraced his ethnic viewpoint instead of erasing it. He demanded that recognition for himself and for his students. In demonstrating a dynamic minority graduate mentoring program, he serves to this day as a model of success to be duplicated.

It is interesting that Samora used family members as participant observers for both his master's thesis and his doctoral dissertation, relying on his own cultural model of family closeness rather than the dominant method of the individual investigator model.[15] Samora's efforts resulted in research that gave the minority perspective rather than the dominant perspective. This is an important difference that Samora carried out all through his long career. By working hard and distinguishing himself early in his career, Samora earned the right (some might say he forced the right) to be perceived from his minority perspective and not from the dominant perspective. He wanted his students to have that choice as well.

Samora saw an opening in the academy, perhaps brought about by the political activism of the 1960s and 1970s, and cracked it as wide as he could, accepting students from all over the country and a few from abroad into his graduate studies program. I think his ultimate goal was to change the academy and broaden the academic culture to appreciate the richness that large numbers of minorities and women would bring. (Remember that Notre Dame was a male bastion until 1972–73, when women were formally enrolled in the freshman class.)

Samora had a four-point comprehensive leadership training program. First, the students admitted to the MAGSP would attend the weekly seminar for at least the first year of their tenure at Notre Dame. The seminar served as the formal training ground for toughening and preparing his students for academic life. Within the context of the seminar, he let his students know they would need to be twice as prepared as their Anglo counterparts and might receive half of the acknowledgments. He encouraged argument, research, discussion, and academic rigor. Samora brought in Latino leaders to speak to his students, encouraging networking between the students and these established leaders. Second, he asked students to act as co-researchers with him on major academic topics, he was generous with any funds he had, and he encouraged student travel for research. Third, Samora infused the Notre Dame Press with monies that enabled the publication of scholarly works by the nation's leading Mexican American scholars. And finally, Samora was on the acquisitions committee for the Notre Dame library, and he made frequent recommendations for purchases. Thus, Samora was able to present a cohesive and comprehensive program to the students who studied under his direction.

When necessary, he went behind the scenes for those students who were not as prepared academically as others and interceded for them to retake tests or whatever was necessary to complete a course. He argued that academic deficiencies did not mean deficiencies in the culture or the person. He argued that the academy had a responsibility to allow a student more time, and his students performed admirably.

More important than the formal mentoring Samora provided was the nurturing provided by him and his wife. The Samoras entertained students at holiday times, baptized their children, hosted graduation parties, located housing, found babysitters, and provided jobs for spouses. The Samoras included students on picnics, travel to Mexico, and impromptu meals at their home; they befriended them in countless ways. This additional step of providing mentoring through friendship was not seen as a hardship by the couple. This was their vocation, their duty, and their pleasure. They knew intimately the difficulties associated with leaving home and setting out on an academic path. They knew all too well the difficulties students would have as they made their way through the gauntlet of academic trials. Of the fifty-seven students who were formally admitted into the program, all but seven completed advanced degrees. Samora created a program that accepted the minority students for who they were as people. He validated their minority experiences within the framework of the larger dominant culture. He did not want them to lose their "otherness." He wanted them to add skills, but he saw them as essentially complete, not needing to change to fit into a dominant model. The acceptance Samora and his wife had for their students allowed another aspect of mentoring to flourish, a spiritual element.

Conclusion

Julian Samora embraced many forms of mentoring his students and colleagues. He provided formal training that was academically rigorous and resulted in a large number of men and women receiving advanced degrees from Notre Dame. He also engaged in informal mentoring through his open office door and frequent invitations to students and colleagues to his home. Samora's efforts serve as a model of mentoring as a vocation and as a proven means to promote leadership training. Women and minorities need to rise in greater numbers into positions of leadership in both the academy and the private sector. Enough women and minorities need to reach the upper levels of power in order to serve as effective mentors to incoming women and minorities to effect real change in their numbers in positions of leadership.

Junior faculty members, minority and women faculty members, women graduate students and graduate students of color need to be supported through mentoring, both formally and informally. Graduate students must find the supportive relationships they need to help them complete their programs of study. Mentoring is recognized as an important component in training the protégé, yet where is the institutional support for the mentor? Successful models of mentoring must be documented and studied to provide the needed inspiration for others to continue mentoring in ever-greater numbers.[16] Mentoring will continue to occur because it is human nature to pass along one's wisdom. But if mentoring were encouraged and supported institutionally, women and minorities could benefit on the scale of their white male counterparts.

The following essays give the reader a comprehensive overview of Samorista-style mentoring. The essayists go beyond the expected topic of becoming confident scholars and professionals. They write about what it means to be valued, to be heard, to be at the center of their school experience rather than on the sidelines. They write about the empowering aspect of being in on the creation of an intellectual community, one that served as home to them in every sense of that compelling word. We are fortunate to be able to offer the reader thoughtfully written firsthand accounts that document what it was like to be part of Samora's leadership training experience, Samoristas @ 57.

Notes

1. Mose Trujillo, interview with Carmen Samora, Golden, Colorado, December 17, 2001; Bridget Olguín, interview with Carmen Samora, San Luis, Colorado, December 18, 2001.

2. See chapters 3 and 13 for discussions of the Mexican American Graduate Studies Program at Notre Dame.

3. Karen S. Cockrell, Rosalita D. Mitchell, Julie N. Middleton, and N. Jo Campbell, "The Holmes Scholars Network: A Study of the Holmes Group Initiative for Recruitment and Retention of Minority Faculty," *Journal of Teacher Education* 50 (2) (1999): 85–93.

4. Ibid.

5. Ibid.

6. Ibid.

7. Ibid.

8. Betty Samora, Olga Villa, and Grace Olivarez are just three of the women who come to mind.

9. Fewer women than men are full professors, leaving a void for female students seeking same gender high-status mentors. Regina M. O'Neill, "Gender and Race in Mentoring Relationships: A Review of the Literature," in *Mentoring and Diversity: An International Perspective*, ed. David Clutterbuck and Belle Rose Ragins (Oxford: Butterworth-Heinnemann, 2002).

10. O'Neill, "Gender and Race in Mentoring Relationships."

11. Cockrell, et al., "The Holmes Scholars Network."

12. Peter J. Lysy, telephone interview with Carmen Samora, September 12, 2005.

13. Shirley Peddy, *The Art of Mentoring: Lead, Follow and Get Out of the Way* (Houston: Bullion Books, 1998).

14. Anthony J. Blasi and Bernard F. Donahoe, *A History of Sociological Research and Teaching at Catholic Notre Dame University, Indiana* (Lewiston, N.Y.: Edwin Mellen Press, 2002), p. 163.

15. Ibid.

16. See Carmen Samora, "Evolution of Mentoring in the Field of Professional Preparation" (unpublished master's thesis, College of Education, University of New Mexico, 2005).

CHAPTER FOUR

Constructive Marginality
En el otro lado
Richard A. Navarro

During a radio call-in show on bilingual education, Julian Samora was
confronted by an angry caller who told him he should go back to where he
came from if he didn't like it in this country. Rather than return the anger,
Julian politely told her, "Madame, I did not cross the border . . . the border crossed me." Julian Samora was always proud of his roots in southern
Colorado. He was also proud of his achievements *en el otro lado*; the side
that made his language and culture a "minority" and was as unwelcoming as the signs in the businesses where he grew up that read "No Dogs,
Indians, or Mexicans ALLOWED."

Anthropologist Victor Turner[1] coined the term "liminality" to describe
the state of "between-ness" of initiates undergoing rites of passage. It is a
threshold state of being no longer a girl or boy, but not yet a woman or
man. The momentary state of liminality can be a brief period in the life
of an individual, or in the history of a society. Educational anthropologist
Steven Arvizu extended the concept of liminality in describing the marginal
status of Chicanos in American society.[2] According to Arvizu, Chicanos are a
people in the "state of becoming." No longer Mexican and not yet accepted
as mainstream American, Chicanos are in a state of liminality as we define
a new identity for ourselves in this society.

Existing in this threshold state can be a liberating and creative experience.
Freed from the burdens of tradition and breaking from the past allows for
a greater freedom of expression and self-determination; "the Chicano is a
highly advantaged person, for he [*sic*] has the benefits of true *constructive*

marginality, the ability to live in more than one culture, and so to enjoy a richness not possible for those limited in understanding and experience to a single ethnic setting."[3] However, by examining the lives of individual Chicano youth in his own family, Arvizu discovered the negative dimensions of liminality, particularly when Chicanos are made to feel inferior because of their language, culture, and class background. In other words, to be in a state of liminality can be self-empowering or self-destroying.

Julian Samora seemed to intuitively understand that he was in a state of liminality as he negotiated life between two worlds and that this is what it meant to be a Chicano. Growing up in the margins of society—a poor mestizo boy raised by his grandmother and mother—he could have allowed his circumstances to define him and his life chances. Instead, through the love and support he received from his maternal guardians, he cultivated an identity that was rooted in his experience, a Chicano experience.

In the spring of 1993, Henry Santiesteven, a contemporary and friend, was interviewing Julian Samora at Michigan State University for the institute named for him, the Julian Samora Research Institute. Santiesteven wanted to know what stood out in Julian's memory as determining his future. He pressed Julian for a single incident or person that made the difference in his decision to pursue education and to eventually become such a significant leader for Chicanos and American society. I remember observing the interview and watching as Dr. Samora demurred, saying there was no one incident or individual that made the difference, but a series of events and people who touched his life during those formative years in Pagosa Springs, Colorado, and beyond that shaped his character.[4] His motto in life is best expressed by the Spanish poet Antonio Machado: *se hace camino al andar* (you make the path by walking).[5] Julian Samora knew poverty and understood its cruelty. He experienced discrimination and committed himself to a lifelong struggle for social justice. And he witnessed the darkness of ignorance and dedicated his life to spreading the light of education. His legacy is an example of *constructive marginality* as seen through the life experiences of his students and colleagues.

The Parra and Villa essay tells the story of two people making a path by walking and the significant influence that Julian Samora had in giving them direction. The 1970 Mexican American Conference organized by Samora and others at the University of Notre Dame and the subsequent establishment of the Midwest Council of La Raza changed their lives personally and professionally. Like Samora, they reflect, "there is not usually a single turning point, but a collection of smaller turns and events that become life-defining."

Julian Samora's role in giving direction to their path was also evident in the community he helped to shape in South Bend. Through the grants and scholarships that brought students and scholars from all over the country, particularly the Southwest, and his social activism that resonated with the spirit of change at the time, South Bend became a dynamic environment for constructing a new identity from the margins. Parra and Villa suggest that although Julian Samora recognized the state of liminality they were in, he was never intimidated by their marginality and never let the negative stereotypes blur his vision of a more just society. Whether shaping the scholarship of Chicano Studies or establishing a new moral standard for social institutions that purport to stand for social justice, he was only too familiar with the barriers, and he understood the institutional contradictions such as those that were revealed in the groundskeepers' dispute at Notre Dame. And it was through this understanding, as Parra and Villa point out, that he also knew how to find the tipping point to achieve a *just* decision.

The Santos essay is a poignant reminder of the vicissitudes of universities like Notre Dame and how little the academy values the Chicano experience. After actively recruiting Santos to the doctoral program in economics, the institution did little to guarantee his success once he arrived. For Santos, like many of Samora's students, South Bend, Indiana, was his first venture outside of the Southwest. There were no Chicano faculty members in economics, or even faculty members of color with whom he might have been able to relate. And the infrastructure that was supposed to support graduate students either did not serve the needs of Chicano students or lumped them all together and treated them as "second-class citizens." Santos did not see himself or his community in his professors, in his fellow students, or in the intellectual discourse in his discipline. The absence of a mentor in economics with an interest in the Chicano experience served to further marginalize him in the institution. This liminal state left him to feel he was to blame for his "failure" rather than the people in the economics department and the university that brought him.

Although Samora was instrumental in finding a just solution to the groundskeepers' dispute, he was not always able to overcome the institutional barriers of mainstream academics and institutions that continue to marginalize Chicano Studies and Chicano scholars. He provided the financial means for many young Chicano students to study at Notre Dame, but he was not always able to shield them from the hostility of unearned privilege[6] that kept them marginalized rather than helping them realize their full potential. Santos's essay is a reminder that liminality can have negative consequences as well.

A theme that runs through all the essays is the importance of the Samora home and family for his students and colleagues. Finding the *caritas* of the Samora hearth through food, company, music, ritual, and friendship was more than a warm refuge from the cold, harsh winters of South Bend. It was an oasis in the cold, harsh, unwelcoming environment of the university and the community that kept Chicanos marginalized. But Samora did more than share his family and home with his students. As Crafton describes Samora so accurately, "A person who lives his life by a philosophy of *ubuntu* experiences his humanity through belonging, participation, and sharing." Whether in his home or in his classroom gathered in a circle with his students in the Mexican American Graduate Studies Program, Samora shared his personal and professional knowledge and experiences and in so doing made them feel that they too belonged.

Julian Samora is most widely recognized as one of the *fathers* of Chicano Studies. In Mata's essay, he refers to this pioneering role as "our community's *Primero Sabios*" and goes on to reflect on how difficult it must have been to be among *Los Primeros* and how important their role is to this day. As Mata points out, during the height of Samora's research and scholarship, there was almost nothing written about the Chicano experience, and what did exist, even that written by "sympathetic" social scientists, were distorted caricatures that served to reinforce stereotypes rather than debunk them. For aspiring scholars like Mata, this environment was alienating. "Through undergraduate and my master's training, I had not yet met a Mexican American professor, much less one who came from circumstances similar to my own," Mata states. So when Samora offered to share his time and willingness to discuss "life-altering possibilities" with him, Mata was impressed. Later, in his own career, pressed by personal and professional demands, Mata is even more appreciative for the "unassuming, genuine, reassuring, respectful, gentle, and yet quietly commanding" demeanor of his mentor. Mata reminds us that however alienating and marginalized he might have felt in his own career, this support and encouragement was not available to *Los Primeros Sabios*.

Echoing the motto of *se hace camino al andar*, Mata notes that Samora's dream was to make a difference to his forgotten peoples. Forged out of his own life experiences, Mata, among others who witnessed Samora at work, observed that his strategy was an evolving one. As the agenda evolved, Samora used his constructive marginality to bridge the world of knowledge to bring about change. Change not just for improving the lives of Mexican Americans but change to bring about a more just society for all Americans.

Samora's impact as a role model differed among his many students, who were experiencing their own states of *liminality*. Madrigal comments in his essay how impressed he was with the example Samora set of applying his discipline of sociology to the documentation and understanding of Latinos in the United States. He credits the "microcosm" of a Chicano community that Samora was able to create in his home and in his graduate seminars as providing him the support and encouragement he needed to persevere. They were safe havens that were instrumental in his own constructive marginality. Today, Madrigal is carrying on the Samora legacy through the impact he is having on tax policies in Texas and other states. Because taxes are as much a part of life as death itself, it is comforting to know that someone with the sense of fairness and social justice of a *Samorista* is helping shape tax policies and their implementation.

Ronquillo picks up on Samora's superior mentoring capabilities and credits him with showing his students that their responsibility was more than making their individual contributions to La Causa, but to recognize that they "were part of the struggle of a community to survive and pursue the American Dream." Although his students' activism sometimes put him in difficult circumstances in relation to the university, Samora relished their energy and growing awareness. Fighting the university to provide better working conditions for gardeners and cafeteria workers, supporting the grape boycott, and bringing critical thinkers and activists to the campus were just a few of the strategies Samora used to give his students real-life lessons of supporting and promoting equal rights for the marginalized. Ronquillo learned from his mentor, Julian Samora, that remaining rooted in the Chicano community is essential for success, whether forging a national civil rights agenda or conducting groundbreaking immigration research.

Martínez also recognizes the importance of remaining rooted in one's community, even when one is geographically removed from it. The essay, which beautifully weaves together the life lessons of his father with Julian's, centers on the importance of service as a lifelong commitment for both men. Martínez was impressed that a person who came from the same village as his own family could be such a significant actor in the U.S. civil rights movement. Through Samora's guidance, Martínez discovered the Chicano community in South Bend and that he could be of service to his community tutoring young people, working with farm workers, and worshipping in the Spanish-language churches.

Perhaps because of their common roots in northern New Mexico and southern Colorado, Martínez makes an important observation about Samora's demeanor and ways of speaking. Always respectful and deliberative in his wording, Samora was never pompous. In fact, through storytelling and exhibiting a self-deprecating style that was also a characteristic of Martínez's father, Samora demonstrated for his students the value of humor and the importance of not taking oneself too seriously. While Samora was serious about his purpose, he understood that change would come not through his actions alone, but through the actions of many.

Martínez observed that Samora and his father "exhibited a combination of altruism and power." In this regard, power is not the ability to dominate others, but "the ability to do good." And over a lifetime of exercising this form of power—the ability to do good—one acquires wisdom instead of money or fame. Those of us who had the privilege of knowing Don Julian know this to be true.

For most in the academy, leaving an impeccable record of pioneering scholarship is a singular achievement alone. But to also leave an army of scholars, activists, and organizations continuing to change society is truly a legacy worth recognizing. I had the privilege of serving as the founding director of the Julian Samora Research Institute at Michigan State University. When the institute was first proposed in 1987, it was given the generic name of the Hispanic Research Center. For obvious reasons, several of us were not comfortable with the name, but more importantly, we felt this new research center should honor our heroes and reflect the values of the land-grant tradition of which Michigan State was so proud. Together with colleagues such as Joseph Spielberg-Benitez and Juan and Diana Marinez, I proposed to the university that the center be named for a Chicano scholar whose name is synonymous with research on the Chicano experience in the Midwest and nationally . . . Julian Samora. I remember traveling to South Bend with Joseph Spielberg-Benitez to discuss the idea with Don Julian. Over a lunch of green chile, which he had so exquisitely prepared for us, we explained the mission of the center and why we wanted to name it for him. Neither Joe nor I had been Samoristas, but we knew that the first academic appointment Samora received after completing his PhD was at Michigan State University. More importantly, his achievements reflected the values upon which we wished to build the center, which also harmonized with MSU's values—pioneering research, educating the next generation of Chicano scholars, and applying the new knowledge to improve the lives of Chicanos and their communities. Above all else, Don Julian wanted assurance that the institute that would bear his name would remain a steadfast advocate for the application of knowledge to further social justice and equal rights for the marginalized in our society. This was the commitment we made to him then in South Bend, and again a year later during the inaugural ceremonies for the Julian Samora Research Institute in East Lansing, and it is a commitment that the contributors herein have reaffirmed.

I believe that as a society we are in a state of liminality. Thanks to Samora and many others, we are no longer the racist and discriminatory society of his childhood. Gone are the signs that proclaim "No Dogs, Indians, or Mexicans ALLOWED." Yet as a society we have not learned the benefits of constructive marginality. Rather than embracing our diversity to bring people together, we are even more segregated and polarized on the basis of language, culture, social class, and immigration status. To me, the legacy of Julian Samora is in showing us that *el otro lado* is a state of mind and borders are barriers that diminish our humanity and our ability to live together in harmony. The path he made by walking gives us reason to hope.

Notes

1. Victor Turner, *The Ritual Process: Structure and Antistructure* (Ithaca, N.Y.: Cornell University Press, 1969).

2. Steven Arvizu, "Education for Constructive Marginality," in *The Cultural Drama*, ed. W. Dillon (Washington, D.C.: The Smithsonian Institute Press, 1974).

3. Ibid., p. 123.

4. There was one person Julian often returned to during more than forty hours of reflective interviews as having been his closest companion in his pioneering life, his wife Betty. Although I did not have the privilege of knowing her personally, it is clear from the essays in this volume that she was a true companion to Julian in every sense of the word. He once said that when they met they were instantly drawn to each other, in part due to the marginality they both felt at Adams State College. Together, they made a pact to pursue education and to use their education and whatever cultural capital they would acquire to serve their community and to promote the cause of justice for all peoples living in the margins of society.

5. Antonio Machado, *Selected Poems*, trans. A. S. Trueblood (Cambridge, Mass.: Harvard University Press, 2007).

6. For a discussion of "unearned privilege," see Peggy McIntosh, "White Privilege and Male Privilege: A Personal Account of Coming to See Correspondences through Work in Women's Studies," Wellesley College, Center for Research on Women, 1988.

CHAPTER FIVE

Serving Our Communities
(1970–1980)

Ricardo Parra and Olga Villa Parra

We want to remember how it all started. Like in nature, life rejuvenates in the spring.

On April 17 and 18, 1970, we attended a historical gathering, the Mexican American Conference at the University of Notre Dame hosted by the Institute for Urban Studies. Mexican Americans and other Latino leaders from the ten midwestern states—Illinois, Indiana, Michigan, Ohio, Minnesota, Wisconsin, Kansas, Iowa, Missouri, and Nebraska—attended. It was the beginning of a life-changing experience for us.

The Mexican American Conference of 1970

Ricardo: I was twenty-four years old in 1970 and searching for ways to help our Mexican American communities in the Midwest. I already had more than six years of experience in working with community groups. I served as a neighborhood and community worker, as a VISTA volunteer, and as a human rights worker; I participated in the civil rights movement, the war on poverty, the farm workers' movement, and the Chicano movement. I learned about the Mexican American Conference and knew that Dr. Julian Samora was going to be one of the speakers at the April Mexican American Conference. I had read his book *La Raza: Forgotten Americans* and wanted to be at that conference. In April of 1970, I flew to Chicago from Kansas City, caught a North Central commuter flight to South Bend, Indiana, and registered at the Morris Inn on the Notre Dame campus. This was the beginning of wonderful friendships, relationships, and experiences that I now treasure and that changed my life. It was at that conference where I first met a young woman from Michigan who became my wife. Her name was Olga Villa and she was from Muskegon. I remember she gave a short yet engaging talk, energetic and enthusiastic.

Olga: Encouraged by my friend Jane Gonzales[1] from my hometown of Muskegon, Michigan, I attended the Mexican American Conference. The conference was organized by Notre Dame's Institute for Urban Studies to explore issues concerning the Spanish-speaking population of the Midwest and to select a site for a "Midwest regional center to service Chicanos in this area."[2] And it changed my life. The seminal Mexican American Conference of April of 1970 held at Notre Dame resulted in an agreement about a new organization, The Midwest Council of La Raza (MCLR).

Ricardo: The 1970 conference highlighted the presence and condition of Mexican Americans in the Midwest and brought together Latino leadership from the Southwest, Washington, D.C., and the Midwest. Enthusiasm was great. More than two hundred leaders from throughout the ten midwestern states attended, including one hundred student leaders. State leaders presented a report on their state. The chief planners, organizers, and presenters at the conference included Dr. Julian Samora and Dr. Ernesto Galarza, two of the co-founders of the Southwest Council of La Raza; Dr. Jorge Prieto, a physician working with Mexicans and Mexican American populations in Chicago; Dr. Thomas Broden, director of the Institute for Urban Studies and a professor in the law school; Graciela Olivarez, the first woman to graduate from the Notre Dame law school, then in her final year; and Ruben Alfaro, an organizer from Lansing, Michigan.

We discussed the needs of the Mexican Americans and other Latino groups in the Midwest. Some of us at the conference hoped we could link up with the Southwest Council of La Raza or replicate many of the same programs or find and share resources for the many needs in the Midwest. Since Dr. Samora, Dr. Gallegos, and Dr. Galarza founded the Southwest Council, maybe an organization to serve the needs of Latinos in the Midwest could be established. It was at this conference of Latino leaders and activists that the Midwest Council of La Raza was formed, a Midwest advocacy, empowerment, and self-determination organization.

Olga: As part of that effort, Dr. Tom Broden at Notre Dame and Graciela Olivarez contacted me by mail to come for an interview to assist in organizing the Midwest Council of La Raza as an umbrella organization under the Institute for Urban Studies. I was hired and started working at the Memorial Library[3] within the office of the Institute for Urban Studies. Within a few days I met Dr. Samora and a graduate student named Gil Cárdenas. Things moved fast those first three months at the new organization. The Midwest Council of La Raza hired its first executive director, Mr. Leo Rivera from Michigan, and I became the administrative assistant.

Ricardo: We were part of that generation of young people ready to take on the world. We were filled with idealism. A movement for greater acceptance and inclusion had begun to unfold in many parts of the country, building on the work of previous generations from the 1940s and 1950s. Little did some of us know that social and institutional change sometimes takes a lifetime.

Midwest Council of La Raza and the Notre Dame Institute for Urban Studies

Olga: The Institute for Urban Studies was established originally as a response by the University of Notre Dame to address urban issues and diversity challenges. At that time, Dr. Broden[4] was a law professor and an advocate for diversity within the university and in the South Bend community. Graciela Olivarez was the chief architect of the implementation of the MCLR. Later she would serve as planning director for the state of New Mexico and eventually be appointed by President Jimmy Carter as director of the Department of Community Service, serving as the highest-ranking Latina in the Carter administration.

My commitment to social justice for farm workers continued after I came to work at Notre Dame. Two weeks after I started working, religious Sisters from Kalamazoo asked me to join them in prayer at the food stamp office in Benton Harbor, Michigan. Local farmers had recruited more than a thousand migrant workers to come to Michigan from Texas, but the farmers miscalculated and the workers had arrived too early to harvest the crops. The families needed food stamps and the local public assistance office would not help them. I went to pray with the Sisters at the food stamp office and was arrested for refusing to leave the premises until there was some resolution to the issue. In some areas, local residents viewed migrant workers suspiciously and only as a source of cheap temporary labor to be discarded when they were no longer of use. At times like this, I think of St. Augustine: "Peace is not the absence of tension but the presence of justice."

What a way to start my job at the university! I called my supervisor, Dr. Tom Broden, to let him know what had happened and that I would not be in the next day. The next thing I knew, Dr. Broden showed up at the jail to bail us out. He became one of our great friends and mentors; we could always count on his support and wise counsel.

Ricardo: In May 1971, I found myself catching another flight to South Bend to accept a job as a regional coordinator and evaluator for Midwest migrant programs under the coordination of the Midwest Council of La Raza. The Midwest Council developed pioneering migrant transition centers throughout the Midwest, some of which served as model programs. Later in 1971, I became the second executive director of the council when Leo Rivera, the first director, resigned.

The Midwest Council was organized under the auspices of the Institute for Urban Studies and housed near them in the Rockne Memorial at the far end of the campus. As you entered the building, you came across a large bust of the legendary Knute Rockne. The location was impressive. Within walking distance were the beautiful paths that wrapped around the two campus lakes. Nearby was the Grotto, a replica of the grotto in Lourdes, France. Dr. Broden and the Institute for Urban Studies assisted us in navigating through the university bureaucracy, and we learned how systems and processes worked both inside and outside of Notre Dame. We learned plenty. Sometimes we made mistakes, but he always stuck by us. We also shared office space with a noted and legendary priest from Chicago, Monsignor Jack Egan, director of the Catholic Committee on Urban Ministry.[5] He was more than willing to help us. From Monsignor Egan we received solid advice about community organizations and fund raising. He had a strong commitment to social justice. He was a good friend to us.

Olga: Though we had a noble mission of focusing attention on the presence and plight of our communities in the Midwest, we soon learned that we faced many obstacles and challenges. The Ford Foundation that had helped the Southwest Council of La Raza was not in a position to help the Midwest Council of La Raza. We had to develop new and innovative strategies to raise money. We had to diversify funding sources, and we turned to the federal and local governments, to religious organizations, to foundations, and to our own fund-raising efforts. We were able to find support from the U.S. Department of Labor, the Office of Economic Opportunity, the Department of Housing and Urban Development, and the Department of Health, Education and Welfare. Our social justice and social action projects received funding from church organizations and foundations; an important supporter was the Catholic Campaign for Human Development (CHD). CHD continues to be the domestic antipoverty, social justice program of the U.S. Catholic bishops, and its mission is to address the root causes of poverty in America through promotion and support of community-controlled self-help organizations and through transformative education. We were fortunate to have the wonderful help and support of José Juárez, who was very knowledgeable about CHD. The Presbyterian, Methodist, Episcopal, Mennonite, and Disciples of Christ churches and the Franciscan and Holy Cross religious orders also helped us.

Ricardo: The staff of the Midwest Council was relatively young. We were in our twenties and although we had much to learn, we built a pretty good team. For example, Cande Marín was our comptroller and effectively crunched the numbers that kept us afloat. He was from the Valley of South Texas and had worked for the United Migrant Opportunities Inc. in Michigan. We had great people helping us as staff members, volunteers, and friends. Odessa Earles, administrative assistant, and Alice Benjamin, secretary at the Institute for Urban Studies, were instrumental in helping to navigate the intricate university system, and we became lifelong friends.

Olga: In time, my community work became central to the Midwest Council of La Raza. Yes, we were housed at Notre Dame, but one always sensed that working or living on campus was really different from living and working out in the South Bend community.

Ricardo: We learned that building trust in our relationships was instrumental. As a new organization, we had to build friendships and reach out for help and advice as we learned about the needs of various midwestern communities. There were many good people willing to help us. But one of our best teachers was on staff. Olga was really helpful in showing us the importance of establishing and maintaining good working relationships. Good proposals could easily go down the drain for the lack of trust or established relationships.

Olga: There were just so many good people that helped us in our work and mission: Gil Cárdenas, Albert Mata, Mike Carranza, Barbara Driscoll, Concepcion and Ignacio Niño, Cande Marín, David Martínez, Raul Carrasco, Ramiro Gómez, Manuel García, Guadalupe and Olga Rocha, Ramon Rodríguez, Fr. Tom Lemos, Fr. John Phalen, Benito and Berta Salazar, José and Joyce Juárez, Jane Gonzáles, Maritza Robles, Yaya Cantu, Velma Garza, Ricardo Chapa, Ismael Alvarez, Jesús Negrete, Rebecca Alvin, Sam Bell, John Terronez, Jorge and Luz Prieto, Marcos Ronquillo, and José and Lydia Bracomonte.[6] Just so many names that the list goes on of countless friends who helped us in big and small ways and identified with us and in what we were trying to accomplish.

Ricardo: My life was always on the go, whether in South Bend or traveling the Midwest and beyond. I know I put many miles on my canary yellow 1967 Pontiac Catalina. I drove to Chicago to meet with funding sources and regional coordinating councils, view other projects and organizations, and discuss the issues with community leaders. Midwest Council had very little money and it had to be used wisely. Fortunately there were people who opened their homes to me. Midwest Council members also drove to Davenport, Toledo, St. Paul, Milwaukee, Lincoln, Indianapolis, Ft. Wayne, and Marion, Indiana, and we were so fortunate to always find wonderful hospitality from friends, churches, and religious organizations. In short, a wonderful network of good-hearted people dispersed throughout the cities or migrants camps of the Midwest offered encouragement and goodwill.

Olga, a people person, never felt alone at the university. She made many friends among the students, groundskeepers, food service people, and the faculty, and she also knew how to cook, which was a big hit, especially with the students. One professor in particular drew her attention, Dr. Julian Samora along with his wife Betty. Olga became close friends with the Samoras. Betty and Olga searched for ways to get children better day care and have the South Bend Community School Corporation (SBCSC) education system respond to the education needs of Latino children in schools.

Olga: Betty and I joined with Mrs. Concepción Niño to start the El Campito Day Care Center after observing that many children were left in cars as their parents worked in agriculture fields outside South Bend. Our concern was for the health, safety, and education of the children. Betty also worked with a migrant resettlement program and taught adult basic education through the Midwest Council of La Raza Migrant Farmworker Program. This was a joint venture between the Midwest Council of La Raza and Ivy Tech College in South Bend, Indiana.

For his part, Dr. Samora worked with community members to improve education for the young Latino students and people of the community. For the Samoras, for us, for the community, and for the Midwest Council, education was the big issue. Whether it was early childhood education, bilingual education, cutting the high school dropout rate, college preparation and admission to higher education, or getting graduate students through school, education was the big issue. Given Dr. Samora's enormous responsibilities at the university and his national work, Betty often was more involved with the local community issues than he was. I recall that she was a strong supporter of Cesar Chavez and the United Farm Workers, and she would join us on the picket line. In 1972, we had a rally and a sit-in at the statehouse in Indianapolis and Betty was there with us. We have a photo of both Betty and Ricardo at the sit-in at the Indiana statehouse.

Ricardo: Olga and I valued our friendship with Betty and Dr. Samora and their family, students, and colleagues. Dr. Samora's life reflected the life of a scholar, researcher, educator, and person actively engaged in the world of action and change. One would not perceive this engagement during a first meeting, or at first glance, as you passed him in the hall, for Dr. Samora had a quiet, unassuming demeanor. Once we got to know him, however, we learned that he had keen instincts, he knew how to read people and situations, and he had compassion for the underdog. He was an advocate for the forgotten and ignored, choosing his own time, ways, and methods to act. Samora was very effective; he showed how the world of knowledge could bring about change.

His life was an example, yet he chose to put the light on others by bringing in other scholars, researchers, and national leaders as part of his seminars and lecture series. These were popular forums attended by the Latino community as well as the university folk.

The Groundskeepers' Dispute at Notre Dame

Ricardo: The groundskeepers' struggle started in 1977 and ended in 1978. Twenty-one Notre Dame groundskeepers wanted to join Teamsters Local 364 to obtain a pay raise. Eventually cafeteria workers on campus joined the struggle for union recognition to improve their working conditions, pay, and benefits. The university administration resisted by threatening to contract those particular services to companies external to Notre Dame and eliminate the jobs on campus. Notre Dame even hired expensive, high-powered, union-busting lawyers to stop unionization on campus.

Olga: Many of the groundskeepers and cafeteria workers were friends and members of our own parish in South Bend, St. Stephen. Their struggle to organize for adequate working conditions left many of us sad and confused. We had experienced good friendships among and between the Holy Cross Community at Notre Dame and the Latino community at St. Stephen's parish, especially regarding issues of social justice. But the groundskeepers' dispute exposed a deep disconnect between the life on campus and the local Latino community. We considered ourselves part of the greater Notre Dame family and so it was painful. But the plight of the groundskeepers and other Notre Dame workers needed to be addressed through implementing a fair and just resolution.[7]

Ricardo: The groundskeepers' dispute attracted attention on and off campus. The student newspaper, *The Observer,* and the local *South Bend Tribune* also ran many articles in 1977 and 1978 about the dispute's origins and evolution. The Midwest Council's own newsletter *Los Desarraigados* included extensive coverage and urged people to support the workers. In short order, the local Teamsters filed complaints of unfair labor practices against Notre Dame with the National Labor Relations Board. In early 1978, Notre Dame accepted an NLRB ruling to abide by certain practices and not interfere with workers seeking to unionize.

Olga: Fr. Theodore Hesburgh's work as a champion of civil rights did not coincide with the university's attitude toward the poorest paid of its workers. We were shocked and surprised when the university so aggressively opposed improving the workers' lot. Where was the social justice?

Ricardo: I remember Dr. Samora attending the organization meetings and

standing with his arms crossed and a stern look on his face. He was one of
the first and one of the few faculty members at Notre Dame that stood with
us in support of the groundskeepers and cafeteria workers in their quest for
fuller inclusion as part of the Notre Dame family as they acquired reasonable working conditions and benefits. Dr. Samora was an advocate within
the faculty and administration to help them arrive at a just decision. He
also started working with local Holy Cross priests at St. Stephen's Church
to gain support for the unionization issues.

Retrospective

Olga: I have been blessed with a certain kind of wisdom and experience. I
don't know where those qualities come from, my parents, Catholic upbringing, or the life lessons of being the oldest of nine siblings. Life appointed me
the role of pathfinder for family, neighbors, church, and community. Indeed,
we were a founding family of St. Thomas Parish in Muskegon, Michigan, and
since that time I have been active in the parish community in both pastoral
and social action concerns, such as organizing migrant farm workers and
their families to better their lives.

Ricardo: Olga has the skill and personality that engenders trust and confidence, a good dose of charisma, a non-threatening manner and common
sense that make people feel at ease with her. And let me tell you, people both
young and old, students, parents, and grandparents seek out her advice on
issues, big and small. Olga is always respectful and when she takes a stand,
she defends herself in a strong and positive way. Although Olga learned
organizing skills, she possesses many qualities essential to building partnerships, and she was generous in teaching. She, like I, was excited about the
1970 April conference at the University of Notre Dame that focused on
Spanish-speaking communities in the Midwest.

We did things as if time was running out—we had a sense of urgency, we
did not know when the window of opportunity would close. Timing was
everything. We were impatient, we believed in action. We had victories, de-
feats, and successes, and we learned many lessons. Those were action years
and established a foundation we built for the future. It was a hands-on
experience, both individually and collectively.

We each had our own individual way of contributing to the cause. It was
a lot of hard work. Sometimes I would feel I had the weight of the whole
world on my shoulders, but I had the tremendous help of a lot of wonderful
people. Knowing this was so encouraging. Sometimes I feared making mistakes. Then I read something that went like this: "There are no assurances

against mistakes. Those who fail to do anything to change unjust conditions or better the world for fear of making a mistake, make no mistakes. But neither do they change anything in the limited time of their lives."

Working at the Midwest Council was a pivotal experience in our lives, a moment in time, a coming of age, a rite of passage into the future, or maybe it was our Don Quixote moment where impossible dreams were possible. Perhaps this shared collective experience was something that only those who went through it fully comprehend and appreciate.

The South Bend community was also an important place for us. Our web of relationships woven through our membership of St. Stephen's Church, Fr. Tom and Fr. John, Benito Salazar, the people of the parish, the Guadalupanas, the Cursillistas,[8] sustained us. These wonderful sources provided us with spiritual support and shared solidarity. I remember the ladies at the church, the men, the youth, and the families. This too was an experience that remains with us to this day.

These experiences changed and shaped our lives. It was a different time, one of idealism that filled and motivated people with hope. The civil rights movement was underway, the war on poverty had been declared, and the Chicano movement was making gains. The words of President Kennedy, "ask not what your country can do for you, ask what you can do for your country" still resonated. The idea that one could effect social change and everyone should try remained the ideal. IBM told us that the system was the solution; our dissenting youth told us that the system was the problem. Martin Luther King Jr. told us that injustice anywhere is a threat to justice everywhere. James Baldwin told us not everything that is faced can be changed, but nothing can be changed until it is faced. Cesar Chavez fasted for strength following the non-violent path of Gandhi. Chavez told us when we are really honest with ourselves we must admit that our lives are all that really belong to us. So it is how we share our lives that determine what kind of people we are. The time has come for people of the Midwest Council generation to tell our stories.

There we were with hope and belief that we could help in building a better world. We were surrounded by a movement calling us to service as a force for good, for something larger than ourselves, and many of us responded. We called this force "La Causa." We learned to work and struggle together. We felt so much affection for those with whom we worked and served. We felt so much support from them when we got married. The friendship and warmth has extended to this day.

Everyone needs heroes, mentors, role models, and guides, and in a great and quiet way Dr. Samora and Betty were among them. Meeting Dr. Samora and Betty, their students, our friends everywhere during the Midwest Council years was the experience of a lifetime. And it changed our lives. We are glad that people remember Dr. Samora. Institutions and societies have memories, but first they are composed of people, people who sometimes ignore, appreciate, or remember. I am thankful that just when I was beginning to think that some had forgotten the rich deeds and legacy of Dr. Samora and the good work he did, I now see others have stepped up with deeds of their own to honor him and the causes that mattered to him. I think he would be absolutely delighted with all the good work going on today.

Notes

1. Olga often refers to Jane Gonzáles as an important influence in her professional and personal development. Gonzáles was a political activist in Muskegon.

2. Information about the Mexican American Conference discussed here comes from documents distributed at the conference and saved by Olga and Ricardo.

3. Now known as the Hesburgh Library.

4. Thomas Broden, still a professor at the law school at Notre Dame, was the first faculty member at Notre Dame to promote involvement in neighborhood-based legal services. He directed the Institute for Urban Studies from 1970 to 1990. Please see http://law.nd/faculty/facultypages/broden.

5. Please see Kamaria Porter, "Egan and Catholic Action Against Segregation in Chicago," *Notre Dame Journal of Undergraduate Research* (2005), http://www .nd.edu/~ujournal/past/2005–6/print/egan.

6. Midwest Council of La Raza actively generated a community off and on campus concerned with issues relating to the well-being of Latinos throughout the Midwest. The agency functioned as a bridge between the academy and the local and regional Latino community.

7. In 1976 I left Midwest Council to work with the Midwest Hispanic Catholic Commission as the social action coordinator. Working for the institutional Catholic Church was a new venture for me, although I had been volunteering since childhood in the Hispanic ministry at Saint Thomas the Apostle Church in Muskegon.

8. The Guadalupanas and Cursillistas are Spanish-speaking women's organizations in the Catholic Church.

CHAPTER SIX

From Uvalde, Texas, to South Bend, Indiana

A Chicano Goes to Notre Dame

Alfredo Rodriguez Santos c/s

"Well no, . . . I don't know of anyone who wants to go to Notre Dame. No sir . . . yes sir, OK. . . . I will keep my eyes open and let you know if I hear of anyone. OK, . . . Yes sir, goodbye."

I put the telephone down and looked out the window of my office on Main Street in Uvalde, Texas. It was July 14th, 1978. I had just finished a conversation with Dr. Charles Wilbur, the chairman of the economics department at the University of Notre Dame.

A few weeks earlier, I had written a letter to the department asking them to send information to my boss, José Uriegas, the executive director of the Mexican American Center for Economic Development (MACED) in Austin, Texas. Mr. Uriegas had expressed an interest in doing graduate work in economics, and I thought I was doing him a favor by making some inquiries. Somehow, Dr. Wilbur had gotten a hold of my telephone number and was looking for students who would be willing to do graduate work in his program.

The following week, Dr. Wilbur called again, *y otra vez*[1] he wanted to know if I knew of anyone who wanted to go to South Bend, Indiana . . . to the University of Notre Dame. Being the polite fellow that I was, once again I told him I still hadn't come across anyone.

"OK," he said. "Well, I am still recruiting. I am looking for three Mexican Americans and I have scholarship money."

"OK, I'll keep my eyes wide open," *le dije otra vez.*[2]

We said our cordial good-byes again and I hung up. It was 10:00 a.m., time for a taco. As I stepped out the door I told Maxine, our secretary, about this professor from Notre Dame. I also told her he might be calling back.

Dicho y hecho,[3] the following week, it was Dr. Wilbur *otra vez!* "There is a Dr. Charles Wilbur on the phone for you Alfredo. Do you want to take the call?" I already knew what he wanted but still I had nothing new to tell him.

I thought for a moment about what to say. "Yes Maxine, put him through." Once again Dr. Wilbur made his pitch, and once again I found myself politely repeating what I had told him the previous week. He went on and on about the need for more Mexican American students at Notre Dame. Back in the 1970s, we were not using the term Hispanic. "Yes Dr. Wilbur . . . You are right Dr. Wilbur . . . que si Dr. Wilbur." *Este vato . . . me está cansado.*[4]

Then he wanted to know about my work in Uvalde and where I went to school. *Le dije poquito de lo que estábamos haciendo*[5] with this new CETA program we were running at Southwest Texas Junior College and what the students were learning.

Then he asked, "Did you go to high school in Uvalde?"

Le dije, "Yes sir, but I didn't graduate." I went on to tell him about the 1970 Uvalde school walkout. I explained that unlike Crystal City,[6] we were not successful in Uvalde with our walkout and as punishment for protesting, many students were flunked back one year. Many of us who were juniors and seniors refused to go back to school, including me. We were either too proud or too embarrassed.

"So did you graduate later?" he asked.

I told him no. "Well, did you go to college later?"

"Yes," *le dije.* "Later that year I was out in California working in the fields when I heard on the radio that a person could go to college for free as long as they were over eighteen years of age. I went to the community college in Stockton, California, to see if it was true. When they told me it was indeed true, I got myself enrolled and started taking classes."

There was a long silence on his end of the telephone. Dr. Wilbur asked me if I had a bachelor's degree.

Le dije, "Yes sir, I went on to graduate from UC Berkeley with a degree in economics in 1974."

Now there was a longer silence on his end of the telephone. It sounded as if he were talking to somebody else in the room. When he began to speak again he said, "How would you like to come to Notre Dame?"

"How would I like to go to Notre Dame? Is that what you asked me?"

"Yes," he said.

Now it was my turn to go silent. I begin with excuses by stammering out, "No . . . not me. I just came back from California not too long ago and I have a real job. No. . . . I am going to stay where I'm at." I thought to myself, after spending three years as a labor organizer in Watsonville, California, for Cesar Chavez and the UFW at $5.00 a week, I was not about to let go of my new $14,000–a-year job with MACED.

Dr. Wilbur continued to talk about the program, the scholarship, and the tradition of Notre Dame. I thought to myself, *este guy, neta que anda en overdrive con su onda.*[7]

Then he said, "Well I have a scholarship that will pay for everything for four years. School will be starting soon and I would sure hate to have to return the money because I couldn't find anyone who wanted to come to Notre Dame."

To this I replied, "Look Dr. Wilbur, it sounds like a great offer but even if I were to tell you 'yes,' I wouldn't be able to go." He asked why not? So I told him, "Well, I would have to order transcripts. And then I would have to take the GRE. There is just not enough time. And then I would . . ."

He cut me off as I was thinking of all the reasons why I couldn't go. "Can I call you Alfredo?" "Yes." "Alfredo, you didn't hear the question. I asked you if you wanted to come to the University of Notre Dame to pursue a doctoral degree in economics? If you say yes . . . then you're in. We can do the paperwork once you get here."

For the purpose of clarity I asked him, "You mean just like that, if I say yes, I'm in?"

"That's right," he said.

I was shocked to say the least. I went silent for about a minute. "Let me call you back in a couple of days,"

"OK, but you understand the offer?"

"Yes I do." I hung up the telephone and stared out the window. It was now early August of 1978.

In the following days, I called Mr. Uriegas in Austin to tell him what Dr. Wilbur had offered. I also told him that I really liked my job with MACED and that I enjoyed what I was doing. Mr. Uriegas said to me, "*No seas pendejo!*[8] Do you know what I would give to be able to go to Notre Dame? Take it! *Al cabo,*[9] you're on soft money. It won't last forever." That weekend I went to Angleton, Texas, where my mother was living and told her what this professor was offering me. She said to think it over carefully and do what I thought was best. The offer was tempting. Other friends I told said to go for it. I thought to myself, I'm twenty-six years old. If I go back to school I wouldn't finish until I am thirty, maybe thirty-one. It seemed like a long time. I liked economics but did I want to get a doctorate in economics? I called Dr. Wilbur the next day.

"Dr. Wilbur, this is Alfredo Santos c/s in Texas."

"Yes Alfredo."

I told him, "OK, I accept your offer."

"That is great. Classes start the last week of August. I will send you a letter and once you get here we will do all of the paperwork. See you soon."

After hanging up the phone I took a deep breath to reflect on what I had just done. Many thoughts raced through my mind. Is this the right decision? Is this the right time to leave Uvalde? I just got back here. What is the winter going to be like up there? I was making a decision based on the word of a man I had never met, to go to a place I had never been, to earn a doctoral degree, which I wasn't even thinking about. This was truly going to be a leap of faith. I left Uvalde, Texas, on August 26th, for South Bend, Indiana, in my 1956 Chevy lowrider with a couple hundred dollars in my pocket and the idea that someday I might be Dr. Alfredo Santos c/s. *¡Qué loco!*

La Llegada (The Arrival)

Arriving in South Bend, Indiana, I stopped at a gas station to ask which was the way to Notre Dame. The guy pointed north, and I followed his directions. It was a Sunday afternoon, not too hot, and there was a good wind blowing. I parked my car, untied my bike from the trunk of my car, and took a ride around the campus. I saw a small lake, the Golden Dome, and a grotto; many of the buildings had ivy growing on the walls. So this is Notre Dame! That evening I checked into a cheap motel just north of the campus.

Arriving on campus early the next morning, I went looking for Dr. Charles Wilbur in the economics department. I found him in his office, and he congratulated me on my arrival. He also shared with me that after all the time and effort recruiting all over the country, he was only able to find one other Mexican American who took him up on his offer. He told me I would soon meet the other fellow who had come in from Colorado with his family. Then he said I should go and see Dr. Julian Samora. "Dr. Samora is the one who is really responsible for you coming to Notre Dame." I was surprised to say the least. I knew Dr. Julian Samora was a professor at Notre Dame, but up to that point I did not know he was involved in my being here. Dr. Wilbur never said anything about Dr. Samora and what I would later learn was the Mexican American Graduate Studies Program.

Meeting Dr. Julian Samora

I found Dr. Samora's office in the library building. I went up and introduced myself to the secretary who was sitting at a desk. She asked me to wait a second and went into another office. When she came out, Dr. Julian Samora was following her. This was my first meeting with him. He shook my hand and smiled and said that he was glad I had made the decision to come to Notre Dame. Then he said something that absolutely floored me. "I spoke to José Uriegas and he was sorry that you left MACED, but he would have done the same thing."

I said, "You know José Uriegas?"

He just smiled back at me. It appears there were a lot of things I didn't know.

Dr. Samora told the secretary to go ahead and have me start filling out some paperwork. I took a seat in a little conference room and began to fill out forms when John Ribal walked into the office. He was the guy from Colorado. I could hear Dr. Samora welcoming John to Notre Dame and making small talk. Then he had John join me in the conference room to fill out paperwork. When we announced that we had finished with the paperwork, Dr. Samora came in and began to tell us about the weekly seminar we would be expected to attend. John and I looked at each other and said fine, we would be there. Dr. Samora chatted with us for a little bit more until he was called away to take a phone call. John and I headed back to the economics department to find out what our class schedule was going to be.

I knew Dr. Julian Samora was the author of books and that he had been at Notre Dame for a long time, but I did not know about all of his behind-the-scenes work in the Chicano movement. I did not know about his role with the Ford Foundation or his role in setting up the National Council of La Raza. And I did not know that he and Mr. Uriegas were friends.

The Economics Program at Notre Dame

John Ribal and I went to our first economics class that very morning. I believe it was a macroeconomics class taught by Professor James Rakowski. Altogether they had us taking five classes that first semester. I remember saying to myself that this was going to be a heavy workload. Before the first class ended I stood up and announced I was looking for housing. As we walked out the door, a student named Jeff Ankrom told me there were rooms at a house where he was staying. He gave me a telephone number to call, and I ended up moving into a small room in the basement of a place where five other graduate students were staying. The rent was $65 a month.

As I settled into my new reality at Notre Dame, I began to meet the other students. One of these students was Rene Perez Rosenbaum. When I first met Rene, he had a cast on his leg. I found out later that he had been in a car accident. But despite the cast, he could still move around. Rene was a second-year student in the economics program. John Ribal and I were a little bit older than Rene, but we quickly realized he had a lot of insight and advice we could benefit from. As John and I went to our other classes, we saw that, besides Rene, we were the only Chicanos in all five of our classes.

The Mexican American Graduate Studies Program

I had not known about the Mexican American Graduate Studies Program at Notre Dame. When Dr. Wilbur was on the telephone with me in Texas, he never mentioned Dr. Samora or the Mexican American Graduate Studies Program. But the opportunity to get together weekly with other Chicano students from other departments was a good idea. As I recall, there were law students in the seminar, students from sociology, English, and of course economics. It was a laid-back seminar and each week Dr. Samora had a different topic we would discuss around the table, and he made sure everyone had a chance to contribute to the discussions. When he detected a flaw in an argument or wanted you to think more critically about what you were saying, he had a gentle way of asking you to explain it again. Sometimes we would move the seminar over to the law school when we had a guest speaker in town. I remember Raul Yzaguirre from the National Council of La Raza came to speak to us, as did Vilma Martínez from the Mexican American Legal Defense and Educational Fund. Each one of the speakers seemed to be good friends with Dr. Samora by the way they interacted with one another.

There was an incident in the seminar with Dr. Samora that got ugly. There was a law student who seemed to think that because he was in law school he had it made in the shade. Over several encounters during the fall semester (translate that into beers), Rene, another law student named Jorge Canales, and I discovered that despite this student's big ego and claims to fame in the Chicano movement in Texas, he didn't speak Spanish hardly at all. During a particular weekly seminar in the spring of 1979, he became very rude and insulting toward Dr. Samora. He kept insisting that Dr. Samora didn't know what he was talking about and that Dr. Samora needed to read this and that. *Una falta de respeto pero tremendo.*[10]

Rene, Jorge, and I looked at each other to see who would be the one to challenge this rude and insulting student and redirect him away from Dr. Samora. The hole in the student's persona was his inability to defend himself in Spanish. I went first. In Spanish and in front of everyone, I told him, "*Oyes cabrón, qué chingaos tienes tú hablando a Dr. Samora en esa forma?*"[11] He was stunned. While he couldn't speak Spanish, he sure as hell understood it. Then Rene came at him from the other side of the table. "*Debes de agredece que estás aquí en Notre Dame por los esfuerzos de Dr. Samora.*[12] When you speak to him, you better show him more respect, you son of a bitch!" Then Jorge told him, "Who the fuck do you think you are?" We were ready to beat the shit out of him right there. Now everybody was stunned. The student could see that it was no longer just him and Dr. Samora, now it was the twelve or thirteen people in the seminar. Realizing that he had crossed the line, he got up and stormed out of the room. I don't remember ever seeing him again. We were not afraid of him because we knew who the real person was after ten beers.

The Samora Family

One day after the seminar, Dr. Samora invited me to come to his house for dinner. I went the following week, and I met his wife, Betty. I believe this was also the first time I met Carmen. As I recall from the conversation around the dinner table that evening, Carmen had come back from Alaska to help care for her mother, who was ill. Dr. Samora didn't talk much that evening. I tried to be careful not to talk too much either since I was the new person in town. From all I could tell, the Samoras were very nice people. I remember I got sick in November with a cold and Carmen and her mother made a soup for me. Living in that house in the basement like a rat with no sunlight did not help me feel better. But that *caldito*[13] sure did warm me up. I will never forget that soup or their gestures of kindness.

Training to Be an Economist

I was taking five economics classes that first semester, and even though I did not have to work, the classes were killing me. As an economics under-graduate at Berkeley, the classes were hard and the math was difficult, but the stuff I was getting at the graduate level was way over my head. We had study groups for different classes and I would attend, but for some reason I just wasn't cutting it, although I do recall that I was doing well in a public finance class that I was taking with Rene. As the first semester wound down, I was having serious reservations about continuing. I drove back to Texas for Christmas in my '56 Chevy thinking I might not come back.

After three weeks off for the Christmas break, I felt better and got ready to drive back to Notre Dame. I had a whole new set of classes and was ready to move forward. But after a few weeks, I started crashing again. Economics at the graduate level just seemed to be too abstract for me. One day I was sitting in Professor Larry Marsh's microeconomic class in O'Shaughnessy Hall watching as he wrote something called a Slutsky equation on the chalkboard. According to Professor Marsh, we were going to study how this equation would relate Marshallian demand and Hicksian demand, which are two demand changes due to price changes that are a result of a substitution effect and an income effect of price results in a change of the consumer's purchasing power.

I was writing all this down in my notebook, and I suddenly stopped. I looked up at the board and at all the students around me who were taking copious notes and said to myself, I am not going to become an economist. I closed my notebook and started making plans to return to Texas. It was now March of 1979.

I went to see Dr. Samora in his office and told him that economics at the graduate level was not for me. I also told him that I would be returning to Texas. He was very quiet and asked me if I had thought this over very carefully. I told him that I had. He suggested that I visit with my advisor in the economics department before making a final decision. I told him I would, and I excused myself.

The Decision to Leave Notre Dame

After visiting with my advisor, Professor Roger Skurski, I turned in my Notre Dame ID card. My '56 Chevy had fallen victim to the harsh South Bend winter, and Rene and I had managed to salvage two Volkswagens from three that we had acquired in the last couple of months. I had learned how to fix vws in an earlier life. I remember saying good-bye to Carmen, to John Ribal, and to Rene. I told them I was going back to Texas. Since I had stopped going to classes, I had been in the library reading for two weeks. The weather was warming up, and I left in mid-April. It was a long, slow drive back to Texas, and I had a lot of time to think. I had met many wonderful people at Notre Dame and was given many, many opportunities. But it wasn't meant to be for me.

Life after Notre Dame

Instead of going back to Uvalde, Texas, I decided to go to Houston. I had been reading in all the magazines that Houston was a jumping town and so I decided to go see for myself. In a previous life I was a certified locksmith, so in three days I found a job as a locksmith in Houston. When September came around, somehow I found out that there was a Catholic School in a barrio called Denver Harbor that was in need of schoolteachers. I applied and was hired on the spot to teach math and science. My salary was going to be $30.00 a day. This was not exactly the economic boom that I had been reading about, but I saw a need and thought I could be of service. To supplement my pay, I got a job as a waiter at a night club called Emiliano's. I would teach in the day and wait tables at night. As a waiter I was making $100 a night. Back then that was good money. For that whole year (1979–80) I worked two jobs.

When my first year was up, Sister Bernice, the principal, had plenty of applicants who wanted to teach, so I bowed out gracefully. Somewhere somebody had told me a great story about being a taxi driver, so I got my license. It was my intention to drive only for a little while. I always figured I would go back to school. But instead, I ended up driving a taxicab in Houston, Texas, for ten years. I got into a fight with the city over a transportation modality called jitney service and became an advocate for the reintroduction of jitneys (in Mexico they are called Peseros). I sued the city of Houston, challenging the 1924 anti-jitney law, and I won a major lawsuit (Santos vs. City of Houston).

In 1985, I did go back to Notre Dame to Dr. Samora's retirement party. Rene and I had remained friends over the years, and we have been in each other's weddings.

I tried graduate school again, this time in a doctoral program in urban affairs and public policy at the University of Delaware. I stayed in that program for three years and, as at Notre Dame, I ended up crashing out. I went back to teaching, earned a master's degree, helped to start a charter school in Uvalde, and got into journalism. Today, I publish newspapers in several cities in Texas (www.lavoznewspapers.com).

When I think about the short time I spent at Notre Dame, sometimes it seems like it was just yesterday. I enjoyed meeting all the people who came into my life while I was there (even the rude law student). With respect to Dr. Samora, I am grateful for all he did to open doors and create opportunities for me and people like me. I believe that everyone who is working on this legacy project should be commended for all the hard work that goes into remembering someone who gave so much to so many.

Notes

The "c/s" means *con safos,* or respectfully.

1. and once again
2. I told him again
3. When all is said and done
4. "well, yes, Dr. Wilbur." This guy is boring me.
5. I told him little about what we were doing.

6. Crystal City, Texas, is thirty-nine miles from Uvalde. Jose Angel Gutierrez organized MAYO (Mexican American Youth Organization) chapters throughout the state in the 1960s. When the students at Crystal High School staged a walkout in 1969, those of us who were MAYO members in Uvalde would cut classes and drive to Crystal City to help them with the marches and picket lines.

7. "this guy is really pushing the idea"

8. Don't be an asshole!

9. In the end,

10. This was a huge failure of respect.

11. Hey, you bastard, what gives you the balls to talk to Dr. Samora that way?

12. You should be grateful, you are here at Notre Dame because of Dr. Samora.

13. soup

CHAPTER SEVEN

Don Julian Samora, *un hombre de Ubuntu*

Lydia Espinosa Crafton

When we want to give high praise to someone we say "*Yu, u no-buntu*"; "Hey so-and-so has *ubuntu.*" Then you are generous, you are hospitable, you are friendly and caring and compassionate. You share what you have. It is to say, "My humanity is caught up, is inextricably bound up in yours." We belong in a bundle of life. We say, "A person is a person through other person." It is not, "I think therefore I am." It says rather: "I am human because I belong. I participate, I share." A person with *ubuntu* is open and available to others, affirming of others, does not feel threatened that others are able and good, for he or she has a proper self-assurance that comes from knowing that he or she belongs in a greater whole and is diminished when others are humiliated and diminished, when others are tortured or oppressed or treated as if they were less than who they are.
—ARCHBISHOP DESMOND TUTU, 1999

By the time I met Dr. Samora he was already a respected scholar in the field of immigration and Mexican American history, a published writer, and a recognized leader, yet he was *un hombre humilde,*[1] never a grandstander, never pretentious. His easy, unhurried manner and welcoming smile made one feel accepted and understood, and it fostered *confianza*.[2] *Así se debe ser*[3] I would think. Years after Notre Dame, when I was reading Archbishop Desmond Tutu's reflective account on South Africa's Truth and Reconciliation Commission, I discovered the name for this rare quality I so liked, admired, and found in Dr. Samora—*ubuntu*.

I recall Dr. Samora as *una persona* that brought people together, in person as well as in dialogue, an expert facilitator of communication and understanding. A most attentive listener, always relaxed in his pose, he was always fully present and curious. Mild of manner and friendly, he was a master of the use of open-ended questions to explore underlying premises or recognize assumptions without sure grounds. An attentive and curious listener, Dr. Samora left a person telling a story or sharing their view with his or her dignity intact and a little wiser.

A person with *ubuntu* is generous, hospitable, friendly, caring, and shares what he or she has with others, as if to say, "My humanity is caught up, is inextricably bound up in yours."[4] When a person lives his or her life this way, each day is full of examples one can point to as reflections of *ubuntu*. The moments we later remember are those of special significance to ourselves.

I do not recall how many times I knocked on his office door, but I do remember the smile of welcome and the feeling that I could speak openly with him regardless of the reason. In retrospect, I recognize him as the ideal mentor for me. His way was not to start sentences with "What you should do," but rather through the use of simple questions he helped guide one to discover deepened understanding of a situation and the best course of action to take. By his manner and his way, he indicated empathy and support, and he cultivated trust.

I don't know how things are now at Notre Dame, but in the Notre Dame of those days Chicanos still experienced incidents that were hurtful and disrespectful. An example was when the Sociology Department served Gallo wine during their Christmas party although a boycott of Gallo wine by the United Farm Workers union was underway. While the choice of wine was later claimed to have been unintentional, an unknowing choice on the part of a secretary, a grievous incident did occur during the party. The professor for whom I was a graduate assistant offended a fellow Chicano by teasing him to drink the wine. I hadn't attended the party because I was studying for a final. Finding out about it set off a powder keg (within me) that landed me at Dr. Samora's door. Fuming, I let loose every unfavorable *sobre nombre*[5] I could think of and a number of choice expletives, repeating several of them many times over. Dr. Samora quietly sat through it all, never trying to stop me or correct me. When the *chubasco*[6] had run its course and I, with final breath, excused my language, Dr. Samora with a small smile said the obvious, "I can see you're pretty upset." He then engaged me in talking over the incident. I remember little of the substance that ensued in that talk we had, but still recall his calm in the face of my anger and plan of revenge, and my confidence in his empathy.

Since all of us (his students) were far away from home, the times Dr. Samora and his wife Betty gathered us into their family circle to celebrate special events enveloped us with special warmth and belonging that is remembered to this day. The stories, photographs, and special items shared with us during these times provided a window into their personal circle of memories and hopes. I recall a heavy handmade adobe brick and photographs of their family making these bricks in New Mexico, where they told us they were hand-building a family home. Happiness and pride flowed from them as they stood there, and it warmed us.

A person who lives his life by a philosophy of *ubuntu* experiences his humanity through belonging, participation, and sharing. The focal point for students in the Mexican American Graduate Studies Program was a weekly gathering for the Chicano seminar. Through the seminar Dr. Samora helped us understand the arena of academia, its expectations, and its rules and tools of engagement. Amid our companions a social community was also created. I learned a key factor of this weekly seminar through an unrelated experience two years ago when conducting focus group research with Latino immigrants.[7] When asked their opinion of what would be most beneficial to Latino immigrants, the first two needs identified across all groups were a place to get information (to have questions answered, for orientation, to help one know what to do to avoid or resolve problems, and to give guidance about how to survive), and a place for social gathering. During one focus group session someone said, "Even though one is far from one's family and his homeland and it appears that one is alone . . . a public gathering about development brings people together with each other . . . to get to know each other." These poignant words touch me deeply. They resonate with a desire to be empowered with sense making, understanding, and connection with others, of the need to belong through participation and sharing . . . especially when one is a stranger in a new land. Now I see it was we—the Chicano seminar students—were once the strangers in a strange land and that the seminar met our needs for belonging, connection, and information.

As I recall, we would sit in a circle. Years later I recognize the wisdom and the expert facilitator's touch in using this group arrangement to foster a sense of community. A group circle welcomes and empowers shared voices—all the stories, experiences, and meanings of those who take part have equal value—thereby fostering respect, understanding, and constructive conflict resolution. As with most gatherings we find ourselves in, we are apt to take essentials for granted, so I never asked why we sat that way, but I do remember the closeness and connection with each of the others who were there then, the liveliness of our dialogue, and synergetic[8] learning that occurred between us. Now across time and experience I see that from the detail of the seating arrangement to his modeling of respectful discourse through inclusion of all voices and basic curious inquiry, Dr. Samora fostered an environment of *ubuntu*.

As part of the Mexican American Graduate Studies Program we were encouraged to focus on our own special area of interest about Mexican Americans. Knowing of my own past in Chicana research and history, Dr. Samora encouraged my interest in the Farah strike and pregnancy practices among Mexican American women before modern medicine. During my stay at Notre Dame the Mexican American Graduate Studies Program also sponsored a Chicana conference.

We may have been impoverished graduate students, but for Dr. Samora we were budding intellectuals, or at least he instilled that belief in us. For example, one of the perks of the program was the opportunity to meet outstanding scholars and other persons prominent in Mexican American/ Chicano affairs who were invited to present at Notre Dame through the Mexican American Graduate Studies Program. Listening to these people firsthand was a special opportunity in itself, but linked to their visit would be an invitation for us (program students) to have either dinner or breakfast with them for a face-to-face informal chat. By his manner and his wording we felt the pride and esteem Dr. Samora felt for us as he introduced us to the speaker, and in that moment we basked in his affirmation.

"A person with *ubuntu* . . . is diminished when others are humiliated and diminished, when others are tortured or oppressed or treated as if they were less than who they are."[9] While it can be said that the greatest part of Dr. Samora's life work was the extensive study of the human experience of immigrants, Mexican Americans, or Hispano/Latinos and the sharing of this knowledge with others, it can also be said that he used his knowledge and life experience as a cornerstone to further the equitable protection of human and civil rights of members of these groups. Through the many lives he touched through his works, he became a *sembrador de ideas*[10] for the common good.

Incredible as it now seems, during the time I was a student of Dr. Samora, I was unaware that a full decade earlier his had been one of the early voices foundational to what would become the Chicano movement. In 1963, when addressing gatherings of community leaders who were meeting to probe the educational problems of Mexican American youth in the Southwest, Dr. Samora named the unfair and prejudicial practices of educational systems toward Mexican Americans as the cause of these problems.[11] He charged "a vicious social system which is detrimental to our society" with depriving Mexican Americans of their civil rights.[12] That same year, in an article in the educational journal *Theory Into Practice*, he again recognized that prejudicial marginalization experienced by Mexican Americans at the social community level reflected the practices in their educational institutions. In his words, "If it is true that the schools reflect the norms and values of the community, then perhaps it is equally true that its prejudices are also reflected, through acts of commission as well as omission."[13]

At this same time in California, Cesar Chavez and Dolores Huerta were beginning to organize farm workers under the United Farm Workers union along issues of safety and exploitation, and on September 16, 1965, Mexican Independence Day, the Delano grape strike began. In New Mexico, the Alianza Federal de Mercedes (Federated Alliance of Land Grants) under Reies Tijerina was challenging the U.S. government for *ejido*[14] lands.[15]

Meanwhile, living on a farm miles away from a small town in Texas, listening to the occasional faraway drone of traffic traveling along Highway 111, I wove schoolgirl dreams of Someday.

By the mid-1960s, from California to Texas, the Chicano movement emerged in a groundswell of grassroots protest, activism, and cultural pride flexing community power in direct challenge to systemic discriminatory practices. In Colorado, the Crusaders for Justice, led by Corky Gonzales, were exposing corruption within the Denver political machinery and unfair practices by city agencies and the legal system, as well as prejudicial reporting of Mexican Americans by the *Rocky Mountain News*.[16] In Texas, the Mexican American Youth Organization (MAYO) was organizing walkouts, marches, and demonstrations challenging unfair and discriminatory educational practices of school districts.

According to Chicano historian and professor emeritus Felipe de Ortego y Gasca, "From 1964 to 1975 Texas A&I[17] was 'Command Central' for Chicano activities throughout South Texas and the state. Major Chicano activities occurred elsewhere, but their genesis had its origins at Texas A&I where many of the Texas Chicano activists were students."[18] The Chicano activism at Texas A&I evolved as a response to real-life "acts of bigotry, oppression and intimidation" that "were daily experiences for Hispanics" attending the university at this time.[19]

I believe that the being we are unfolds through the choices we make—these choices being shaped both by the core beliefs that underlie what sense we make of the world and how we see and wish ourselves to be in relationship with others. In the summer of '69, out of curiosity, I was drawn to an advertised MAYO meeting at A&I where I was an undergraduate student. Questions led me there. What are Chicanos? Am I one? Why? What's going on here?

At that meeting people who attended were invited to the MAYO headquarters, a little ramshackle house in the barrio where, to be honest, I first entered with a pang of trepidation but came to return to again and again. Through the shared stories and explanations of these first MAYO members (Mage y Rene Treviño, Chito, and others) who gathered there, I came to first know and embrace the spirit of *carnalismo*[20] and my identity as a Chicana. This experience fueled my sense of personal responsibility to fight social injustice for my community, my people—*La Raza*.

> *Yo soy Chicana tengo color, Americana pero con honor,*
> *Cuando me dicen que hay revolución, defiendo a mi Raza*
> *con mucho valor.*[21]

It was an exciting time to be part of the Chicano movement. So many were awakening at the same time, connecting, exploring, and creating new ways, new expressions, a new social reality. Women were an integral part of the movement in organizing and speaking out, and in time many of us came to form special bonds, referring to each other as *comadres* and sharing our views on the role of women.

While the Chicano movement was happening, the women's movement had also been growing, with white women primarily at its forefront. Within the context of that time, still holding a critical and wary view of the motives of (and manipulation by) whites, activist Chicanas (I among them) became engaged in clarifying our own platform as Chicana feminists and the nature of our alliance with feminist (primarily white) political activists. While we agreed with them on equal opportunity for women, we also saw the women's movement as highly individualistic. We foresaw the individual liberation of women as having a profound effect on *familia* and requiring a new construct among Chicano men of what it means to be a man in a relationship with this new type of woman. And as we sensed the historical nature of our own moment we also wondered about the women who had come before us.

Just as Chicanos were reconnecting with their heritage, we (Chicanas) felt a desire to know the roles, accomplishments, and *sufrimientos*[22] of Mexican and Chicana females who had traveled life's path before us. The quest for this knowledge and the need for a vehicle to assist other Chicanas in clarifying their own life vision led to our founding of the Chicana Research and Learning Center (of which I served as its first research director). Perhaps because of a deepened desire for knowledge or because of the influence of Chicano friends already in academia that happened during this time, I applied for and was granted a fellowship in the Notre Dame Mexican American Graduate Studies Program. And so I came to cross life's paths with Dr. Samora.

I only stayed a year at Notre Dame before I returned to Texas. Why did I not remain there and continue my studies and mentorship by someone I highly valued? While I recognized the value of the opportunity of both studying at Notre Dame, a prestigious school of learning, and the on-hand access to a special scholar and relationships with others whose interests ran parallel to my own, I had a strong feeling that this was not the right path for me. The objective sociological lens felt alien, too detached.

The lenses with which we view a situation vary, shaped by time, life experience, and accumulated knowledge. While now I can with some detachment view the person I was back in those days and name the reason why I left, back then all I knew was "this is not right for me." So I walked away from Notre Dame, but I still had the friends I met there and the learning of that year, the most valuable being Dr. Samora and his modeling of how to be with others and how to engage in constructive dialogue.

Many years later, when introduced to the process of mediation, I recognized within its practice a reflection of Dr. Samora's way of being in interaction with others. His attentive and active listening and his use of open-ended questions are fundamental mediator tools used to clarify and deepen awareness of how a situation is being viewed and what underlies that view. Similarly, his use of the circular seating arrangement, the care he took to include all voices, and his openness to listening to different views all give evidence of both a mediator and a humanist.

Through his works, Dr. Julian Samora will be remembered as a scholar, mentor, and civil rights advocate. It was my privilege to have known him as a friend, a mentor, and a supreme example of *ubuntu.*

Notes

Desmond Tutu, *No Future Without Forgiveness* (New York: Doubleday, 1999), p. 31.

1. a humble man
2. confidence in trustworthiness

3. That's the way for one to be.

4. Tutu, *No Future Without Forgiveness.*

5. nickname

6. storm

7. Lydia Espinosa Crafton, "Exploring the Diverse Worldviews of Latino Immigrants in a Community in Maryland Through Meanings Attached to Interpersonal Conflict Events" (*Capstone Project for Master's Program:* Antioch-McGregor University, 2005), p. 41.

8. Learning from interaction whose combined effect is greater than the sum of the individual parts.

9. Tutu, *No Future Without Forgiveness.*

10. Someone who scatters or plants seeds.

11. Ruben Salazar, a popular Chicano journalist for the *Los Angeles Times,* was known for his articulate and forthright reporting on issues related to the marginalization of Chicanos. His death in 1970 at the hands of police during an anti–Vietnam War protest in East L.A. and the lack of punishment for his killing represented (for Chicanos) police abuse and unequal American justice for Mexican Americans. Considered a martyr within the Chicano movement, in 1971 he was posthumously awarded a special Robert F. Kennedy Journalism Award. Since then, Laguna Park—the site of the 1970 rally—has been renamed Salazar Park in his honor, and a portion of State Route 5 similarly been named the Ruben Salazar Memorial Highway. Ruben Salazar and Mario T. García, *Border Correspondent: Selected Writings, 1955–1970* (Berkeley: University of California Press, 1998).

12. Salazar and García, *Border Correspondent: Selected Writings, 1955–1970.* Retrieved June 29, 2007, from http://ark.cdlib.org/ark:/13030/ft058002v2/.

13. Julian Samora, "The Educational Status of a Minority: Theory into Practice," *Intergroup-Relations Education* 2 (3) (1963): 44–150.

14. communal lands

15. Elizabeth Sutherland-Martínez and Enriqueta Longeaux y Vasquez, *Viva La Raza* (New York: Doubleday and Company, 1974).

16. Martínez and Longeaux y Vasquez, *Viva La Raza.*

17. Now Texas A&M-Kingsville.

18. Carlos Guerra, "Activist Reunion Held Amid Changes and Need for More Change," *San Antonio Express-News.* Web Posted: 10/16/2005 12:00 AM CDT. Retrieved June 28, 2007, from www.mysanantonio.com/news/metro/stories/MYSA101605.1B.guerra.2fa5c17.html.

19. Mari Saugier, "Activist: Chicano Civil Rights Fight Not Over," *Corpus Christi Caller-Times,* Thursday, October 13, 2005. Retrieved June 30, 2007, from: http://www.caller.com/ccct/local_news/article/0,1641,CCCT_811_4154750,00.html.

20. brotherhood

21. *Yo Soy Chicano/a* was the most popular song of the Chicano movement; this is the first stanza of the version we recited often.

22. sufferings

CHAPTER EIGHT

Julian Samora

Uno de los primeros sabios

Alberto Mata Jr.

When one speaks of Mexican American academic pioneers, Dr. Julian Samora will long be remembered with *Los Primeros Sabios:* George I. Sánchez, Ernesto Galarza, and Américo Paredes. These are but a few of the major *lideres*[1] that will long be remembered as our community's *Primeros Sabios.*[2] Although the number of Mexican American scholars, as well as other Latino scholars and professionals serving our communities has increased, the need for the role remains, especially for those in the mold of *Los Primeros Sabios.*

In this essay, I seek to share what first drew me to study with Dr. Julian Samora, my experiences with him and the Mexican American Graduate Studies Program (MAGSP) at the University of Notre Dame (UND), and the impact he has had on my own research, teaching, and service endeavors. In doing so I will also share my observations of his place in the academy as a *Primero Sabio,* his collaborative efforts in the making of Mexican American Studies, and why he remains a model for future first-generation Mexican American scholars and professionals. First-generation scholars are those who are first in their families to begin and complete college and perhaps do advanced doctoral graduate studies. Dr. Samora symbolizes for me a most important model of academic and professional leadership for first-generation scholars, then and now. In sharing these observations I underscore why he and *los otros Primero Sabios* provided examples that need to be continued.

As *Los Primeros Sabios* were themselves the first to complete high school, attend college, and complete advanced graduate studies—the sense of acting as a bridge between two distinct social worlds became second nature. *Los Primeros* were sensitive to and aware of the many challenges faced by vulnerable students and communities, and they recognized the need for advocacy and measured actions with an eye on long-term goals. They took their role as *maestros* and mentors seriously and gladly. But they understood the limits of their agendas and efforts. Thus Mexican American Studies was a vehicle to meet that wider agenda and effect its promise. This meant attention to recruiting and training the next generation of Raza scholars and professionals who would provide alternative voices and *ejemplos*[3] for those in need.

For me, only after embarking on my career did I come to better appreciate the contributions and sacrifices of Dr. Samora and the other *Sabios*. They were the first and on their own. They knew about breaking new ground in the academy as well as in the professions. And they did this with the knowledge and sense that *if not now, when? If not oneself, who?* We, their students, benefited from their support, from each other, and possibly from the winds of change. Their *ejemplo* is found in their commitment to teaching and mentoring the next generation. Their *ejemplo* and *maneras* allowed and expected their students to build upon and even surpass their work. Their *ejemplo* and *maneras* call for us to make our academies responsive, our peers more civically engaged, and our operating institutions more just and respectful to the needs of others. I remember that their comportment with us reflected their worldview that simple decent courtesies were the rule and not the exception.

On First-Generation Scholars

When I first began my graduate studies, I was full of motivation and commitment. As a first-generation college student, I was aware of the *terra nova* on which I was treading, but I was not fully apprised of the many challenges awaiting me. There were a few administrators and faculty members who had a limited sense of what we non-traditional students faced, and there were some few student services designed to aid us. Through my undergraduate and master's training, I had not yet met a Mexican American professor, much less one who came from circumstances similar to my own. I was drawn to those non-Latino *simpático*[4] professors who possessed a strong interest and knowledge about the lives of those from what Michael Harrington termed "the Other America."[5] While *The Other America* touched on realities outside the view of many Americans, it brought me to thinking about many key dynamics of the Mexican American experience in the United States missing from the view of the dominant culture. In much that I had read in academic texts, we were a small historical footnote at best, or overdrawn caricatures at worst. The "Other America" that I was from was so much more than the limited stereotypes represented in popular media. As I wrote a paper or pursued research in some aspect of the Mexican American experience, I discovered only a few journal articles, monographs, and government reports that touched on the questions of Mexican Americans in the United States. Whether the works were written by *simpáticos* or Chicanos, there was a dearth of published materials on the Mexican American experience in the United States, especially in the areas I was interested in pursuing. As I completed my master's I opted for a career in teaching. I wanted to do this in a field that I expected to help address key issues facing our families and communities. But after completing my master's, where to go to pursue advanced studies?

I was first introduced to Dr. Samora in 1971 by the then chair of the Sociology Department and two other professors at the University of Texas-Austin. They heralded him as a first-rate sociologist working on issues relevant and important to low-income Mexican-origin populations in the United States. Fortunately for me, Dr. Samora was a visiting scholar at UT Austin. He was in the middle of a field project and would return to Notre Dame at the end of the summer. I asked for an appointment and mailed my materials. In that appointment with him I was only expecting to establish contact and explore other possible study venues that he might share. Instead, I found in him *un maestro y sabio*.[6] His persona and *manera* were unassuming, genuine, reassuring, respectful, and gentle yet quietly commanding.

He had made time for me even though his work schedule was pressing. Yet this meeting and others like it I had with him were part of his daily agenda. He had reviewed the materials I sent to him, and he asked me about my areas of sociological interests as well as my long-term professional goals. Then we turned to the questions and discussion of others involved in developing Mexican American Studies and venues to pursue my sociological interests. He mentioned a few principals and a couple of programs on other campuses that were in their beginning phases. While he spoke well of the hosting department, he mentioned a possible fit within his own department and a new programming effort at Notre Dame. He told me about his research and the Notre Dame students' research efforts and his launching of the MAGSP. He asked me to consider and get back to him.

While this first meeting was brief, I was impressed by this working Mexican American scholar in the middle of a field study. Here, in this seemingly casual meeting, we were discussing important career options. In this encounter he posed new life-altering possibilities to me. To this day, I remain appreciative of the time he took, his measured and thoughtful questions, and his willingness to share his working knowledge on my behalf.

The hand and time he extended to me that day was his custom with other students and young faculty members. While this was a chance meeting for me, it was an activity that expressed his raison d'être as a professor and as a link to the academy. As my own schedule meets the pressing demands of my professional and personal duties, I remain impressed with this *ejemplo* of reaching out to a young student. Moreover, I remain ever mindful of the value of common courtesies and honesty in all meetings and exchanges with others—even the chance ones. This I encountered in all my own meetings with Julian. I found this to be the case, as well, in my few exchanges with *los otros Sabios.*

On the Mexican American Graduate Studies Program

Then, as now, the urgent need for sociological, anthropological, political, economic, legal, and theological research on and for La Raza was apparent to Dr. Samora. The MAGSP provided a vehicle to train the next generation of scholars who would fill that need. Through the program, we students came to better know Dr. Samora, his agenda, and his dreams of making a difference through service to then forgotten peoples. His agenda was grounded in his own biography and in his lessons learned while becoming a member of the academy. This dream was an evolving one as he sought to academically address the longstanding and pressing issues of the day. But, it was his persona, his *maneras,* and his outreach that captured my interest and drew me to his example. But no less inviting were his efforts to establish and promote national as well as regional Raza advocacy organizations, forums and leadership.

During my first two years at Notre Dame, we met many key researchers and fellow travelers through meetings and lectures that allowed us to get a sense of the range of issues across the nation. Dr. Samora encouraged each of us to seek out and develop direct contacts and working relationships with persons who had special expertise related to our own personal research agendas. He did all this with the aim of pushing us toward direct interaction with other researchers to broaden our academic perspective.

The third year and summer were preparation for my comps and work on my dissertation thesis topic. As each of us in the 1971 cohort was coming into our own, Dr. Samora was appropriately supportive and facilitated our growth. In my own work, this meant going into the field and working on Mexican American youth drug use in a midwestern, blue-collar, steel mill community. Here, I used a methodology and approach he was fond of in his own fieldwork in Colorado and Texas communities. The approach and methodology had to be retooled for an urban, inner-city, blue-collar community field study. While the social worlds of the homies and *cholos* were not on his agenda, Dr. Samora saw these worlds as ever-looming problems for many of our communities and their respective families. He encouraged and facilitated my seeking out Drs. Juan Ramos, Armando Morales, and Elliott Liebow.[7]

The topic for substantive research was left for each student to choose as well as the method to be undertaken for gathering data. Yet Samora underscored that our personal choice and scholarly commitment was to inform the field and to help build Mexican American Studies. While each of us was subject to our own discipline's requirements, the MAGSP helped focus our work and served as a key source of support and encouragement. I am mindful that this support and encouragement was not available to Professors Sánchez, Galarza, Paredes, and Samora when they undertook their own doctoral studies and undertook their first academic work. Again I remain duly impressed by their lone steady and unwavering efforts to *cumplir*[8] and break new ground.

Today, the growth and spread of Mexican American populations out of the Southwest and the joining of other Latino populations have served to create new and emerging communities in the northwestern, southeastern, north central and northeastern United States. Julian personally knew what it meant to be *uno de los desarraigados*—uprooted and resettled. These experiences were a part of his own efforts to complete his studies and assume his first professional posting after completing his PhD in St. Louis. Our work was to inform our respective professions, but also to help shape an interdisciplinary area involving Mexican American experiences. Moreover, we were driven by the example that Samora set before us.

Dr. Samora believed it was part of our academic training to study and to interact with other scholars and to seek out those closest to the issues that concerned our research. But Dr. Samora also recognized the value of interaction and involvement with community and policy leaders for his graduate students. Ultimately, his values are reflected in his firm belief that each MAGSP fellow would make a solid contribution to his or her field.

On Friendships and Collaboration

Dr. Samora is best understood when one sees him in one of his three social spheres of action and influence: his professional associates; his intimate friends; and his wife and family. Julian's energies seemed to be interlocked into these three. The drive of his work ethic and character strength were clearly evident, yet the source of his resilience was not. Yet I am sure that he was ever mindful and appreciative of the supportive environment that his wife, family, circle of intimates, and associates provided him. It was this loyalty, support, and *amistad*[9] that he in turn gave to them.

As a doctoral student, I gained insight as to how one builds community. In his relationships with his Notre Dame colleagues, Bill Liu, Arthur Rubel,

Andy Weigert, Tom Sasaki, and Joe Scott, I got to see the importance of friendships—not just working relationships. Good working relationships can come from one doing one's collegial duties and responsibilities. They help in earning respect, trust, and confidence. But the abiding *confianza*[10] resulting from deep friendships allows one to just be oneself and relax. Today, I better understand why he worked at developing and maintaining these working relationships and friendships. I came to see this in the relationships that he had with Herman Gallegos, Joe Bernal, and Juan Ramos. These were *amistades* and bridge-building relationships that they cultivated and maintained.

In later meetings with Charles Loomis, Lyle Saunders, and William D'Antonio, they would share with me their experiences with Julian and their appreciation of their relationship with him. When I moved to Chicago, the friendship and collegial relationship he had with Drs. Jorge Prieto and Año Nuevo Kerr helped pave my way.

Still to this day rarely do I think of Julian without really thinking about Julian and his wife, Betty. He and Betty shared their *casa y familia*—a home away from home and a reminder of what grounded them. We all knew Betty, their five children, and their support of his work. The Samoras' *casa* and *familia* were our respite. The visits were a source of rejuvenation. While he was supportive, friendly, and caring—I came to count on Betty's optimistic energy. They complemented each other and served as a reminder of what good teamwork could do.

Informally and through his seminars we came to meet the pioneers, the rising stars, and trailblazers of the field. Also, we occasionally found ourselves in working sessions with Mexican American political and community leaders. Samora was always gracious and attentive with them. It was typical for him to involve us in those visits. He was generous to each of us with his personal and professional networks.

On Service and Advocacy

Samora was always mindful of his need to be an active contributing participant in his academic and professional community. But the need for leadership could only be addressed when the professional met the grassroots and acted through national advocacy organizations and even our own service organizations. Julian intuitively understood the role and value of mediating agencies advocating for marginal and emerging populations and communities in American society.

Moreover, he was rejuvenated through his involvement with ethnic organizations, especially those involving local communities or those with a national campaign. As co-founder, along with Ernesto Galarza and Herman Gallegos, of the Southwest Council of La Raza, now the National Council of La Raza, his sense of the need for a state, regional, and national leadership organization was prophetic and I am sure one of his proudest investments.

Samora signaled the need for us to make our voices heard and contribute to our corresponding third sector organizations and forums. He instilled in us the need to bring along the next generation of voice and leaders, some who would surpass his and our own contributions, and enhance existing ones. He always saw a need to serve those who were not at the table and press these organizations to further their service efforts to include the underserved and minority communities.

This service would take him away from his own research, his duties on campus, and from his own family, but he rarely shirked his responsibility. He always voiced the needs of the underserved and spoke for the voiceless.

Occasionally, there were days when I would see him drawn into deep thought, drained and tired, and at times frustrated and demoralized. But those days were few. Samora handled and resolved these issues himself or possibly with a few intimates. Never were there angry outbursts that would attract others. He showed us how to handle the roadblocks, dismissals, and rejections that we, too, would have to face. His service model is one that now becomes clearer to me. I hope I act with the same dignity and presence of mind that he demonstrated.

Notes

1. exemplars and leaders
2. The first Mexican Americans in their respective fields who served as models for peers and students.
3. examples
4. *Simpáticos* were individuals who were not Latino but through their vision and comportment demonstrated a natural ethnic sensitivity and appreciation to the "Other America."
5. This monograph helped to rediscover poverty in Appalachia, the Mississippi Delta, and on Indian reservations, and it engaged some policymakers to make them part of their agenda.
6. A model of an accomplished professor and one who possesses the wisdom of one's elders.
7. Juan Ramos was the first in his field to obtain a doctorate of social work from Brandeis's Heller School of Social Welfare and assisted the MAGSP in obtaining National Institute of Mental Health (NIMH) doctoral fellowship money. Armando

Morales' monograph *Ando Sangrando* (Los Angeles: Perspectiva Publications, 1972) detailed the death of *Los Angeles Times* reporter Rubén Salazár and the longstanding problem of police brutality of Mexican Americans in East Los Angeles. Elliot Liebow is an NIMH analyst and anthropologist whose works include E. Liebow, "Tally's Corner" (PhD diss., Catholic University of America, 1967); and Elliot Liebow, *Tell Them Who I Am* (New York: Penguin Group, 1993). Both of these works are shaped as participant observer studies of people in poor areas. All three men offered key guidance and suggestions to me as I entered the field.

8. Fulfill their tasks or duties, and in a broader sense, meet an obligation.

9. friendship

10. confidence

CHAPTER NINE

Fair Taxes and the Social Contract
The Samora Influence on a Chicano Economist
Sergio X. Madrigal

A friend of mine buys sneakers for his children at the local discount store. Another friend of mine, with fewer children and a higher income, buys his top-of-the-line running shoes on the Internet. In the former case, the friend contributes to the sales tax revenue of our state. In the latter case, our state receives no tax revenue. So even though the two purchases were for similar products, in the second case my friend did not contribute to the state funds available to provide the public services that our state residents desire, such as highways and state parks, public schools and universities, the state's National Guard, and much more.

I have been making observations like these and the follow-up research they engender in a little-known area of economics called tax incidence analysis, sometimes better known as tax burden analysis, for more than twenty years now. This is directly attributable to my being able to complete my PhD in economics at Notre Dame. In retrospect, I was lucky to have come across this opportunity. The circumstances that led to my higher education were a series of serendipitous happenstances. In my twenties, I had continually sought to find a way to attend graduate school to supplement my under-graduate bachelor's degree in mathematics from the University of Texas at

Austin and return to the academic world, a world that had attracted me since my youth, when my parents had instilled in me an appreciation of both the material and intellectual rewards of education. Working as a programmer analyst, I was enjoying my work developing computerized business systems for a couple of state agencies in Austin.

But I was resisting doing graduate work in either mathematics or computer science, as these disciplines felt to me more as methodologies to accomplish something rather than as actual subjects of inquiry into the human condition. Due to my work on business systems, I was also developing an interest in business; I looked into the possibility of a Master's in Business Administration, but this degree seemed to me more focused on making money in the business world than in doing one's bit to improve the world. Just about that time, a good friend who had returned to college to finish his long-postponed bachelor's degree suggested I go talk to a professor of his whom he had found to be very helpful and supportive of Latino students. He was a professor of economics at the University of Texas named Dr. Richard Santos. Dr. Santos was sympathetic and informed me about the program of graduate studies being sponsored and cultivated by Dr. Samora at the University of Notre Dame that provided fellowship grants for those pursuing a master's degree or a doctoral degree or a law degree at that institution. One of the available options was a graduate degree in economics. Dr. Santos encouraged me to apply.

Economics appealed to me highly, as it allowed me to use my abilities in mathematics and computer science and business, but instead of merely applying economics for pecuniary benefit, economics further empowered me, in my mind, to focus on it as a social science and seek to apply it for social benefit, which was more my inclination. I applied forthwith and was accepted, and within a few months I was driving with a fellow intern from Austin, Texas, to the University of Notre Dame in South Bend, Indiana. We drove the twelve hundred miles almost non-stop for twenty-four hours, as we did not have much extra money for niceties like motels.

But I recall embarking on this academic venture with some trepidation. Here I was, in my late twenties, starting graduate-level classes in economics with other students who were not only much younger but who nearly all had bachelor's degrees in economics, while my sole background in economics consisted of one meager undergraduate class in macroeconomics, which I had taken about eight years before and, worse even, received a grade of D, the only grade below B that I had ever earned in my whole academic career. Though it is not a good excuse, I had found this topic boring to tears.

Now, here I was, commencing a graduate program in economics. How a person matures and changes over the years I still find amazing. But to finish this anecdote on a positive note, a month or two into the first semester, I found myself tutoring some of my fellow economics students who lacked as thorough a background in mathematics as I had. I found that most of the mathematics used in our more quantitative economics courses was mathematics I had already seen, but now it was being presented with names and concepts attached to the x's and y's.

As the semesters rolled on and I was exposed to more aspects of economics, I found the subject increasingly absorbing. Especially motivating was listening to professors and students and engaging them on the impact of economics and similar disciplines not just in the abstract, but also on the lives of people. One particular professor in the department of economics, Dr. Thomas R. Swartz, saw my potential and encouraged me to continue beyond earning my master's, which is all I had hoped to achieve when I first came to Notre Dame. I subsequently did decide to continue and pursue the doctoral degree, and Dr. Swartz became my dissertation director. So in 1983, almost four years after pulling into South Bend, I completed my dissertation, titled "Racial/Ethnic/Gender Wage Differentials in the Early Labor Career: The Case of Hispanic, Black, and White Youth," and was awarded the PhD.

In retrospect, I can say that a lot of my interest and motivation in my professional life as an economist stemmed from the early years of my career as I worked on my doctorate in economics at the University of Notre Dame. This was largely due to the influence of a professor there named Dr. Julian Samora. He was one of the first influences in my life to expand my intellectual horizons from the purely academic to the more broadly humanitarian. In his lectures and books, I continually saw his motivation to apply the discipline of sociology to the documentation and understanding of the Latino people and culture in the United States.

His quiet but strong determination to study and document a people previously not meriting much scholarly attention spilled over into both a broader and a more direct involvement in Latino affairs for me. I don't believe I would have ever achieved a doctorate were it not for the fellowship program that Dr. Samora started and nurtured at Notre Dame to bring in young Latino and Latina scholars and provide the funding and encouraging environment to allow them to pursue advanced academic degrees. I was very heartened and stimulated by his implicit attitude of scholarly research into social and economic issues that affect Latinos, so much so that instead of leaving Notre Dame with the master's in economics that I had come to pursue, I decided to stay and continue with my studies and finish with a doctorate in economics.

An example of the encouraging environment Dr. Samora fostered was his ability to create a microcosm of the Latino community in his personal and academic environs. He was always available at his campus office to help a student iron out personal and academic problems and challenges. Dr. Samora would also host a few parties and get-togethers at his house throughout the year that would substitute for a lot of us students as our home-away-from-home family. When the cold weather of South Bend at Thanksgiving would roll around and one's family home was too many miles and too many dollars away, as it was for a lot of us at Notre Dame, a Thanksgiving get-together at Dr. Samora's home would always re-energize one through the end-of-term papers and finals and help many a student get through until the reprieve of the winter holidays.

Another example of this encouraging environment was his graduate seminar, required for participants in the graduate fellowship program. I found these seminars quite enlightening. He would bring up both research and topical issues that would not only be thought-provoking, but that seemed to infiltrate the very prism of one's mental construction of the world and that would somehow over time shift that prism into a clearer reflection of the world.

One instance comes to mind. One semester, in one of those required graduate seminars of his, he challenged the students with a research project of our own devising, with the stipulated goal that it should attempt to bridge our diverse, semidetached academic disciplines with the community. That is, we were supposed to formulate a project based on our own ideas for reaching out to the community, whatever that community meant for us. For my own project, I came up with the idea of a monthly column in the student newspaper. My goal was to engage the small, fledgling Latino student community of the early 1980s at Notre Dame and perhaps move us out a little from the near invisibility and isolation we seemed to be in at the time.

The editors of the student newspaper, *The Observer,* readily agreed to my proposal, and I soon submitted my first effort. It was a piece on my perception of how a typical Latino student, newly arrived at Notre Dame, might find himself or herself at odds, or at least at some unease, in a new world with such different climate, culture, and especially sustenance (that is, a lack of Mexican food). The column was titled "Al Alba" (meaning in South Texas Chicano-speak: beware, or be alert) and was aimed mainly at generating some reader response with which to continue a dialogue with the student community for the rest of the semester. The following week I eagerly picked up the next edition to see my first-ever achievement of being published, which I was excited about mailing immediately to my family back home in South Texas. And there it was: A Chicano at Notre Dame by Al Alba. My much anticipated byline was gone in a puff of cultural misunderstanding. I was chagrined and bemused at the same time.

I would also like to quote from the acknowledgments section of my dissertation: "Professor Julian Samora should also be highly commended for his life-long work to assist and develop Chicano scholars; his untiring efforts to provide fellowship support have produced a number of Mexican-American scholars. In addition, his graduate colloquium on the Chicano movement has stimulated discussion on the Chicano experience that has served to enlighten and motivate many of his students. I have been greatly inspired by his work and have benefited much from his advice and friendship."

I tend to think the rich variety of experience and academic challenges made possible by the visionary efforts of Dr. Samora bore fruit by greatly increasing the quantity and quality of Latino scholars and professionals. That is certainly the case with me. I was always attracted to the academic life but was wary of its itinerant nature in its early, pre-tenure phase, so I migrated toward work in the applied economics of a professional economist. I started out as a tax economist for the U.S. Treasury, analyzing the effects of Reaganomics on the tax burden of households and industries, and have turned that into a long and intellectually rewarding career that impacts on social fiscal policy.

Beginning with Reaganomics and continuing with the prevailing neo-liberalism of the past quarter-century, I believe it has become especially important to analyze the impact of fiscal and tax policy because capitalism, as good a system as it is, does, like all systems devised by humans, need to be monitored and adjusted, lest it again produce excesses such as the Great Depression, the savings and loan scandal of the 1980s, and the deep recession of 2008–09, to name a few problems. For example, the reasons for the first major economic crisis of the millennium will be debated for a long time, but early on many economists are citing the deregulation and non-regulation of lending practices and exotic financial instruments, along with lax monetary and tax policy, as the principal causes for the exacerbation of the normal business cycle. It seems we must relearn the lesson that government must play an essential role in setting and monitoring the rules, so that the economic games people play do not go out of bounds.

After working at the Treasury Department, I worked in the private sector for a decade with a consulting company in the Washington, D.C., area that provided these same tax revenue estimates and tax burden analyses to various state governments in the United States and also various foreign countries, such as Egypt, Guatemala, and El Salvador. These countries had contracted with the U.S. Agency for International Development (USAID) to bring in consultants to help them develop the data and studies needed to further develop their systems of taxation in a fair and equitable manner.

Back to the Future

After that decade, I returned to Texas and have done the same kind of work for the Texas legislature. In the group of analysts supporting a standing committee of the Texas legislature for which I currently work, we analyze the impact of current and proposed legislation on the economic welfare of households by income level, to ensure that taxation does not unduly burden one group or another. We also analyze the effects on business by industry sector to attempt to create a level playing field for all businesses and industries. It is very interesting and rewarding work that I realize I am fortunate to be able to do due to the opportunities made available a couple of decades ago by the foresight of Dr. Samora.

The incidence of tax burdens is the effort by economists to study how the burden of taxes falls, in the final analysis, on households, categorized by income classes. (Economists agree that all taxes, including those initially paid by business, are eventually passed on to consumers. Since, for businesses, taxes are just another of the costs incurred in doing business, the taxes paid by business are usually passed on to consumers in the form of higher prices or sometimes in the form of lower returns, lower profits, to investors in the business.) Then, by sorting all households from those receiving the lowest income to those receiving the highest income and partitioning all these households into, for example, ten income groups or deciles, one can then analyze what share of total taxes is paid by each income group.

Thus, these analyses usually show that the percentage share of taxes paid rises from the lowest income group to the highest, not unexpectedly. But for many taxes, the ratio of taxes to household income actually decreases from the lowest group to the highest. Such is the case with the property tax and the sales tax. These are called regressive taxes, when lower and middle-income groups pay a higher percentage of their income in taxes than do upper-income groups.

An understanding of the analysis of tax incidence is not difficult to grasp, but it is challenging to execute. The study of tax incidence is merely the study of how tax burdens fall on different groups. Tax burden analysis endeavors to calculate the effective tax rates for all households at all income levels and study how the effective tax rates vary for households from the lowest income groups to the highest income groups.

My career goal has become to further develop and document the methodologies used in the analysis of tax burden incidence, so that other states can more easily analyze their tax burdens and can make their tax systems more equitable for their citizens of all income levels. In the near future, I am planning to develop software tax models that would be readily customizable by state so that any state bureaucracy can produce timely analyses of their state's tax burden on its residents, from either its current tax law or proposed tax legislation. This can only strengthen the social contract that makes our democracy a leader in the world and enhance the transparency that gives government credibility with its citizens. I can only thank Dr. Julian Samora for the great influence he had on developing my sense of social justice during the years I knew him at Notre Dame.

CHAPTER TEN

Circles of Commitment

Marcos Ronquillo

Dr. Julian Samora's lifelong commitment to academic scholarship as a vehicle for social change is widely recognized in Mexican American Studies; his was a life dedicated to promoting research and teaching in the field. However, the personal impact he had on his colleagues, the Latino community, and particularly his students remains largely unknown. He left us all a legacy embracing academic scholarship and advocacy as tools to serve those striving to become part of the American Dream.

From 1971 to 1975, as an undergraduate at Notre Dame, I had the unexpected and wonderful opportunity to participate in a host of activities sponsored by the good work and generous spirit of Julian Samora. Little did I know or understand at the time that those experiences would shape my commitment to pursue social activism as an integral part of my life.

As a Mexican American student from Tucson who had lived in Cuba and graduated from high school in San Juan, Puerto Rico, my undergraduate education at Notre Dame offered me the opportunity to broaden my horizons. I had been heavily recruited for academic and athletic scholarships by small colleges, regional schools, and Ivy League institutions in the Northeast. Both my high school wrestling coaches hailed from the Midwest, and they highly recommended the University of Notre Dame; the endorsement of one influenced me in particular since he was a graduate of a Catholic high school in South Chicago.

Undergraduate Days at Notre Dame

I was ultimately attracted to Notre Dame by the opportunity to wrestle on the university's varsity wrestling team. My experience confirmed the wrestling coach's admonition that athletes were not bestowed special privileges at Notre Dame. Other than training tables and an academic schedule that guaranteed no classes after 3 p.m., varsity athletes received no special treatment. Then, as now, Notre Dame had no athletic dorms.

As a work-study student and a recipient of the Holy Cross Scholarship, I worked with Gilberto Cárdenas, who had organized the Centro de Estudios Chicanos e Investigaciones Sociales, the research center. Cárdenas was pursuing a doctorate in the multidisciplinary Mexican American Graduate Studies Program under the direction of Dr. Julian Samora. Through my friendship with Cárdenas, I developed a close bond with many other Mexican American undergraduate and graduate students and was exposed to many intellectual and political currents from the theology of liberation, to guerrilla theater, and to the migrant farm labor and civil rights movements of the Midwest. I participated in the Notre Dame chapter of MEChA,[1] sold tacos to raise funds, and was invited to pen reviews of the "*teatro campesino*" and several "guerrilla theater" performances for the campus newspaper and the *South Bend Tribune*. In time, we turned our advocacy to unionizing campus cafeteria workers and gardeners, many of whom were Mexican American or Mexican immigrants.

My senior year afforded me a "ringside seat" observing Dr. Samora and his work. I spent many fascinating hours visiting with Dr. Samora in the library office, querying him about his work, what issues he considered to be priorities, and, more importantly, with which local, state, and national organizations he was collaborating in his support of La Causa. At the time, I could not appreciate that Dr. Samora was pivotal in developing a national agenda for Latinos. Nor could I realize that the Chicano movement or "El Movimiento" was just beginning to define itself and coalesce through the formation of national organizations and platforms. Now I recognize that I was in the midst of these important developments and learning from a pioneering Mexican American scholar activist at the height of his career.

I was a direct beneficiary of Dr. Samora's extraordinary vision and commitment to educate my generation of scholars and professionals. Through

my discussions with Dr. Samora, my involvement with MEChA, and friendships with the MAGSP students, I had the unique opportunity to witness a
parade of accomplished intellectuals, artists, political activists, and community leaders whose energies were already converging in many ways to form
the nucleus of *La Lucha*[2] for equality and justice. I worked with community
leaders and union organizers to support the grape and lettuce boycotts and
the promotion of equal rights for migrant workers. I participated in protests
and other forms of civil disobedience on and off campus, in South Bend
and in South Chicago. So profound was Dr. Samora's influence on me and
so life changing was my involvement in his world that I altered my focus
during my remaining time at Notre Dame.

At the time, I did not fully understand the transformation that was taking place, not only at Notre Dame, but throughout American society. It
was gratifying to see people of color obtain undergraduate and graduate
degrees and become lawyers, doctors, accountants, and even full-tenured
college professors. Dr. Samora's use of scholarship for advocacy left us a
lasting legacy and his fatherly instincts provided great insights for those of
us he mentored. Indeed, we began to see that we were part of the nationwide struggle of communities to achieve more than survival. We wanted to
pursue the American Dream, and we did.

Dr. Samora was a member of that small group of Latino intellectuals and
activists that helped define the platform for a national civil rights agenda for
Latinos and plan its implementation through new organizations focused on
issues of civil rights and equality. At the same time, we, as individuals and
undergraduate students of Dr. Samora, came to understand the relationship
between the new Latino civil rights agenda and our roles in the Latino community and in the larger American society. Bridging that gulf between understanding and action was our dilemma and challenge as his students during this
new era of civil rights. Dr. Samora's groundbreaking research, dedication to
social justice, and determination to address community problems taught many
of us the valuable, lifelong lesson—how to give back to the community.

As we completed our undergraduate experience at Notre Dame, many of
us moved on to professional schools to pursue careers in business, academia,
and law. We celebrated our graduations with family and friends at the home
of Betty and Julian Samora. This became almost an annual tradition, and I
remember attending several graduation parties at their home. Not only did
graduation reward us with diplomas but, as undergraduates, observing Dr.
Samora and his graduate students empowered us with the "burden of leadership"; as we left Notre Dame we came to appreciate the personal challenge to
succeed in our respective fields without giving up our roots, language, or cul-

ture. We learned the power of information and the use of knowledge to attack problems and positions, not people or personalities. Dr. Samora established the highest standards for hard work, problem solving, focused discipline, and an intense, heightened sense of responsibility for our community.

Our second lesson from Dr. Samora centered on developing scholarly research that translates into real advocacy for the betterment of our community in particular and society as a whole. Education should not be pursued in a vacuum or exclusively for one's own benefit. This lesson manifested itself in seminars, conferences, papers, articles, art, theater, and media events that analyzed immigration, civil rights, bilingual education, housing, political access, employment, and economic development in the growing Latino community, not only in South Bend, but also the Midwest and throughout the country.

Many of us completed our undergraduate education with a growing appreciation of the art of political activism, community development, and advocacy. But I wanted more, and I was presented with the opportunity to further develop that aspect of my education at Notre Dame. Rather than continuing directly to law school, I worked for a year as the director of the Centro de Estudios Chicanos e Investigaciones Sociales. During that year, I applied the principles of political activism by collaborating with the Midwest Council of La Raza as a counselor and grant writer under the direction of Olga Villa and Ricardo Parra. Honing my skills in political activism meant using them to better our community, developing my network of lifelong friends and associates committed to *La Lucha,* and cultivating an extended family in the Samoras, graduate students, and others in the South Bend community.

During this time, Betty and Julian Samora's home served as a personal place of refuge, debate, and dialogue. I worked with Betty on activities promoting and supporting "El Campito," a day care center in South Bend dedicated to serving the needs of children of migrant workers. I also spent a summer in South Chicago's Proyecto Venceremos[3] teaching ESL to Latino steel workers seeking to exit the migrant stream and settle in the well-established Mexican American community there.

My experiences at Notre Dame developed a sense of urgency and compassion in me and led me to appreciate the need for solid research and scholarship to support the political, economic, and social agendas that would benefit a growing Latino community. Dr. Samora was the role model who set the standard for many of us as we embarked on our postgraduate and professional experiences. Dr. Samora's groundbreaking research, his dedication to social justice, and his commitment to find solutions for community problems inspired many of us to embrace the lesson—give back to the community no matter where life takes you.

After Notre Dame

My desire to help people motivated me to earn a degree in law. I obtained a full academic scholarship as the 1976 Dean Kramer Scholar at the National Law Center of The George Washington University. My political activism continued at law school; I led the local chapter of "La Raza" law students association and later the "Movimiento Legal Latino." I was also chosen by fellow students of color to serve as the student advocate on the admissions committee at the National Law Center, and I continued to promote and participate in national conferences hosted by "La Raza" law students association and other Washington, D.C., activist groups.

After my graduation from George Washington, a referral from José Luis Gonzalez, a fellow Notre Dame student and Georgetown graduate, led to employment as a civil rights attorney in the Dallas office for Civil Rights in the U.S. Department of Health, Education, and Welfare.

In 1983, I joined Callejo & Callejo Law, a firm in Dallas, to continue representing individuals in their complaints of discrimination against public entities and private companies. I worked with long-time Dallas community activists Adelfa and Bill Callejo as counsel, partner, and finally name partner; they encouraged my interest in community service, and I became active in the Mexican American Bar Association[4] and the Greater Dallas Hispanic Chamber of Commerce. Eventually, I assumed the leadership of both these organizations so pivotal for our Latino community here in North Texas, and to date I am the only Latino in Dallas to have done so.

Later on, I established my own law firm, which gave me the opportunity to represent major public entities, political subdivisions, and Fortune 500 companies in complex litigation in state and federal courts, thus broadening my service to the community. In retrospect, the legacy of Dr. Samora and other Hispanic leaders such as Mr. and Mrs. Callejo impacted my drive to give back to the community and honed my ability to do so. This dedication and commitment began at Notre Dame and still continues to grow and develop today.

Notre Dame

I have come full circle. Several years ago I renewed my relationship with the University of Notre Dame by serving as a member of the Hispanic Alumni Board of Directors, and later I was elected chairman of the Hispanic Alumni Association. My collaboration with the Hispanic alumni facilitated collaborations with Dr. Gilberto Cárdenas and former chairs of the Hispanic

Alumni Association, which resulted in the establishment of the Institute for Latino Studies at Notre Dame. The institute is pivotal in honoring the legacy, scholarship, and advocacy of Dr. Julian Samora. Further, it is important for us, the Hispanic alumni, that the effort be institutionalized and articulated so that younger generations of Notre Dame students and future alumni be prepared to carry Dr. Samora's legacy with them. Dr. Cárdenas and the Institute for Latino Studies could serve no better purpose.

The gathering of Chicano intellectuals and Latino intelligentsia at Notre Dame in the early 1970s nurtured a social movement with far-reaching results. In those days many of us were seeking roots, exploring identities, and forging the directions and purposes of our lives. This pursuit assumed many forms, followed many paths, and embraced a myriad of intellectual, academic, political, cultural, and spiritual activities as we interfaced with the only Latino scholar and professor on campus, Dr. Julian Samora.

During a MALDEF[5] board meeting in Albuquerque, New Mexico, in 1995, Dr. Cárdenas and I visited with Julian Samora, who was already frail and confined to a wheelchair. It would turn out to be the last time I would ever see him. Seeing Dr. Samora once again reminded me of how great this man had been and that his contributions had already left this world a different place. Years before, I had been a young undergraduate student, seated in his office, asking him what I am sure were very basic questions. Now, as a seasoned lawyer with thirty-plus years in private practice, it is clear to me that that day in Albuquerque I was witnessing the passing of a hero in our community. The "Father of Chicano Studies" had indeed bequeathed his work and legacy to my generation and to me.

As Gilberto and I sat with Dr. Samora for the last time, I realized that as my mentor and friend he had profoundly impacted many aspects of my life. I further felt that this visit was reconnecting me with the Notre Dame community and that I was completing a circle that joined what I had learned as an undergraduate through Dr. Samora's mentoring with what I had accomplished since leaving the university. I felt peace and deep understanding.

Eight years later my eldest son Marcos Javier also graduated from Notre Dame. My youngest son, Adrian Luis, as a junior math major at Notre Dame, took a course in the fall of 2005 titled "An Introduction to Latinos in Society" taught by Gilberto Cárdenas. My son now tells me he wants to minor in Latino Studies! Once again, the struggle on behalf of our community encircles and embraces and incorporates the lessons that Dr. Samora left.

Today I'm proud to call myself a Samorista! I am sure in time my sons will too.

Notes

1. MEChA is an acronym for "Movimiento Estudiantil Chicano de Aztlán" or "Chicano Student Movement of Aztlán." Founded in 1969, this student political organization has chapters in high schools and colleges all over the country.

2. The fight or the struggle for social and civic justice.

3. Proyecto Venceremos was a model community education project in South Chicago under the aegis of the Midwest Council of La Raza that provided classes in English, GED classes, and eventually basic college courses.

4. The Mexican American Bar Association is now the Dallas Hispanic Bar Association.

5. Founded in 1968 in San Antonio, Texas, the Mexican American Legal Defense and Educational Fund (MALDEF) is the leading nonprofit Latino litigation, advocacy, and educational outreach institution in the United States. Its headquarters are now in Los Angeles, California. www.maldef.org.

CHAPTER ELEVEN

Common Geographies

Ken Martínez

I had never heard of Julian Samora. I applied to Notre Dame because it was a Catholic school. I had never been east of Amarillo, Texas, and I thought I was going to be the only Mexican east of the Mississippi. I knew there were probably other Hispanics, like Cubans and Puerto Ricans, but I didn't know there were going to be a lot of southwestern Mexican Americans in the program. When I first arrived, I thought I was the darkest person in the world and then I met Professor Samora, who was darker than I was. Most interesting was that Professor Samora and I were basically from the same area. His mother was from Los Ojos, a village just a few miles from my dad's village of Tierra Amarilla. He spoke the same kind of Spanish I spoke, and his message of service was very like my father's.

I recognized in Professor Samora the same calm that my father had. I think it comes from life in the villages. There is a rhythm to life there that is so primordial. The village is up against a mountain and next to a river. No one has a lot of land—everybody has a little bit of land, but it is enough to feed your family if you know how to work it. There are well-respected rules of behavior about who used the water and when, about sharing with your neighbors. It was considered to be in poor taste to stand out from your neighbors. Everybody wanted to try to be the same, to be together. There was a long tradition of stories—*cuentos*—that were told over and over again that inculcated not just the story and the entertainment of it, but the social mores, and it was just really magical. The smells, the foods, the way the neighbors got along, the stories, the humor, there is a dry humor that is also self-deprecating. You would make fun of yourself before you made fun of anyone else. But it was tremendous fun. It was just kind of a joy in life that you see up there—you still see it today. We were so poor and there was nothing else but each other, so there was a tremendous appreciation for one another. The people from those villages had a very deliberate way of speaking. Professor Samora had that too, a deliberate, slow speech with a measured cadence. No one was in a hurry and people considered every possible ramification of what they may say next, including making sure they didn't offend. And now it seems like we all say anything without regard to whether we offend people or not. Those traditions are a lost art.

My father, Walter K. Martínez, had a lot of influence in my life. He was an attorney who was elected to the New Mexico State Legislature, where he served about twenty years and was Speaker of the House for twelve years. What impressed me about him was his vocation of service. He told me once that as a lawyer in a small town he could help one person at a time with their individual problems, but in the state legislature he could help many people. At the time of his service, the 1960s to the 1980s, there was a kind of realigning political movement in New Mexico. Up until then, New Mexico was controlled by a group of southern conservatives who were referred to as the cowboys.[1] But that changed with the Supreme Court decision Baker v. Carr that provided for one person, one vote. Before that decision, minorities across the country had been relegated to districts that were either too populated or too thinly spread out; in either case, there were not many minority representatives. The Supreme Court decision said each district should be roughly the same size, and my father was elected the term before that 1962 decision. After the 1962 decision there was an influx of both northern New Mexico Hispanics and urban intellectuals into the legislature. They were much more liberal and they combined to become a new political force nicknamed the Mama Lucies. The name was coined when Mama Lucy, a lady who ran a coffee shop in Las Vegas, New Mexico, fed poor college kids attending Highlands University in Las Vegas. They became known as the Mama Lucy group. A cohort of intellectual state legislators attended New Mexico Highlands together and benefited from the Mama Lucy tradition of kindness to those in need. Through a series of legislative maneuvers, they came to control the House, a goal that included installing my father as Speaker and then gradually dominating the chairmanships.

My father was from the small northern New Mexico village of Tierra Amarilla (TA).[2] We kids went there every summer, so we knew our relatives, and we knew the terrain. My dad came from a huge family, eleven children. They were a poor but very tight-knit family, and they were well-educated because they turned to their books for entertainment. They all had voracious appetites for reading. My father went to law school from 1952 to 1955 at the University of New Mexico (UNM).

My father never told me to go to law school. But when I graduated with a degree in Spanish and political science from UNM, I was unsure of my next move. A professor of political science, Dr. Chris García, who later became president of UNM, suggested that I apply to the national schools. Graduate and Professional Opportunities Program (GPOP) fellowships,[3] which Professor Samora's efforts made available at Notre Dame, supported my education. Unlike at many other universities, Samora included law students among the allotted GPOP fellowships.

My dad thought it was fantastic that I was accepted to Notre Dame. He had graduated from UNM as one of the first Hispanics and had done well, but I wanted to make my own way. My dad had been so independent and I wanted to be independent, too. Both my father and Professor Samora regarded education as paramount. And both believed that if you are given the opportunity to be educated, you have the responsibility to do good things and to help those less fortunate. At Notre Dame I found an affirmation through Professor Samora of the attitudes regarding social justice I had learned from my father. I saw my father respond at the local level, and I saw Professor Samora as a national and international actor. Frankly, I was kind of star-struck. Julian Samora was an actor in the United States civil rights movement and yet he was from the same village as my people. That had a big impact on me.

I resented attending the Mexican American seminar, which was a condition of the fellowship. Notre Dame Law School was competitive and the reading was technical, and I felt a tremendous amount of pressure to survive it. When I understood I was going to have another graduate course on top of all that . . . I just dreaded it. The law school supported a different kind of ethics about work and study compared to my undergraduate experience studying literature and Spanish. Law school was a real paper chase. People stole volumes from the library and hid them so others could not complete their assignments, just because perhaps they thought, "If I'm tenth in the class and you're twelfth, I'm going to get the better job." That amazed me because I had never seen that before, and at a Catholic University! When we did trial advocacy, people sabotaged each other's advocacy and it made me laugh because it was all so silly. The colloquium was a nice change where we all collaborated on papers and our social justice work. And we had fun—a lot of fun.

The law school also lumped all the Chicano students together and told us we had to take a remedial English course to help us with our writing. It was a non-credit course we attended with the black students. Notre Dame was concerned about our writing and they just wanted us to succeed. But it was kind of funny that they just assumed that we all needed it. They didn't do any testing or placement; we were just assigned to the class. After I handed in the first assignment, I was told I didn't need to return.

Three of us in the seminar studied for law degrees, while the rest were PhD students. Samora designed the seminar to be multidisciplinary, and he assigned a project in which the law students teamed with the PhD students. There were legal components to the project and perhaps a historical component, a sociological component, and so forth. For me it was fascinating because we collaborated on papers and I really enjoyed the non-legal research. That approach also kept it real. I realized how the law affects human beings at the most basic level.

We law students in the seminar took a different path from the other Notre Dame law students. Professor Samora encouraged collaboration in contrast to the competition in the law school. At that time, intense competition for the big corporate jobs permeated the law school because Notre Dame was fairly well-recognized. Law students trod a well-worn and generally recognized path to corporate success that included making straight A's and writing law review articles. Doing legal work for the poor was not what the corporate world wanted to see on your resume. Samora introduced us to the local Hispanic population and involved us in legal assistance projects. We went to Michigan and worked with the farm workers and actually built a class-action lawsuit. We tutored high school students at the Casa de Amistad.[4] We often attended Mass at St. Stephen's instead of Notre Dame, because it was a Hispanic congregation and had a Spanish Mass. I had had no idea of the extent of the Latino community in South Bend and the Midwest, and I would not have found it were it not for Professor Samora.

Samora created an atmosphere of learning that extended beyond the classroom. We had roundtable discussions in class, but we also had very lively parties. He got us all involved—not just academically, but directly with public service through Casa de Amistad and with the migrant farm workers, and in the process created this tremendous fellowship. Many of us were too poor to travel home for Thanksgiving, so we all went over to his house. I remember Professor Samora would tell a little story and he'd have a little laugh at the end of it—it was a very little laugh. That laugh was punctuation at the end of a story about an epic struggle. He knew he had prevailed and that laugh was always the punctuation. He took a lot of delight in telling those stories and he seemed pretty much at peace.

As an example of the collaborative atmosphere supported by Dr. Samora and the seminar, Rick Siller and Jorge Canales, members of the colloquium and then second-year law students, gave me the summaries so necessary to understand the first-year course material. They handed me a sheaf of papers that was about five hundred pages deep. These summaries not only helped to understand the cases, but they also showed what we were supposed to be gleaning from the cases, because we had no idea. I don't know why they chose to give those golden documents to me, but I guess I was the first Chicano they ran into in the first-year class. I have always suspected that Samora was behind it as a way to draw the law students into the colloquium.

Another aspect of my education that I really enjoyed was borrowing books from Dr. Samora's office library. Professor Samora gave us a reading list that really broadened my understanding. I read about Ernesto Galarza and a Chicano movement literature I had never seen before. The readings helped to contextualize what was happening in the world. When the groundskeepers struck,[5] I remember Professor Samora conducting meetings on their behalf and helping to lead the strike. I found it really interesting that one of our professors was leading a strike against his own university.

When I was in my third year of law school, my father was diagnosed with Lou Gehrig's disease, and at first the family wasn't sure what it was. I had thought about doing something national when I graduated. My knowledge of Spanish made me attractive to the national firms, and I was also thinking about being a union organizer. I wasn't sure I wanted to practice law, but when we found out my dad was sick I figured it was time to go home and help. So I helped with his practice and then helped take care of him in his illness.

The year I graduated, 1984, was his last session in the House. I was approached to run when Dad didn't run for re-election, but I wasn't even admitted to the bar yet. I stayed out of politics for a few years trying to keep the practice alive, but he passed away two years later. A group of the New Mexico politicos approached me just before my father died. So I ran for the Grants, New Mexico, schoolboard and served for eight years.

At the time, the most pressing issue in Grants was declining school enrollment. Grants had been a uranium mining community, but after Three Mile Island, uranium demand fell and mining was no longer feasible. My hometown was closing down. In one year we lost 5,000 jobs in a county of about 20,000 people. As board president, declining enrollment forced us to close schools. We had to shut down schools in small Spanish-speaking villages and bus the children twenty-five miles to larger schools. These were really difficult decisions, both personally and professionally.

Both Professor Samora and my father exhibited a combination of altruism and power. My dad always said that a person could seek money, power, or wisdom. Both money and power are fleeting, but wisdom is forever. Professor Samora's life mirrored my father's observations; Samora could have been very rich I'm sure, and he could have been very powerful. Wisdom comes to you from interacting with people, and it's much more valuable than money. I think there is nothing wrong with power as long as you define the power that you're seeking. Both my father and Professor Samora always defined power in their lives as the ability to do good. I learned from them not to shy away from power as long as it involves the ability to do good. Samora echoed my father's maxim about helping more than one person at a time.

Professor Samora suggested that you can create a legacy and affect many people, who then pass it on to others. I could have remained a country lawyer, an effective advocate for my clients, but as a legislator, I have a much broader sweep. Sometimes I can shift the paradigm. Currently the national and state debate about immigration has an underlying meanness brought about by fear of actual brown hordes coming in and changing the face of America. In New Mexico, we took a different approach to the issue. In the House, for instance, we introduced a bill, which passed, stating that the state of New Mexico could not enforce a federal immigration law. The debate about not enforcing federal immigration laws became ugly and people started speaking in jingoistic and patriotic terms about America. So I just read a list of names of people, all undocumented Hispanics from Mexico, Guatemala, and other places, who had died fighting for this country and were awarded citizenship posthumously.

There has been some fallout about my stance on these difficult and emotional issues. But I tell people that I wasn't elected to be re-elected. I was elected to do the right thing and if that means I will not be re-elected then so be it. I learned that from Professor Samora. He always did the right thing. I don't know how much trouble he got into his life. . . . I imagine that it was quite a bit—but I think he always kind of enjoyed the debate. I think he died knowing he'd done a good job. He had a tremendous wisdom. Most of us recognize that when you are in the presence of a wise man, if you are willing to sit and be quiet and then if you are willing to just listen, it is a nice opportunity.

I watched both my father and Professor Samora pass on their wisdom through mentoring. I believe that I am meant to engage in passing on what

I learned from them and the knowledge I have developed. When I was practicing law exclusively, I mentored young lawyers who were coming after me. When I was on the schoolboard I mentored new board members, and now I mentor the new legislative members. I call them my legislative *hijitos*.[6] Every year there will be a young freshman who just looks both bright and bewildered, and I adopt him or her. I sometimes give the junior legislator a big bill I have worked on, but instead of trying to get the credit myself, I give it away and work behind the scenes to get it passed. Then the junior legislator is on the front page of the paper and that helps with name recognition. I also try to model standing my ground for issues I believe in. If there is a "sin" in politics, it is being timid about the core issues that define a person. It is not so much about being courageous; it is just about being true to your core beliefs. It is an interesting counterbalance to the collaborative ideas I learned from Samora.

After Professor Samora became ill, he fell out of circulation. He came to Albuquerque to die, and it's ironic that we would both end up back in New Mexico. He had pulled in a little bit; my dad did the same thing when he became ill. I think that more than anything, Professor Samora didn't want other people to be hurt at the sight of his illness. And my dad did the same thing. Both of them worried more about other people than themselves.

For some reason, I don't know why, Professor Samora called me and we had coffee in a little café close to his house in Albuquerque. I think we had eggs and chile, and it was just the most pleasant hour. Obviously it was close to the end although I didn't know that. He didn't seem as healthy as he'd always been before, but we just sat and had coffee and eggs. He was just at peace. Tremendous peace. I really enjoyed being with him. That's the last time I saw him.

Notes

1. Many observers of New Mexico divide the state into three distinct regions: northern, eastern, and southern.

2. Tierra Amarilla is the seat of Rio Arriba County in northern New Mexico.

3. The Graduate and Professional Opportunities Program was initiated by the U.S. Department of Education to fund minority and women graduate students. It was a 1976 amendment to Title IX of the Higher Education Act of 1965.

4. Casa de Amistad is a community center for Mexican Americans on the west side of South Bend.

5. See the essay by Ricardo Parra and Olga Villa in this volume for more information about the groundskeepers' strike.

6. Spanish diminutive for son.

B. The Pedagogy of Julian Samora

CHAPTER TWELVE

Reflections on Education
Post-Samora

Teresita E. Aguilar

Five of Julian Samora's former students and a colleague offer their reflections on how Dr. Samora influenced their careers in higher education and how they came to appreciate their educational experiences with their former mentor. Their paths all differed, yet their reflections repeat themes that would likely please the good teacher immensely. It is clear from reading the following reflections that Dr. Samora had a vision and hope for creating a more *inclusive and vibrant academy,* an academy that would gain immensely from legitimizing the study of the Mexican cultures of the United States and in preparing more Mexican American/Chicano scholars and academic leaders. This change in the academy would occur one scholar at a time. Samora's vision clearly integrated *the human element*—one not expected of or by Mexican Americans within the often foreign place of higher education.

In accepting the invitation to name Samora's *pedagogy* and how it shaped his students' lives and careers, I have relied primarily on the words of his students and colleagues. What was at the base of Samora's pedagogy? How was it? In bell hooks' reflection of engaged pedagogy,[1] she speaks of the need for the professor to be human, to engage in dialogue with students, to connect learning with life, and to encourage making the connection between knowing and taking action. These are precisely the descriptors gleaned from these reflective essays written by his former students.

Victor Rios reflects on Samora's impact on his teaching career of nearly three decades. Though clearly prepared for a faculty position at a research university, Rios found his calling to be in a teaching institution serving students from socioeconomically disadvantaged backgrounds. Similarly, José Hinojosa reflects on Samora's impact on his teaching career in higher education, many of those on the border of South Texas. He recalls a message acquired in graduate school that persisted through his academic career: "You will not be considered equal by the majority of your Anglo colleagues . . . get used to it." Unfortunately, Hinojosa witnessed this throughout his career. But he also took with him Samora's survivor's message: "You will have the self-assurance and self-confidence to take on anything and everybody."

Barbara Driscoll de Alvarado took the path of researcher, with a particular calling to a deeper understanding of Mexico as a means to enrich her appreciation of Mexican Americans and Mexican cultures in the United States. She spent many years throughout her academic career in Mexican institutions of higher education. This calling and journey were clearly influenced by a trip she shared with Julian and Betty Samora during her first year as a graduate student. Her observations of his teaching style in this experience in Mexico confirmed his ability to expand the classroom. She describes Dr. Samora's keen ability to nurture students' minds and spirits as only a few dedicated and competent academicians are able to do across cultural contexts.

Rios recognizes his own teaching as an effort to emulate his mentor. Samora was unquestionably student-centered or learner-centered before either term was so frequently used in academic circles. Samora promoted critical thinking and multiple perspectives. Hinojosa adds that Samora demanded that scholarly arguments were expected to be supported by "expert testimony, documentation, and verifiable information," rather than mere anecdotal opinions.

A fourth student, Phillip Gallegos, describes his journey from a naïve eighteen-year-old first-year student to a professional architect with a commitment to social justice. The Catholic institution was a factor in his decision to attend Notre Dame. It was Dr. Samora's reputation that further reinforced that decision. What Gallegos and other students would come to find was that Dr. Samora's pedagogy and mentorship illustrated and gave life to the mission of the university.[2] Though the mission statement cited is the current one, I suspect it has not changed significantly since the time of Julian Samora's presence. To have had a faculty member with Samora's vision and commitment could only reinforce this mission statement so grounded in the Catholic tradition of higher education.

While Anthony Cortese's reflections on the impact of Samora on his own academic career continue with many of the same observations as previous essays in this section, he adds a unique dimension in terms of self-discovery as a bicultural individual. Cortese was able to learn more about the plight of Chicanos from the distance provided by his own mixed racial/ethnic experience. All the while, Dr. Samora approached Cortese as a family member, welcoming him with open arms. Consequently, Cortese takes his experience as a guide to how he mentors his students, regardless of race, gender, or ethnic background.

Dr. Samora's students consistently recognized that he did not assume a position of the all-knowing scholar who was to fill the minds of his students with the knowledge he had and that they could only get from him. His teaching style placed him as facilitator, mediator, resource, and guide. According to Rios, his professor's questions served to challenge them while demonstrating a "pedagogy that was liberating, democratic, and learner centered." Though Samora was committed to enhancing competent and intellectual scholars, he managed to approach teaching in a non-traditional, unassuming way, as would an elder, a godparent, or a highly respected community leader.

Driscoll de Alvarado sheds light on the Wednesday seminar, noting that it provided a forum for interdisciplinary reflection on matters affecting Mexican American people, communities, and conditions. The seminar provided an opportunity to supplement and give greater relevance and meaning to his students' specific disciplines or fields of study. The seminar provided a space in which peer mentoring, networking, and the building of a cohort model were nurtured. This space was critical given the otherwise isolated experiences likely within students' home departments or disciplines.

Dr. Samora further enhanced the Wednesday seminars by inviting nationally known scholars and activists who were committed to advancing the knowledge and advocacy of Mexican Americans. This strategy served to value voices that were less common to the traditional academy. He understood that a more inclusive academy was needed to prepare effective academic leaders for the future. As Driscoll de Alvarado observed, this would also require the development of both academic and leadership skills to serve as a liaison between the academy and the Mexican American communities. Such development of skills, however, would not be possible so long as the academy held a narrow definition of legitimate scholarship (which too often excluded the study of Mexican American experiences or people) across disciplines. Further, unless the academy recognized and valued Mexican/ Mexican American/Chicano Studies topics, these areas would not find their way into the scholarly literature or professional practice, which would limit long-term academic opportunities (e.g., tenure) for those committed to these research areas. He knew there was a need to move beyond unspoken and unwritten perceptions of illegitimacy or insignificance of Mexican American scholars and scholarship within the academy. He openly and unapologetically challenged the practice of treating such scholars as illegal or unwanted immigrants to institutions of higher education.

Gallegos also witnessed Samora's challenge to Notre Dame as a Catholic institution that to that date had failed to be more inclusive and welcoming to Latino Catholics. As a result of coordinated strategies and informed activism, the institution responded in a manner that significantly increased in enrollment of Latino/a students. Again, Samora was providing Notre Dame an opportunity to live up to its university mission through his proactive leadership on the issue of inclusion.

That three of the five reflections are written by former students preparing to retire from long, successful careers in teaching in the academy speaks to Samora's successful impact in challenging the status quo in the academy.

The element of cultural bridging is also supported in the reflections provided. Literally from the border crossings and bridges between Mexico and the United States to the concern for bridging the academy with the Mexican/Mexican American community, Samora reminded his students of their roles in serving in this capacity. He modeled it. He lived it. And they witnessed it.

According to his students, Julian Samora was incredibly human. His former students consistently talk about how they were welcomed to Samora's home and treated as extended family members. They were treated as human beings with lives beyond graduate school. Many of his students were keenly aware of the challenges Samora faced in his day as a pioneer in a time when persons of Mexican descent were simply not welcomed in public spaces, much less in more exclusive settings such as institutions of higher education. In his teaching and in his mentoring, he gave life to humility while remaining clearly committed to social justice. His hope for a better plight for persons of Mexican descent was far bigger than his anger toward the inequities and his personal experiences with discrimination. Samora offered a pedagogy of hope[3] to his students, which is clearly visible in their careers and reflections.

He challenged the academy to acknowledge the place for studying a growing segment of our nation's population—not simply as a matter of demographics, but as a matter of social, political, and academic significance. Further, he was a master at desegregating university and community through his more engaging and culturally centered pedagogy. He could imagine an academy that would gain from moving Mexican cultures from the margins to a more significant place in higher education. Rudy Sandoval speaks to us as a former colleague of Julian Samora when they were both on the faculty of Notre Dame. He recognized the many roles played by Samora in their relationship. "Don Julian" was a friend, colleague, historian, teacher, and mentor to Sandoval.

He witnessed Samora's unique blend of the roles of scholar and community activist. Perhaps in making his decision to accept his current administrative position in higher education, Sandoval recalled Samora's vision and "idea of promoting and producing Mexican American leadership for academia."

As I reflect on the long-term impact of Julian Samora in and beyond the university classroom, I am reminded of David Trend's concluding thoughts on the critical role of pedagogy within a democracy. He suggests that cultural pedagogy holds a dual function. "It is both the means by which the oppressed come to know their oppression and the vehicle through which they struggle to find methods for change."[4] Dr. Samora contributed to a movement in higher education that was designed to accomplish what Trend suggests. That is, Samora effectively taught and mentored Chicano/as and non-Chicano/as to recognize historical oppression within higher education and the nation, and he did so in and beyond the university classrooms. Julian Samora's pedagogy was unquestionably transformative in its impact upon his students. As a transformative educator and intellectual, he served as a "catalyst for change" in how Chicano/as who studied with him came to understand their history.

No, I never had the pleasure of meeting Dr. Julian Samora. But I have had the pleasure of meeting, teaching with, and learning from those who knew him well. It is through meeting those individuals who were clearly influenced by Dr. Samora that I have come to know him as a radical or revolutionary teacher and caring mentor. His vision is one we must continue to hold if we are to create inclusive institutions of higher education that recognize the enrichment rather than a deficit in celebrating the Mexican cultures of our society. This shall be the legacy of Dr. Julian Samora, the "godfather of Chicano Studies."

Notes

1. bell hooks, *Teaching to Transgress: Education as the Practice of Freedom* (New York: Routledge, 1994).

2. The current university mission statement reads, "The University prides itself on being in an environment of teaching and learning which fosters the development in its students of those disciplined habits of mind, body and spirit which characterize educated, skilled and free human beings. In addition, the University seeks to cultivate in its students not only an appreciation for the great achievements of human beings but also a disciplined sensibility to the poverty, injustice and oppression that burden the lives of so many. The aim is to create a sense of human solidarity and concern for the common good that will bear fruit as learning becomes service to justice" (Notre Dame website, July 2007).

3. Paulo Freire, *Pedagogy of Hope: Reliving Pedagogy of the Oppressed* (New York: Continuum, 1997).

4. David Trend, *Cultural Pedagogy: Art/Education/Politics* (New York: Bergin and Garvey, 1992).

CHAPTER THIRTEEN

Julian Samora's Pedagogy of Empowerment

Victor Rios

As I observe the current pedagogical transition from "teaching-centered" to "learning-centered" in higher education, I cannot help but notice that my personal teaching style already incorporates and has for some time now incorporated theoretical and practical elements of the "new" learning-centered methodology. I see myself more as a facilitator than as sole authority in the classroom. I try to create an environment in which students feel comfortable speaking out and participating. I feel that putting the students at ease and reducing the inherent anxiety of the classroom situation helps fuel interaction and learning in the classroom. In my classes learning occurs through a variety of teaching methods and activities. Students are expected to tease out answers from each other, critically question the information they are receiving, and learn to think about the decisions they make and why they make them. Upon reflection, I realize that those elements were instilled in large part by the tutelage and mentorship of Julian Samora at the University of Notre Dame, three decades ago. Dr. Samora's influence on my outlook occurred in three different areas: (1) his approach in the classroom, (2) his personal interaction style, and (3) his direct advice as a mentor.

In 1974, when I was recruited by the sociology graduate studies program at the University of Notre Dame, I was not aware that my fellowship was through the Mexican American Graduate Studies Program (MAGSP), which was funded by the Ford Foundation and was under the direction of Dr. Julian Samora. In fact, I was not even aware of the existence of the MAGSP, even though I had directed my graduate school inquiries and applications to schools that I thought might provide funding support for Mexican Americans. Northern Indiana did not register as a place to go to study about and with Chicanos, and I had only a vague sense of who Julian Samora was. I was familiar with his books, *La Raza: Forgotten Americans* (1966) and *Los Mojados: The Wetback Story* (1971), and I considered him one of the "old guard" of Mexican American scholars. Other than being aware of his scholarship in the field of Chicano Studies, I had no idea whether Samora was a psychologist, sociologist, historian, or political scientist. Even though I had never met Julian Samora, I had formed a judgment that in comparison with other Chicano activists, he was too conservative in asserting and agitating for the rights of Chicanos. Much as the young black nationalists of the 1960s had become impatient with the non-violent, seemingly appeasing nature of Martin Luther King's approach to gaining social justice for African Americans, so were many young Chicanos (including myself) in the late 1960s and early 1970s becoming impatient and disenchanted with the older generation of Chicano scholar/activists, who we felt were not doing justice to the activist part of their title. What we did not realize, of course, was that just because they were not out on the streets spouting rhetoric and leading demonstrations did not mean that this older, original generation of scholars had abdicated their responsibilities to the cause of *la raza*. In fact, to the contrary, they were paving the way for many of the societal changes that improved educational, political, and economic access for Chicanos across the country. But we were enamored of the fiery rhetoric and alternative disciplinary analyses offered by younger, more charismatic intellectuals. So, although Julian Samora was doing great things for the Chicano people, he seemed passé in comparison to the leading lights of the new intellectual and ideological fronts. Therefore, it was with mixed feelings that I approached my first year at Notre Dame.

It did not take long, however, for my impression of Julian Samora to change and my respect for him to grow. The first thing that jumped out at me about him was his down-to-earth nature and lack of self-importance. At the same time, I was impressed by the serious demeanor that did not suffer fools gladly. These characteristics were evident both in the classroom and in his personal interactions. In the sociology classes I took with Dr. Samora, but especially in the multidisciplinary colloquium we were required to attend as part of the Mexican American Graduate Studies Program, I began to be exposed to a style of teaching and professor-student interaction that I would eventually adopt as my own instructional classroom method. Dr. Samora had a way of allowing the class to teach itself. Oftentimes he would throw out a concept, issue, or event for the colloquium to discuss and then he would sit back and allow the students to go at it and form their own ideas and opinions about the issue. Although the students carried forward the learning dynamic, Dr. Samora was not completely detached from the scene. When needed, Dr. Samora would intercede to clarify concepts, guide with critical commentary, and provide historical perspective.

Dr. Samora was always open to new interpretations and others' contributions. For example, several of the students in the colloquium held ideological and/or disciplinary perspectives that were at odds with Dr. Samora's approach.[1] Although Dr. Samora was not trained in these approaches and did not adopt their analyses in his research, he was nonetheless open to hearing the arguments in the colloquium and supporting the efforts of those students who did adopt newer, alternative approaches. In this role of facilitator/teacher Dr. Samora was practicing a pedagogy that was liberating, democratic, and learner-centered. We as students found ourselves in a learning environment in which we were free to express our opinions without fear of negative criticism and in which our opinions and suggestions were welcomed by all and especially by the authority figure in class. Although Dr. Samora was obviously an "authority" in the fields he specialized in, he was always approachable, never condescending, and always open to other viewpoints. This minimization of ego was a central lesson I learned from Julian Samora. I resolved that if this great academic had no problem subsuming his ego and interacting with his students on a personal, humane, and equal level, I, at whatever level I taught, would strive to do the same. I don't know whether any of his students realized it at the time, but Julian Samora was offering us a model to emulate without directly telling us how to teach or help people learn.

Dr. Samora demystified the authority/non-authority dynamic in other ways also. He provided the students with the opportunity to meet and interact with nationally renowned academics and intellectuals on a face-to-face level. We were included as equal participants and encouraged to engage in conversations and discussions with the activists and intellectuals that were part of the various programs and events sponsored by the Mexican American Graduate Studies Program. To be able to have a personal conversation with Cesar Chavez, Ernesto Galarza, and other writers and academics whose works were part of our curriculum was particularly empowering. As a person becomes more personally accessible, his or her work becomes more accessible. This is a great learning tool—to reduce the divide between the consumer (student) of knowledge and the producer/distributor (authority/teacher) of knowledge.

Dr. Samora also allowed students glimpses of his personal life and welcomed the students into his home. A "sense of family" was established with the cookouts and dinners that Dr. Samora hosted at his home. Many of us students were far from our own families, but Julian and Betty Samora welcomed us into their home and made us feel as if we were part of their extended family. This personalization and leveling of the student/teacher interaction reduces some of the stress and tension that is inherent in the situation of teaching and being taught. This reduction of stress, in turn, increases the learner's self-confidence, willingness to participate, and overall sense of competence. Somehow, mostly unconsciously I suppose, I was internalizing these lessons.

The most direct example of Julian Samora's mentorship was his personal guidance and help as an advisor. Before I left Notre Dame, I had co-authored two publications with Dr. Samora. Unlike other professors who might ask you to collaborate on some work and then credit you in the footnotes, Dr. Samora insisted that I be listed as co-author of the published articles. In another example, shortly after another faculty member in the Sociology Department at Notre Dame had nominated one of my course papers to be accepted as the equivalent of a master's thesis, Dr. Samora called me into his office and asked me what my career goals were. I knew I was in the graduate program to get my doctorate, but I was not completely clear on what I would do once I achieved the degree. Dr. Samora explained to me that I had the option of leaving the program with a master's degree or staying on to pursue the PhD. He mentioned that with a master's degree there would be certain job avenues open to me, with the federal bureaucracy being one possibility. A master's degree would probably not be sufficient for positions at most universities, however. He noted that, in essence, doctorate programs are for producing the next generation of intellectuals and specialists in the various academic disciplines. As a PhD, I would most likely find myself teaching and/or doing research at a college, university, or research institution.

When I started graduate school, I had a vague notion that I wanted to teach at the university level, but I was not too clear on the concept or about the politics of academia. What I did know was that I wanted to influence and encourage students from disadvantaged backgrounds, particularly Mexican Americans. Now, in a matter of a few minutes, Dr. Samora's personal counsel helped me to reaffirm my initial notion and to understand what path I would pursue once I obtained my doctorate. Thus, even before I left Notre Dame, I turned down a research position at Michigan State University because there was no opportunity for classroom teaching.

When I applied for academic positions, I focused my attention on teaching-centered institutions and eventually taught at two very similar and highly selective liberal arts colleges that are known for individualized student attention. I was teaching very bright, well-prepared, and enthusiastic students in a seminar-like ambience that provided the perfect setting for encouraging and guiding young minds. The only problem was that the students from disadvantaged backgrounds, especially racial/ethnic minorities, that I had hoped to be a facilitator and role model for were few and far between in these settings.

I am now teaching at an institution where I can be of service to the community and students I have always been particularly concerned about. The majority of our students are from socioeconomically disadvantaged backgrounds. Many are the first generation in their family to aspire to college, some are adult learners returning to education after a hiatus of ten to twenty years, and the majority are of Mexican American or Mexican heritage. It is particularly gratifying when many of these same students contact me later to announce that they wish to apply their degrees as educators, lawyers, and engineers to benefit the population they came from and serve as role models for younger generations. To me, this is a true manifestation of Julian Samora's legacy.

Needless to say, this is the culmination of what almost three decades ago Julian Samora helped me understand I wanted to do. I am influencing lives, serving as a role model, dispensing knowledge, opening up possibilities, lifting aspirations, and facilitating intellectual growth in a population of students that too often are forgotten and neglected by our society. I try to honor Julian Samora by using personal and classroom techniques and methods designed to emphasize inclusiveness and fairness, create a non-threatening classroom environment, increase motivation and participation, promote learning instead of rote teaching, minimize teacher ego, and challenge the students to think critically, not just about the subject matter, but about their personal lives as well.

Notes

1. Dr. Samora had come of academic age in sociology before C. Wright Mills's challenge to structural-functionalist sociology inspired the turn toward Europe and Marx for paradigmatic guidance. The influence of neo-Marxist theory and the critical school of sociology were already quite evident in the writings of the first sociology graduate students in the MAGSP, however. By the mid-1970s two sociology PhD theses, J. Bustamante, "Mexican Immigration and the Social Relations of Capitalism" (PhD diss., University of Notre Dame, 1975); and G. Cárdenas, "A Theoretical Approach to the Sociology of Mexican Labor Migration" (PhD diss., University of Notre Dame, 1977), analyzing undocumented immigration from a critical sociology perspective, had been completed by MAGSP students. C. Wright Mills, *The Power Elite* (New York: Oxford University Press, 1956).

CHAPTER FOURTEEN

Personal Reflections on Education

José R. Hinojosa

As I prepare to retire after nearly forty years in the teaching profession, I am asked to reflect on the contribution that Dr. Julian Samora made to my career. This has been a difficult task for me, as I had never made the time to think out what my teaching career had been like and especially the impact that Dr. Samora had on me and my family. The experiences I had with Dr. Samora and his family, the University of Notre Dame, and the many individuals I met there have been an integral part of my life. I had never attempted to separate them and to look at them as an independent part of my journey through this life. I will attempt to do so now.

My first awareness of Dr. Samora was when I found a book edited by him, *La Raza: Forgotten Americans* (1966), while browsing through a college library. I was familiar with the works of other Chicano pioneers in academia, like Carlos Castañeda (history), George I. Sánchez (education), and Américo Paredes (folklore) at the University of Texas in Austin, and the works of Ernesto Galarza and Ralph Guzmán in California, but Dr. Samora was new to me. The name Samora intrigued me because my father's mother, Amelita, was a Zamora. I had many uncles and aunts and cousins with that last name. My father, Teodulo Hinojosa, often signed his name Zamora in the traditional Mexican manner of listing both parents' last names.

So I began to find out as much as I could about Julian Samora. Most of the information was on his background: born in Pagosa Springs, Colorado, attended Adams State College, Colorado State University in Ft. Collins, Colorado, and received his doctorate from Washington University in St. Louis, Missouri. But there really wasn't much else.

The fact that he taught at the University of Notre Dame also interested me, for like many young Catholics, I was quite familiar with the university through its football teams. I, too, was very familiar with the Four Horsemen, Knute Rockne, the Gipper (George Gipp), Frank Leahy, Ara Parseghian, Johnny Lujack, Paul Hornung, Leon Hart, Mike McCoy, Alan Page, and many others whom any good Fighting Irish fan will quickly name. But a professor with the last name of Samora was new to me.

Like many other American Catholic youth I, too, had dreamed of going to Notre Dame. But for a poor Mexican American from the brush county of South Texas, that was a fantasy beyond imagination. So I attended Texas A & I University, now Texas A & M University–Kingsville. I graduated in 1959 with a bachelor's degree in government and history, and I earned a master's degree in 1960. Then I was able to get a teaching job in Great Bend, Kansas.

I taught there for three years and then came back to Texas and obtained a job teaching at the Gary Job Corps Center in San Marcos, Texas. From there I was able to get a job as an instructor of government and supervisor of student teachers at Southwest Texas State University, now Texas State University in San Marcos. Participating in the anti–Vietnam War and Chicano movements of the late 1960s did not endear me to the college administration, and I was not offered a contract in 1970. I made an effort at public office by running for county judge of Hays County against a thirty-year incumbent. I lost by 1,200 votes at a time when we still had the poll tax in Texas and the voting age was twenty-one. It was a great experience but now I was at a crossroads. I was married in 1967 to a wonderful young woman named Irene, whom I met while working at the Job Corps Center, and we now had a son. I worked at several community action agencies, in San Marcos, Victoria, and New Braunfels, but my true calling was in education. I recalled the great times I had in the classroom and the constant interaction with the students and my colleagues. I loved the exchange of ideas, debating different issues, and researching for information to use, both in the classroom and in the coffee shops. So I started to look for a graduate school to work on my doctorate. I decided that a career in college teaching was what I wanted. I applied to and was accepted by several schools in the state of Texas. I decided to attend the University of Texas at Austin since I was familiar with some of the faculty and the campus. It was also close to my wife's family in San Marcos and we had many friends in the area. But something intervened. I found the book by Julian Samora of Notre Dame, and I was intrigued by him and the university. Also, a colleague at Southwest Texas State University, Randall Bland, who had graduated from Notre Dame, introduced me to Dr. Paul Bartholomew, who was at the time a visiting professor at the University of Texas in Austin. In our conversation I mentioned Dr. Samora, and Dr. Bartholomew stated that Dr. Samora was a well-known colleague. At the same time a very close friend, Roberto Garza, a former roommate and friend at Texas A & I, was doing postdoctorate work at Notre Dame, working on a book on Chicano theater. He convinced me to apply to Notre Dame and to write to Dr. Samora and ask for assistance. I wrote to Dr. Samora after

I had been accepted by the Government Department but with no financial assistance until I could prove myself. Dr. Samora wrote back saying that I would be given financial assistance with a Ford Foundation fellowship the first year, if I attended. Still figuring I would need more money, I wrote Dr. Samora and asked if he could help find a job as a secretary for my wife, Irene. He returned my inquiry by saying that Irene had a job as his secretary when we got there. There was no going back. We started planning our trip to South Bend and Notre Dame.

We arrived at Notre Dame in August of 1974 and moved into an apartment at the University Village, the married students' housing on campus. We found a nearby elementary school, Darden, for our first son, José. Javier, our second son, was three years old and attended Mother Goose Day Care Center. Irene and I went to the university to look up Dr. Samora and to find out what our lives were going to be like for the next four years. Dr. Samora was very gracious, introduced us to some of the other students, and more or less told us to make ourselves at home. And home it was. From the very beginning, we felt at home. The friendliness of the people who attended and worked at the university was amazing. We met some of the other students: Gilberto Cárdenas, Miguel Carranza, Joe Mosqueda, Danny Valdez, Barbara Driscoll, Julie Leininger, Lydia Espinoza, Victor Rios, Ken Barber, Juan García, Salvador Acosta, and Ciro Sepulveda. They were the students involved in the Mexican American Graduate Studies Program when we got there. They quickly became like family. We met other students as they came back, like Jorge Bustamante and Alberto Mata, or as they arrived in later years.

But Dr. Samora, his wife Betty, and the Samora family became the center of our lives. We met the Samora children, Geoff and his wife Mary, Dave and his wife, and Johnny the youngest. Later we also met Carmen, their only daughter.

As soon as we had settled down and started classes, the Samoras invited us to go with them on a weekend picnic at Indiana Dunes State Park by Lake Michigan. It was at occasions like this and the many get-togethers at the Samoras' home that we got to know each other. We ate, we drank, we talked, and we became a big family.

The university was a friendly place; faculty and staff would introduce themselves and ask us where we were from and welcomed us. We attended Mass either at Sacred Heart or in the Crypt. The boys, José and Javier, became altar boys. The priests we congregated the most often with were Father Saleta and Father McGregor. My teachers were Dr. Bartholomew, Father Raymond Cours, Professors Brinkely, Krommers, Francis, Kennedy,

Goerner, Arnold, Roos, and Ivanus. The university had many things to offer. At the beginning of the school year they would have the main quad's family picnic and we would eat hot dogs and hamburgers and talk to other students, faculty members, and staff members, and we even met Fr. Ted Hesburgh, president of the university, Raymond Joyce, vice president, and Moose Krause, athletic director.

But the real focus for us was the Mexican American Graduate Studies Program and the Chicano seminar. The seminar was where I learned to study and participate at a graduate school level. Most of us had already had successful undergraduate careers, so we thought we were already prepared for graduate school. But it was here at the Chicano seminar that Dr. Samora showed us his teaching skills and slowly socialized us into academia. The seminar was held at the library/conference room next to his office on the eleventh floor of the Hesburgh Library. All Chicano students were expected to attend, but some would, at times, not show up. I tried to attend every time it was held. The routine we followed was pretty much the same every time we met, except on special occasions. We would discuss current events and what was happening in our home states. Since the students were from throughout the country, from Boston to California, to Chicago or Michigan, to Texas or to Florida, we became acquainted with events nationally. We did not only discuss Chicano or Latino issues but anything that was brought up. But the trick was that we had to do our homework and be prepared to discuss the various issues with knowledge and facts. We were expected to be able to cite our source of information and to back up our opinion by supporting it with expert testimony, documentation, and verifiable information. Dr. Samora would never lecture; instead he would ask questions and expect us to support our arguments with facts. Occasionally Dr. Samora would assign a manuscript that had been sent to him from the University of Notre Dame Press for review, and we were expected to read it, critique it, and analyze it. We were introduced to materials that had not yet been released to the public, and if it were to be published by the press it would have to be approved by the majority of the students and other readers. These peer review sessions of the new manuscripts and articles taught us a lot about doing research and writing for publication.

On special occasions, Dr. Samora invited speakers or guests who would make seminar presentations and university-wide speeches. Some of the most active scholars, political activists, and experts came to campus. Normally, after their presentation to the university, we would gather for an informal dinner and discussion with the speaker at the Morris Inn or the Samora home. Some of the speakers I remember most are Ernesto Galarza, Ed Roybal, Leo

Estrada, Leonel Castillo, Cesar Chavez, Raul Yzaguirre, Raúl Fernández, and Armando Navarro.

Two other events that Dr. Samora organized and brought to the university that I remember very well were the Latino Women's Conference and the Hispanic Bishops Conference. There were many other events, and students were expected to attend and participate actively in each of them. My wife, Irene, played a big role in organizing these conferences.

The Chicano seminar was a three-hour credit course mandated by the terms of the fellowship, to be taken only once during our tenure at Notre Dame, but most students attended it every semester we were there. This was in addition to what we had to do in our major department. If we majored in sociology, economics, history, psychology, or government, like I did, we were also expected to be full-time active graduate students in our individual majors. Our colleagues in the major department did not have the same double expectations. But Dr. Samora argued that much more was expected from us, so we might as well get used to it. And he was right. If you are a Chicano/Chicana or a student of Chicano Studies, you are expected to do twice as much as your mainstream colleagues. In my twenty-six years at the University of Texas–Pan American, I was expected to do at least twice as much as my Anglo colleagues. No matter how much work you do, how much you publish, or how exceptional is your teaching, you will not be considered an equal by the majority of your Anglo colleagues. You better get used to it. Dr. Samora prepared us for this by insisting on our attending the Chicano seminars along with majoring in a mainstream subject at the same time. But the reward for this double load was the self-assurance and self-confidence to take on anything and everybody.

In the last fifteen years of my teaching career at the University of Texas–Pan American, along the U.S.-Mexico border, despite my many health problems from heart disease to throat cancer to renal failure, I have tried to emulate Dr. Samora's example, in both the classroom and the community. I have been able to assist more than fifty graduate students to receive their Master of Public Administration degree; more than thirty former students attended law school and now practice in our region; and countless former students now work as teachers, businesspersons, and politicians and are active contributors to the development of South Texas.

But more important, I am a graduate of the University of Notre Dame. We have friends all over the United States, and Irene and I were able to raise two wonderful sons. José is now a medical doctor in Fort Collins, Colorado, planning to go into academic medicine. And Javier is director of a home health care agency in McAllen, Texas. Between them both we now have six granddaughters. Hopefully one of them will be as lucky as I and attend Notre Dame. All this was possible because of Dr. Julian Samora, who taught me what a real education can do.

CHAPTER FIFTEEN

Crossing Disciplines and Boundaries
From South Bend to Mexico City
Barbara Driscoll de Alvarado

The return plane trip to Chicago from Mexico City on a dark and stormy afternoon in June of 1973 ended a trip organized by Don Julian Samora for his graduate students to visit and experience Mexico. Don Julian and his wife, Betty, invited us, the graduate students enrolled in the Mexican American Graduate Studies Program (MAGSP), to accompany them on a week of seeing and experiencing Mexico. Fortunately for me, only a couple of us were free to go, thereby providing me an opportunity to spend close time with Betty and Julian while they transmitted to us their passion for Mexico and Mexican culture. We toured Mexico City, climbed the pyramids at Tenochtitlán, met academic colleagues of Julian's, and sampled the culinary riches of Mexico (I ate my first artichoke at Las Mañanitas in Cuernavaca!). Our trip was an extraordinary conclusion to the first academic year in my graduate career at Notre Dame, and in a real sense a continuation of the dynamic and mul-tidimensional program that constituted the core of Dr. Samora's Mexican American Graduate Studies Program. It was to be the first of many trips to Mexico for me.

Our field trip to Mexico reflected Julian's commitment to teach and men-tor not only through formal classes but to nurture his students' minds and spirits via doors of inspiration and reaffirmation wherever they might be found. Julian's appreciation for the complex and dynamic relationship be-tween Mexican Americans and Mexico introduced an important element to Mexican American Studies. Few academics then or now have lived and understood the way that Julian did the *telaraña* (spiderweb) that conjoins Mexico with Mexican Americans. In short, Julian constantly broadened and challenged the parameters of Mexican American Studies.

I was a graduate student of Latin American history, particularly Mexican history, and a visit to Mexico afforded me the opportunity to experience the country firsthand. Although I would later return to Mexico to live, I was fortunate that my first time in the country was guided by Betty and Julian. Through their eyes, I saw the beauty, the inequality, the majesty, and the poverty of Mexico.

Enrollment in the MAGSP entailed a commitment not only to follow a standard graduate program in an academic department (sociology, history, etc.), but to focus original dissertation research on a topic related to Mexican American Studies and further to participate in the weekly Chicano Studies seminar held on Wednesdays in Memorial Library. We met, discussed, and critiqued each other's work, and we frequently had the opportunity to meet with accomplished and recognized scholars and activists Julian invited to Notre Dame. Frequent exposure to accomplished Mexican American scholars and activists and their ideas through the seminar generated ideas, controversies, and new intellectual parameters. We greatly benefited from learning the state of knowledge in many fields, the strategies useful in applying knowledge to political causes, and research methodologies. The Chicano seminar brought us in personal contact with such notables as Ramón Eduardo Ruíz, Jesús Chavarría, Carey McWilliams, and Paul Taylor, all of whose careers exemplified innovative research and provocative intellectual inquiry.

The decade of the 1970s was an exciting time to be part of a Chicano Studies seminar! Chicano scholarship exploded. As new and provocative research circulated and was published mostly from the Southwest, we dissected it, analyzed it, and then digested it. We spent many sessions critiquing academic and non-academic literature about Mexican Americans, from the earliest monographs written by Victor Clark to the most recent works authored by militant Chicano academics. Julian encouraged us to use the seminar to formulate academic discussions and many of us also took the initiative to generate original research. We learned the language of the academy through this engagement.

Since we were a diverse group and the seminar was independent of our academic programs, our infamous freewheeling Wednesday meetings at the library were stimulating, even raucous. Julian presided over the seminar and structured it so that we had a safe environment to exchange ideas and opinions and learn the ropes of academic discourse. Since then I have come to believe that Don Julian designed the Wednesday seminars to prepare us for the life of a professional. Those afternoon sessions served as a venue for us to exercise and broaden our intellects under his tutelage, but also as a space to network, explore ideas, and vent frustrations. Further, the content of the Chicano seminar complemented the curricula of participating academic departments.

Julian's research and teaching experience in the Southwest and Midwest had convinced him that simply promoting an academic Mexican American Studies isolated from a broader sense of community would have limited impact. Indeed, during the life of MAGSP in the 1970s to the mid-1980s, Mexican American Studies was so new that U.S. universities did not and perhaps could not provide infrastructure, library support, or teaching resources so pivotal for a graduate program. The Wednesday seminars provided a much-needed source of reinforcement, nurturing, and intellectual repast for the students, a flexible vehicle for Julian to interact with MAGSP graduate students, and a venue to demonstrate to the academic community that Mexican American Studies was a legitimate albeit new area of study that merited the support of the university.

Further, Julian's approach to Mexican American Studies was inclusive. He freely interchanged many sometimes politically charged terms, such as Mexican Americans, Chicanos, and Spanish-speaking. Moreover, he sought to include men and women as invitees, students, and other collaborators who represented diverse disciplines and occupations, political orientations, ethnic backgrounds, and geographic regions; the common thread was a commitment to advancing the knowledge and advocacy of Mexican Americans. Julian also believed that Mexican American Studies should not exclude non–Mexican Americans; using knowledge to secure social and political change can involve many groups and individuals.

It came then as a surprise to me during my first year at Notre Dame that after a Wednesday seminar, the invited, widely recognized male scholar privately pinned me against a wall to warn me that as an Anglo woman I would never survive in Chicano Studies. At the time I did not have either the personal confidence or power to challenge him, and indeed the identity of the scholar is irrelevant. But the effect of the encounter remained with me. True, I was among the first female students at Notre Dame, but if it had not been for the nurturing environment of the MAGSP, I may not have had the wherewithal to continue my graduate studies. The incident humiliated me, generated a long internal dialogue about my status in the academy, and threatened to become an obstacle to my graduate education. Since I had just met Don Julian and the other participants in the program, I did not yet have the *confianza* (confidence) to share what had happened. Until I developed what would become strong friendships with colleagues at Notre Dame, the incident isolated me.

Julian's ultimate goal was to form leaders. His research on local bicultural leadership in Colorado early in his career and his own networking in the 1950s, also in Colorado, had shown him that effective leadership does not always arise from the isolated energy and effort of an individual but often from a critical juncture of training, consciousness raising, context, and networking. Inexperienced or misdirected leadership sometimes negates the effects of collective actions. Julian's emphasis on graduate and professional education reflected his lifelong concern that higher education respond to the community's need for informed and responsive leaders. To be sure, it was an innovative approach to graduate training in the 1970s.

I looked forward to spending Wednesday afternoons with the other students; our discussions and disagreements sparkled with intellectual energy. Of course, we really did not understand that Julian was mentoring us, but that did not matter. The Wednesday seminars turned out to be the core of our graduate education, and I do not exaggerate to say that they affected me more than any other educational experience in my life. And they were fun!!

The research topic that galvanized us was immigration. Samora's then recently published study *Los Mojados: The Wetback Story*, which he co-authored with then students Jorge Bustamante and Gilbert Cárdenas, *ipso facto* made him a prominent immigration scholar. Importantly, as the first academic book-length study of undocumented Mexican immigration, *Los Mojados* contributed to establishing the Chicano seminar as a legitimate venue for analyzing issues relating to the immigration of Mexican workers, migrant workers, and the problems they faced.

Moreover, controversies surrounding undocumented immigration and immigration policy politicized the Chicano movement, and indeed many of us involved in Mexican American/Chicano Studies. We followed closely the rise and fall of legislative proposals in Congress, although it would not be until the passage of the Immigration Reform and Control Act of 1986 that Congress would actually act.

It is no coincidence that many of us chose immigration-related topics for our doctoral dissertations, topics discussed in the Wednesday seminar. In political science, José Hinojosa studied the discretionary power of the Immigration and Naturalization Service; in sociology, Jorge Bustamante, Gilbert Cárdenas, Victor Rios, and Paul López studied theory-related questions; in history, Juan R. García documented Operation Wetback of 1954, and I documented the railroad Bracero Program of World War II. Still others developed research relevant to the adjustment and incorporation processes that Mexican immigrants faced upon their arrival in the United States. Much of this research has since been published in academic and non-academic form, thereby, in a sense, extending the circle of Chicano seminar discussions. I would venture to say that we can speak of a Samora School of Immigration Studies.

Julian encouraged students to generate original data for their dissertations, and to that end, he generously made whatever funds he had available to us to conduct original research. For example, in November of 1974, Julian provided funding for Gilbert Cárdenas, Juan García, and me to do immigration research in the National Archives and the Immigration and Naturalization Service in Washington, D.C. Accordingly, the three of us drove to Washington, D.C., presented ourselves at the National Archives, and surveyed various record groups in search of material on immigration. We had also contacted the Immigration and Naturalization Service to request access to internal files in their central office in Washington, D.C. They placed the three of us in a room under the supervision of a bureaucrat; we reviewed some files while the INS representative duly interrogated us. Although I did identify files on that trip that would later be useful in my dissertation, of greater importance was experiencing the process of locating data and confronting the animosity of the Immigration Service.

On a more personal note, our return to South Bend from Washington, D.C., coincided with Thanksgiving. We actually arrived the night before, and of course Gilbert and I had not made plans for dinner. Betty anticipated our disorganization and invited us to their house to share Thanksgiving at their big, round table with the lazy Susan. The meal, of course, was scrumptious and plentiful, although I remember clearly that Betty wanted to do a light dessert that year. So our dessert was a delicious crustless pumpkin pie.

As a corollary, several of us collaborated with the Centro de Estudios Chicano e Investigaciones Sociales, a research center founded by sociology graduate student Gilbert Cárdenas with an office on the eleventh floor of the library. Gilbert generated original research in Chicano Studies, particularly regarding the greatly underresearched Midwest community. In fact, in 1975 Gilbert commissioned a three-part study of Mexican Americans in South Bend. Jim Faught prepared a socioeconomic study of the Mexican American community of South Bend, Julie Leininger Pycior conducted oral histories, and I developed a newspaper documentary history. Taken together, the three studies represent a unique and original multidisciplinary view of the barrio in South Bend.[1]

I left Notre Dame in the summer of 1975 to use my graduate stipend to finance my dissertation research. I spent time in Chicago, Washington, D.C., and Mexico City to identify information for my study of the railroad Bracero Program. I also worked for a time at Texas A & M University as a researcher, but decided to return to Notre Dame in 1978 to write my dissertation. Like he did with other students, Don Julian kept track of me through correspondence.

As part of my return to Notre Dame in 1978, I worked as Don Julian's secretary for nine months in his MAGSP office in the library, from September 1979 to May 1980, to support myself while I finished my dissertation. My daily routine for that time coincided with Julian's and I came to know him from a much closer vantage point. I opened the office in the morning, made coffee, answered the phone, and attended to whoever came to the office. Julian arrived usually sometime during the middle of the day, signed the letters I prepared the afternoon before, and made and received many calls. He would actually not remain at the library office long since he conducted classes in other parts of the campus and studied and wrote in his office in the basement of the library. As he left the library office for the day, Julian left the cassette with the day's correspondence that he had dictated at home and during his stay at the office. After he left, I typed the correspondence for his signature.

I should mention the electric typewriter Julian's secretaries used (we still distinguished between manual and electric typewriters in those days!). Although today typewriters are virtually unknown, Julian's Executive IBM bears special mention. Unlike any other typewriter I had seen before or since, the letters of the typeset occupied different spaces. The "i's" were slivers next to the "m's," which meant in practical terms that correcting mistakes with no mechanical assistance from the machine or a "spellcheck" was nightmarish. The carbon copies of his Notre Dame correspondence now available in his papers are replete with white painted splotched corrections!!

Soon I discovered that Dr. Samora's file cabinets housed a veritable gold mine of correspondence and other documents that spanned his career from the early 1940s to the late 1970s. Chronological letter books that he had started in the 1950s contain his correspondence with organizations and with colleagues, potential colleagues, friends, and relatives. Don Julian particularly valued his longstanding network of individuals active in the study and advocacy of Mexican Americans and Spanish-speaking communities. Down time in the office, especially early in the morning and just before locking up late in the afternoon, provided time for me to peruse his papers, time that I greatly enjoyed.

Former students and others who visited will remember that Julian's office in the library was a suite of three rooms. The inner room he used as his office had a window that overlooked the street that passed in front of the library. Some will remember that he collected matches in a huge fish bowl on a table in back of his desk. The outer room with no window contained his file cabinets and the secretary's desk. Further, there was a windowless room parallel to the two offices that held bookcases, and a long green table where students often met to read or to discuss. In fact, Julian greatly liked that his suite could accommodate informal student *tertulias* (gatherings), another way of engaging them and fomenting networks. Indeed, Julian's office facilitated contact among undergraduate, graduate, and professional students, some of whom may not have had occasion to meet. In fact, during my tenure as Julian's secretary, Victor Rios, then a sociology graduate student, and I organized a regional midwestern meeting of the National Association of Chicano/Chicana Studies.

I resigned as secretary in May of 1980 to finally finish my dissertation, but my relationship with Julian had changed. Being his secretary had opened a window onto his life and career that permitted a fuller appreciation of his achievements and the times in which he lived. Those correspondence files of his! Julian had maintained communications with recognized as well as unknown pioneers of Mexican American Studies and political activism. I am delighted that they are now organized and available for researchers.

My deepened relationship with Don Julian prepared me to pursue research about the first cohort of U.S.-Mexican border and Mexican American researchers, to which he belonged. While a researcher based at El Colegio de la Frontera Norte in Tijuana and subsequently at the Universidad Nacional Autónoma de México in Mexico City, I interviewed Julian on several occasions in Tijuana and South Bend from the mid-1980s to the early 1990s. The interviews in Tijuana were conducted collectively as a discussion with Charles Loomis and Gilbert Cárdenas about the origins of U.S.-Mexican Border Studies, and they resulted in a manuscript later published as a Working Paper at the Julian Samora Research Institute (JSRI) of Michigan State University. In that manuscript we explored his early life and education and the myriad challenges he faced as he struggled to develop an academic career focused on research, mentoring, and inevitably advocacy. Julian clearly understood that the challenges of his early life inspired and informed his professional goals. The discrimination and hardships he experienced and witnessed were obstacles to Mexican Americans claiming their rightful place in U.S. society. JSRI also sponsored additional interviews with Julian later in his life.

As my own academic career evolved at the Colegio de la Frontera Norte[2] and Universidad Nacional Autónoma de México[3] over a span of almost twenty years, I again turned to Julian's professional trajectory *por el otro lado* (on the other side) as inspiration. Julian had worked in Mexico City and Bogotá before we knew him as the director of MAGSP. Few Mexican American academics active in the 1980s had actually taught or published in Mexico or Latin America, yet Don Julian brought to our training an understanding of the connection between Mexican Americans and Mexico. Even less evident were publications or research about Mexican immigrants or Mexican Americans. With the important exceptions of Manuel Gamio in the 1920s and later Jorge Bustamante in the 1970s, Mexican society took little public interest in the plight of the Mexican-origin community of the United States until the ascent of Prop 187 in California in 1994. Nonetheless, over time I developed courses and conferences in Mexico in Mexican American history and culture, and I published in Spanish.

My life in Mexico as a permanent resident frequently gave me cause to recall my first trip to Mexico City that I shared with Betty and Julian. Their knowledge and love of Mexico was based on experience and intellectual curiosity, not just on third-hand reminiscences. Both Betty and Julian felt their lives had been enriched through their multifaceted relationship with Mexico and further understood that Mexico constitutes one of the essential concentric circles that leads to understanding the complexity of Mexican Americans and Mexican American history. Their example set a path for me in seeking professional challenges, exploring international borders and boundaries, and identifying injustices.

Notes

1. Copies of the three studies are housed in the Rare Book Room in the Hesburgh Library at the University of Notre Dame.

2. El Colegio de la Frontera Norte is a multidisciplinary teaching and research institute dedicated to the study of the U.S.-Mexico border located in Tijuana, Baja California. I worked as a researcher in the Social Studies Department.

3. The Universidad Nacional Autónoma de México is the oldest and largest university in Mexico. For fifteen years, I worked as a researcher at the Centro de Investigaciones sobre América del Norte.

CHAPTER SIXTEEN

In the Autumn of His Life

Rudy Sandoval

As a fledging law professor, I arrived at the University of Notre Dame during one of the coldest winters the small town of South Bend had ever seen, yet the kind reception I received from Julian Samora was certainly one of the warmest. I was just starting my career as a professor; he was at the peak of his as a full professor. He had received his bachelor's degree the same year I was born. Julian belonged to that famous generation of Mexican American academicians that opened the doors to colleges and universities for the rest of us. That was the courageous generation that tolerated the isolation, the hardships, and the discrimination in academia so that others like myself could have the opportunity to participate as equal partners in classrooms across this nation. They were the academic voice and champions of the Mexican Americans who had been socially, politically, and economically left behind after World War II. How could I not admire him for his outstanding academic and personal accomplishments? How could I not admire and respect him for his personal convictions? This chapter elucidates Dr. Samora's life during the time we were at Notre Dame together, the period when I knew him best. I optimistically hope that my words portray the deep impact Julian had on my life and personal development, as he has surely had on countless others.

When I arrived at Notre Dame in 1976, Julian was at the height of his professional career. He was a professor and the director of the Mexican American Graduate Studies Program, while I was a professor at the Notre Dame Law School. We were the only two Mexican American professors at the university. In the evenings, either I would go to his office or he would come to mine. We would spend long hours together talking about the past, the present, and the future of the status of the Mexican American.

Julian was a quiet, unassuming type of person who projected a sense of controlled confidence. On the surface his appearance seemed serene, as if nothing distressed him. He bore that gentlemanly, stoic, and courteous manner of respectful conversation that is rarely found anymore, except in a few isolated rural parts of the Southwest. He had a quiet disposition about him that made you feel at ease. His movements were slow and purposeful, his speech was precise but calming, and his quiet manner of speaking was disarming. He had a fascinating manner of talking to students. I recall one time when after speaking with a student about his academic work, the student wasn't quite sure whether he had just been chastised or commended, but he still felt good about himself.

Don Julian is what I liked to call him. He had the type of universal wisdom that used to be more common in the old days when, for example, people in a village would visit with "Don Emiliano" to get his advice on marriage, illness, or other family matters.

My father used to say it is one thing to be educated, but it is quite a different matter to be *educado*. To be educated means to have a formal education, to have knowledge of the world around you. To be *educado* means to be honorable and noble, to be considerate, to know how to act in public, to treat people with dignity, and, above all, to be respectful. One could be educated without being *educado,* but he would be considered *un mal creado,* or someone without class. Alternatively, one could be *educado* without being educated, which was perfectly acceptable. Julian was one of those rare individuals who was both educated and *educado.* He had knowledge, wisdom, and class.

Over the years, as we strolled through the snow-covered campus grounds illuminated by the Golden Dome, and during the passing season as winter turned to spring, and summer turned to fall, Julian and I became good friends as well as colleagues. Our conversations seemed endless. Somehow I had discovered a bottomless reservoir of fascinating experiences, stories, and wisdom. In the evenings as I strolled back from his office on the slippery sidewalks, I would replay our conversations, experiencing the world anew, with new perspectives and insights, and I always felt enriched because of him.

Sometimes Julian and I would walk to the south dining hall on campus for lunch and he would share his experiences and the realities of his time as a teenager during the Depression and as a young adult during World War II. He lived through some of the roughest periods in history, when discrimination against Mexican Americans was arguably at its worst, yet his emotional scars were barely visible. Perhaps that is the reason he always had a sense of perspective on history and the kind of wisdom that comes from those experiences. I always had a sense that he was a door through time for me. His was a comprehensive living experience for me and I relished his experiences and his insights. Sometimes I felt I was living vicariously through him. As we talked, he always prefaced his answer with a historical background so that I would understand the true meaning of his answer. He had managed to enlist his experiences, his knowledge, and his education to inform his vision of what we could become. The legal profession had taught me to look at the worst scenario so we could prepare ourselves for the future. He was always looking for the best circumstances with hope beyond the horizon.

Julian had an unlimited reservoir of personal stories and a profound understanding of Mexican American history in the Southwest. I was particularly surprised by his knowledge of Texas and California Mexican American history, since he was from Colorado and New Mexico. His conversation often shifted to the idea of promoting and producing Mexican American leadership for academia. He used to say, "If I can only have my students understand the past, they can learn to appreciate the present and prepare themselves for the future."

Julian also had a strong sense of justice and of right and wrong that seemed to come naturally to him. He didn't have to shout or demonstrate against the injustice before him; his quiet persona projected it. I suppose this characteristic emerged from his painful experiences in the 1940s and 1950s. He often reminded me of the signs on restaurant doors as he traveled through the Southwest that said "no dogs or Mexicans allowed." But the scars he bore from these experiences did not overtly affect him. You had to carefully listen to his comments or read his works to know how these experiences had impacted him, because he was never personally abrasive, confrontational, or bitter. I suppose, too, that by the time I met him he had mellowed with age. His comments were always well-measured and calculated not to offend anyone. This is not to gainsay the passion for justice and equality he had for issues that were important to him. With respect to these, he had strong profound philosophical convictions.

After a while, I also got to know his interesting nuances. There were the times, for example, when I knew he was going to disagree with me even as I was making my point because he had a gentle, timely laugh that would immediately disarm me. His listening skills were something I grew to appreciate and later adopt. He would listen with such intensity that it appeared as if he was looking right through me. From time to time he would stop me in midsentence to get clarification. His intellectual positions were almost irrefutable, for he would first outline them with historical facts, then insert his personal experiences, and finally come to a conclusion by recommending several books to read on the subject, which of course I always felt obliged to read.

When I met Julian he was already a giant in his field and was well known all over the United States and parts of Mexico. On several occasions, I had the opportunity to travel with him to conventions. His only baggage was a brown and red tote bag with a shoulder strap where he carried, among other things, his reading material and pipe. Being with Julian at a convention was quite an experience. Upon entering the reception room, colleagues gravitated toward him, not in the same manner as they would to a celebrity, but toward someone whom they respected, esteemed, and admired. They would reach out to shake his hand and give him an *abrazo*. His contemporaries loved him. The new faculty members would respectfully listen to him, and the uninitiated would ask to have a picture taken with him. Of course he would say yes, and people would crowd around to have their picture taken with Dr. Samora. I could tell he was uncomfortable being in the spotlight, but he was happy to be among friends. He had a quiet, gentle manner about him when he was in a group setting, which I tried to emulate, without much success. While he purposefully and methodically moved about the business of his profession, he was a man in a hurry pursuing the issues he cared about most passionately. And he cared most passionately about the future of Mexican Americans.

Julian was extremely productive during the time we were together at Notre Dame. He had received a half-million-dollar grant from the Ford Foundation to produce scholars and scholarly materials in the field of Mexican American Studies. He also received funding from the John Hay Whitney Foundation to fund original research on the Texas Rangers. I remember he was so exited about this area of study that it consumed him completely. From that work, Julian, Joe Bernal, and Albert Peña produced *Gunpowder Justice: A Reassessment of the Texas Rangers*, which was published by Notre Dame Press. Simultaneously, within a period of two years he was involved with Eugene Nelson's *Pablo Cruz and the American Dream*, for which he wrote the introduction, in addition to "Mexican Immigration," a chapter in *Mexican-Americans Tomorrow*, edited by Gus Tyler, which was published by the University of New Mexico Press. He also collaborated with the other giants in his field, writing "George Sánchez and Testing" (with R. López) in Americo Paredes, ed., *Humanidad: Essays in Memory of George I. Sánchez,* published by Aztlán Publications.

Issues dealing with the United States and Mexico also fascinated him. In 1971, before I knew Julian, he had written *Los Mojados; The Wetback Story.* He followed up with a new grant, which culminated with *Dilemmas and Issues of the U.S.-Mexico Border.* By 1977 he had published, along with P. V. Simon, *A History of the Mexican American People.* After I left Notre Dame, Julian continued to research and write fruitfully about the Mexican American experience for two more decades.

Julian's commitment to the Mexican American community extended beyond intellectual exercise, beyond research, teaching, and writing. One morning he called me at the office and asked me to join him. He said he was going to downtown South Bend to meet some friends who needed our support, and he was sure they would appreciate it if they got support from the Hispanic Notre Dame faculty. Since he and I were the only Mexican Americans at Notre Dame, we obviously had 100 percent representation. Since I'm in the legal profession, I thought he wanted me to help him articulate some point of view at a meeting in support of his friend. When we arrived, I saw at least a hundred people holding up signs and marching in protest in front of a building. When we got out of the car, several people came toward us and started to talk to Julian. Before I knew it I was holding a sign and walking alongside Julian and a hundred other protestors outside the building. I was really getting into the swing of things when suddenly I realized I was the only one wearing a three-piece suit.

Being with Julian meant staying loose and learning on the fly. He was also at the forefront of the strike for higher wages by the university groundskeepers and cafeteria workers, and he was certainly not hesitant about confronting the university president on these issues. On another day he called me at my office in the law school to ask me to come by his office because there was someone he wanted me to meet. When I arrived, he proudly introduced me to Cesar Chavez. It was quite an incredible moment for me, to say the least. Seeing them talk and joke together made me realize how similar they were in character and how their humbleness made them giants. The breadth and depth of his involvement in the local and national community, and his connection to both the grassroots and the national Mexican American leadership, was absolutely amazing.

I cannot even begin to imagine the things he was involved with before I met him *in the autumn of his life,* and the personal contributions that he had made toward the enhancement of Mexican Americans that are not even recorded in his résumé or any other place. By the time I met Julian, his children, whom I grew to respect and love, were all grown up. He and his wife had already lived a lifetime. I only knew Julian for a short period of time, but for me it was one of the most educational, one of the most enlightening, and one of the most humbling experiences of my life. I would like to think that because of my beloved friend Julian, I am a better human being.

CHAPTER SEVENTEEN

Early Mentor

Phillip Gallegos

There was a time early in the life of Dr. Julian Samora when Mexican American scholars and PhDs did not exist in academia. As he opened doors, first for himself and then for others, his journey has become the guiding ethic of my professional career. We each are the sum total of our interactions with others, and I remember the guideposts of my life that marked a clear and compelling path. Julian Samora was renowned as a scholar and researcher, but he also provided a clear marker to the future for me and for a generation of undergraduates he mentored. His accomplishments as a mentor to young students were derived from a deep-seated and strong humanist core.

As I think of the early mentors in my life, there are teachers, family members, colleagues, and surprising strangers. In my undergraduate career at Notre Dame, Dr. Julian Samora was each of these. As a teacher, aside from his highly influential research work, he was an early mentor, the proverbial role model, and one that empowered the undergraduate student intellect. I sensed that he knew he could propel us, as a teacher and mentor, to a life focused on community issues and to focus on others; in other words, he modeled leadership. Like Dr. Samora's experience, when I was a freshman in 1966, there were not many Mexican American role models to be found in college. At that time, to find anyone who looked like me and had similar histories, student or teacher, was essential for survival at Notre Dame and life in Indiana.

So many people have affected and driven my life's work. Among the many people with great souls at crucial crossroads in my life stood Richard Castro of Denver; my mother, Antonia, the most joyful woman I have ever known; my father, the strongest man I have ever known; Graciela Olivarez of Arizona; Dwayne Nuzum of Colorado University; John Rosales of Pueblo; and Dr. Julian Samora of Notre Dame. Of these, the quality and style of leadership I have come to value came primarily from John Rosales and Julian Samora. It was through John Rosales that I came to learn about Julian Samora.

At the beginning of my high school senior year in Pueblo, Colorado, in 1965, my teacher, John Rosales, took an interest in my impending graduation. He encouraged me to seek opportunities in the university. "Such a novel idea" was my first thought, since only one of my parents had graduated from high school. John Rosales was instrumental in helping me secure a nomination to the Naval Academy in 1966, and the University of Colorado had also granted acceptance. Then, in what was a turning point in my life, he asked me to apply to the University of Notre Dame. He said he had heard about "a guy there by the name of Julian Samora who was doing great things" and that I might get special financial assistance. Even before the days of the Internet and electronic searching, there was a small and growing network of Latino whisperers sending information about the works of *Raza* throughout the communities. John Rosales was so certain I could go to Notre Dame that he offered to pay the application fee of $25, a king's ransom in those days. The only condition was that I had to find and meet this person John Rosales kept hearing about from his contacts. When I got accepted to Notre Dame, there was no other choice given my Catholic background, and I accepted the assignment given by John Rosales to find Julian Samora at Notre Dame.

In the fall of 1966 I set off for Notre Dame, Indiana, away from my home in Colorado for only the second time. At Notre Dame, I enrolled in the professional five-year architecture program. Architecture was a world apart from the central campus, and freshman year studies had their own demanding schedule. There was little opportunity to encounter the humanities and Dr. Samora. It was October before I made the special trip across campus required to find Dr. Julian Samora. The Indiana landscape was changing rapidly to wet and cold, decidedly different from the Southwest. The Midwest, I was discovering, had its own patterns of life and I had yet to understand them. When I entered the Sociology Department office, the traditional receptionists, who always seemed to question the validity of your presence, screened me. Dr. Samora passed me on his way to class. This man, who was chair of the department at the time, was firm and direct and had smiling eyes. As a young eighteen-year-old, I was mesmerized both with the scene and this surprisingly interesting stranger. Without much time to talk, he introduced himself and simply invited me to his house for dinner along with other invited students.

He struck me as a man in control, but not controlling, kind yet firm, and clearly in an arena of work in which he excelled. I remember thinking "what a role model." All my family was poor, workers all in the fields and factories without a college degree among us. Yet this man seemed to be strong, without arrogance, in the white world of academia that I was yet to understand. I was enthralled.

And of course, what a family and home he introduced me to. I was immediately jealous of his sons, wishing I could be one. Then other Latino students showed up and it turned out that I was not entirely alone. We were from Colorado, New Mexico, California, Arizona, and Texas. There were at least eight of us there, mostly undergraduates but at least one graduate student. The smell of the tortillas and chile immediately reintroduced each of us to a recognizable sense of home. Betty, his wife, was cooking and greeting, and she was filled with the love a mother uses to shower her children in those moments of family fiestas. I was destined to know and appreciate not only the man's work, but also his remarkable family and their sense of duty through critical community work. I knew I could exist in that land so depleted of the Chicano nature. It was a most compelling evening.

It was a time when terminology and nomenclature for Mexican Americans was becoming hotly debated. But it was not yet viciously expressed in a manner that signaled ideology. Dr. Samora did speak of the term we were still whispering only in our homes or late at night in cars: Chicanos. When he spoke about Chicanos, it was with carefully chosen words and multiple understandings, as an academic could do and still allow one to implant meanings of one's own choice. For an eighteen-year-old with many self-esteem issues, it was like music, full of wonder and possibilities. The term was still considered crude and vulgar by many in my family. Others, however, saw it as an affirmation of a new political era. With this kind of discussion occurring at Notre Dame, away from the political fires of the Southwest, it became possible for this eighteen-year-old kid to examine the questions of self-esteem arising from the changing political and social environment.

There were others like me who sought him out. I did not understand it at the time, but I came to appreciate Dr. Samora as a central figure who drew people to him. He drew intellectuals, politicians, students, artisans, and especially activists. I came to realize the strength of his draw was not flamboyance. It was his genuine interest in people and his commitment to his discipline, research and writing.

It was clearly going to take work to stay connected to this constellation of Chicanos in exile. I was an architecture student with many sleepless nights ahead of me and a universe away from the real world of Chicano social issues. Indeed, on more than one occasion, my architecture classmates asked me if I was an "Indian chief." My psychological survival was at stake at Notre Dame in 1966. Then at the end of my sophomore year I got married and brought my young bride with me to South Bend. Of course, Betty welcomed her and created an emotional safety net for us. Julian provided my wife with a job to help us out. In appreciation, when our first child, Beatrice, was born, we asked and were honored to have them as *padrinos*. In our midwestern exile, he and Betty became surrogate family.

While in my fourth year at Notre Dame, Fr. Ted Hesburgh, president of Notre Dame, brought Graciela Olivarez from Phoenix, whom he had met during the hearings conducted by the U.S. Civil Rights Commission.[1] She was the first woman to attend the law school, and she had neither an undergraduate degree nor a high school diploma. Of course, she was also drawn into the universe of activism surrounding Dr. Samora. Within a year, Graciela had secured funding and had organized a conference at Notre Dame seeking to reveal the conditions of Chicanos in the Midwest.[2] Participants were drawn from Kansas to Michigan, with Chicago the seeming epicenter of Midwest activists, a strange notion for me at the time. We still seemed largely invisible as a people in the Midwest. There were legislators from Illinois and farm worker organizers from Ohio joining communities hidden from the mainstream of Midwest daily life. Betty Samora and I became central figures in organizing the conference.

In that age of impending activism, during the last night of the conference, a confrontation ensued between more vocal participants and Fr. Edmund

Joyce, the second ranking official at the university. The group demanded that Fr. Hesburgh "clean up his own house" and enroll more Chicanos before he continued with the Civil Rights Commission. During the confrontation, the campus police were called but the crowd dispersed. In the morning, a petition was started and the group carried the petition and a memorial to the main altar during the principal Sunday morning Mass at Sacred Heart Church on campus. The group was voicing its frustration with Notre Dame and the Catholic Church and their slow response to issues of social justice. Betty Samora was with the group and was recognized. The congregation was outraged by our presence, but the priests were accepting and placed the memorial up on the altar.

However, the public demonstration came with a price to the conference and those attending the meeting. The Mass that was selected occurred at the same time as the final presentations of the conference. The state representative from Gary, Indiana, Joe Arredondo, was scheduled to speak, and when many of the conference attendees chose to leave his talk and demonstrate at the Mass, a shouting match erupted. Campaign workers for Representative Arredondo were deeply offended and told the crowd preparing to leave, "We have an elected Chicano. What do you have?" The confusion and shouting in the conference was intense. Grace Olivarez became angry and frustrated by the unplanned developments, but in the end, the demonstrators left the conference for the church. As a young man becoming an activist, the choices required of me at that moment were very difficult and confusing. In the end, I followed the group to the church and photographed from the back. Differences in ideology and strategy were as confusing in the Midwest as in the Southwest, and they forced me to make quick choices. Did I choose well and what would my mentor think?

At the time I was working for Dr. Samora. When I reported for work Monday morning, we all faced the stern looks of Dr. Samora. I was given that disapproving look fathers are required to give. Apparently, he had already heard complaints from the South Bend community and Notre Dame. Dr. Samora said, "I told you and Betty not to sign anything." Although I did not know exactly how, Dr. Samora was clearly bearing the brunt of the collective wrath from the Notre Dame community. It was not an easy moment for us Mexican Americans, yet before it was too late, he used this event to set a meeting with admissions to secure a commitment for significant Latino enrollment. At the luncheon meeting, I saw him argue convincingly for the linkages between a Catholic institution and Latino Catholics specifically excluded from educational opportunities, including Chicanos. The following year, our numbers on campus grew from about ten to more than fifty

Chicano students. The numbers of Latino students have grown since that small band of fifty to become a significant part of Notre Dame.

The program I entered, architecture, is a professional undergraduate program with a five-year requirement for graduation. As it was outside the norm, the required fifth year was going to be without financial support for me. It would not be possible to complete a degree at Notre Dame, and I talked to Dr. Samora. He personally appealed to the John Hay Whitney Foundation, which underwrote graduate education and research, on my behalf. Making the case for graduate level work while still technically an undergraduate, he provided the final link to a network of support required to complete my professional degree. Even better, in the final fifth year of college, I was at last provided the opportunity to study with him and take his class, Chicanos in the U.S.

During my final year as an undergraduate, I came to know Dr. Samora truly as a mentor, no longer the superstar or surrogate father figure of my earlier encounters. I was twenty-three years old in 1971. The country was in the midst of the Vietnam War and the civil rights movement of browns, blacks, and women. His class provided a laboratory to engage the dialogue of dissent and views alternative to the mainstream. More importantly, I was struggling with this new profession I was about to engage, architecture. What role in this chaotic world could I play while entering in a profession that was totally, and is still today largely, a white male domain? It was here that Samora became more than a teacher, he became a mentor, a trusted advisor. With his understanding of the professional domains and the world of work coming into sharp conflict with the developing social environment, he once remarked to me, "There is no such thing as Chicano physics or Chicano chemistry, there is only good physics and good chemistry." He understood that intellectual ideas and research come from people and required the discipline of sound thinking to become useful to our community.

For the class, he had me research social art and architecture programs, and I discovered the world of Mexican muralists as they were transferred to Chicano communities in the Southwest and the Midwest as an outgrowth of the civil right movement. He knew that I had an interest in socially responsive architecture and not just service to the wealthy few. Samora led me to understand the need for sound foundations in my discipline. It was critical for my career to establish linkages from an elite profession to the practice of architecture with a socially responsible purpose, such as indigent housing or health care.

The visual aesthetics of art and design were important to architects and the school, but I was more interested in when to apply design principles to a rigorous and socially responsive building program. A formal path in ethnically sensitive architectural design did not exist in the architecture program at that time, but I was still determined to establish a kind of manifesto, or orientation toward designing within cultural frameworks different from the Western European design ethics. While the architecture faculty did not object to this interest, expertise did not exist there to help me research the hypothesis relating use and organization of spaces to cultural values, the subject of my thesis.

My fifth-year architecture thesis was based upon design principles responsive to a worldview as Chicanos. The thesis was a direct outgrowth of Dr. Samora's class, Chicanos in the U.S. This thesis became my personal and seminal work guiding much of my career. Today, students in architecture are required to understand the nature of architecture as an enhancer of social fabric. I was fortunate enough to find in Dr. Samora a disciplined teacher who showed me a way to both ground myself in my community and my profession simultaneously. In 1971, that was a revolutionary idea.

I since have designed and built with community and multidisciplinary design teams such projects as child care centers, health clinics, affordable housing, farm worker migrant housing, housing for the elderly, churches, and schools. Notably absent from my portfolio of work are individual houses, banks, and corporate facilities, structures for the empowered. Additionally, Dr. Samora's guidance fueled a life working with dedicated activists such as Richard Castro in Denver, important programs such as the Campaign for Human Development in the Catholic Church, and higher education issues with the Colorado Commission on Higher Education. In 1974, when I became a licensed architect in Colorado, I was one of three Spanish-surnamed licensees and the only native-born one. As the only Chicano architect in Colorado in 1974, I was a product of two teachers and my family. Today, both my teachers and my influential family are gone. Of them all, Dr. Julian Samora was the intellectual giant that I have come to admire and respect as my early mentor. I have tried to model my academic and professional career after his example.

Samora's quiet sense of ethics and commitment to Chicano issues was drawn from forceful convictions about immigration and civil rights. As a teacher and a writer, he proved to me that those convictions were required for professional and community work needed in our communities. If Dr. Samora could research and teach about Latino issues such as immigration when politicians spoke from myth, then I could use architecture to address socially responsive programs important to Latinos and not be seduced by self-absorbed design imagery. At the end of my undergraduate years, I had a foundation to direct my work toward the Chicano community. The mentor I needed to enter this career in architecture was right there in plain sight.

I have often thought that with the strength of his convictions and his calm manner, Dr. Samora was in the right place at Notre Dame. The Catholic practice of meditation and prayer at Notre Dame provided a place where he and his family could prosper. Yet the Catholic Church is no stranger to controversy and is a site for debates about the nature of roles, authority, and dogmatic convictions. Dr. Samora could not only be quiet and meditative, but, also like the Catholic Church, he could be controversial, determined, and ready for debate. The Catholic Church, for better or worse, has always been an important element in the Chicano community.

Notre Dame was, if not perfect, a very good place for him to write and research on national issues critical to our community as well as influence the career directions of young undergraduates. His personal work among undergraduates insured a continuity of strong and dedicated professionals, intellectuals, and socially conscious Chicano workers.

We still have that compelling need for many mentors.

Notes

1. Fr. Theodore Hesburgh was the chairman of the U.S. Civil Rights Commission from 1969 to 1972.

2. The name of the conference was The Mexican American Conference, and it was held at Notre Dame on April 18 and 19, 1970. See the essay by Ricardo Parra and Olga Villa in this volume.

CHAPTER EIGHTEEN

Vessels of the Samora Legacy
Mentoring the Third Generation
Anthony J. Cortese

Imagine you serve on the admissions committee of a major medical school in the United States, where only one position remains open for the entering class. You must choose between two candidates: one Mexican American, one Anglo—both qualified. Both candidates have the same MCAT score and GPA. Jamie, the Anglo student, is the son of an affluent physician. He graduated from UCLA in four years. Carlos, the son of a poor immigrant from Mexico, took five years to graduate from a smaller public state school.

Whom do you choose? Under the principle of affirmative action—the effort to expand opportunities for minorities to compensate for past discrimination—should you choose Carlos?

"Affirmative action is reverse discrimination," one committee member responds. "I think we should choose the most qualified person, and I don't think we should discriminate against an applicant just because he is not a minority and his parents have money."

"I'm tired of these social programs being shoved down our throats," says another. "The government has no right meddling in the affairs of private institutions."

"But Carlos has grown up with fewer opportunities than Jamie," a third committee member says. "Given the same privileges, he would have graduated from a school as good as Jamie's and in the same amount of time, and he really is qualified for medical school."

"Because there are so few minorities in the medical profession," another member argues, "I feel we must give Carlos the chance."

The debate continues, the dialogue filled with emotion, sometimes outrage. No consensus emerges.

The "committee members" are actually my students engaged in role playing as part of a case study on affirmative action in my course called Minority Dominant Relations. The sociology course is part of the interdisciplinary Ethnic Studies program. I focus on ethnic groups with unequal social and economic power in the United States, but to get inside the social and economic issues of ethnicity, my students have to delve into their own assumptions, stereotypes, and even prejudices.

"It was a tense and painful discussion," one of my black students told me. "Some of us carried on our arguments after class and even the next day in the student center. Some students started to see attitudes in themselves that they didn't know were there. Others were clearly confused about affirmative action."

One of my Chicano students told me, "It did bother me to hear some stereotypes about minorities being expressed by other students, but that's part of the learning process in this course."

As my students debate, I remain in the background, walking quietly among the discussion groups, watching, listening, making mental notes.

In 1989, I was hired by Southern Methodist University to help raise awareness of ethnic issues (through my teaching, research, and service) at a university that is mostly white and located in a virtually all-white upper-class community. Mexican Americans make up about 20 percent of all Dallas residents. By 2030, 46 percent of the state of Texas will be Latino; the overwhelming majority of those will be Mexican Americans. Because Texas once belonged to Mexico and much of Texas's heritage derives from its Mexican past, there is common ground for both understanding and misunderstanding to take place.

The need for ethnic diversity extends beyond state or regional interests. By the year 2025, an estimated 40 percent of the eighteen- to twenty-four-year-olds in the United States will be minorities. United States society is becoming more multiethnic, and our education must reflect that changing demographic reality. My courses expose students to the similarities and differences among Mexican Americans and other Latinos, African Americans, Native Americans, and Asian Americans. They fill the gap sometimes left by traditional liberal arts, with their focus on the Euro-American culture.

Those of us who were fortunate enough to be mentored by Julian Samora (indeed, we have been given a name: *Samoristas*) have become vessels of the Samora legacy in our mentoring the next generation of young scholars in Chicano social science research and applied fields, art, literature, history, and law. Julian was a charismatic role model dedicated to the cause of social justice and the alleviation of social inequality. My extensive work in Chicano and Mexican American Studies all starts with his mentoring, scholarship, and teaching. Julian led by example, not by edict. He was a wonderful facilitator, interviewer, and communicator. I watched how comfortable he was with people from all types of racial, ethnic, and cultural backgrounds. Julian also had a keen ability to make others comfortable. I have tried to model this behavior and attitude in my relations with my students and those whom I mentor. Clearly, it is in mentoring others that one carries on the formidable legacy of Julian Samora. Julian is my model and his work has had a tremendous personal impact on me. In this narrative essay, I will focus on the impact of Samora's life and teaching methods on my worldview, perspectives, and experiences regarding education, and, most important, how I mentor and teach others. During my nearly thirty years of teaching at the university level, I have mentored many students. One particular student comes to mind. I shall call him Miguel.

Miguel was born into poverty in Guadalajara, Mexico. Miguel's father, Hector, was a drug dealer who was killed by rival drug dealers when Miguel was only five years old. Hector, who usually traveled with friends for protection, was attending a dance alone in a nearby town. While no weapons were allowed in the dance hall, Hector's rivals ganged up on him. Several held him down while one thug repeatedly stabbed him in the throat with the tiny file from a fingernail clipper. As he pleaded for his life, no one came to his aid. He slowly and painfully bled to death. Fearing further retribution, Miguel's mother, Josefa, took her four young children to live in Texas.

Despite being brought up in an environment of drugs, gangs, and violence, Miguel somehow managed to stay out of trouble and graduate from high school. He then enrolled at Southern Methodist University. I first came to know him as a student in my Minority Dominant Relations class. He was quiet and unassuming. But I made a point of getting to know him and he gradually opened up to me. Miguel struggled with his courses and was placed on academic probation after his first year of college.

Miguel came back the next fall and enrolled in another of my classes. Furthermore, he decided to major in sociology. Near mid-semester, Miguel stopped coming to my class. This was very uncharacteristic of him, for he never missed class. I became more alarmed when I learned that he also stopped attending his other classes. I called him and he was embarrassed to tell me that he had dropped out. Miguel often became discouraged when he did not do well on exams and assignments. Moreover, he had decided to get married at the young age of nineteen. His wife, Rosa, had recently given birth to their first child. They were struggling financially and Miguel and his long-time amigo, Alejandro, had recently started a landscaping business.

As much as I wanted to, I did not tell Miguel that I thought he was making a big mistake. I told him only to ask his professors for grades of "Incomplete" in case he one day decided to return to school. I was disappointed because he had a lot of potential. I had helped Miguel write papers, giving him ideas and providing encouragement. English was not his first language and writing was difficult for him.

The next semester, Miguel returned to school and was more determined than ever to graduate. At the time of writing this essay I recognize that the struggle is not over for Miguel, but I am proud to say that I have played a critical role in his life as Julian Samora did in mine. I continue to mentor him, as I do so many others. I am proud that I have made a difference. Julian would be proud as well, I feel.

Another area where I believe I mentor is through my research and publications. I carry on Julian's legacy of using social research to frame social policy and as an impetus toward social justice. My scholarly research focuses on Mexican American education, and it provides educational policy implications based on the relationship between education, culture, Mexican American family structure, and social factors. Dr. Samora's legacy continues to affect my current and former students in their academic and professional work. He once told me, "Anyone can be an activist, but not everyone can be a scholar." Similarly, I emphasize scientific knowledge as the foundation of both social policy and self-discovery.

As an effective teacher and inspiring mentor, Julian Samora stimulated my interest in Chicano Studies. For me, the journey was also autobiographical. My ethnic background is half Mexican American and half Italian. My mother's family is from Jalisco, Mexico, while my father's is from Carlentini, Sicily. This biethnic background had both positive and negative effects. On the positive side, I was able to move freely and easily between the dominant mainstream culture and the minority Chicano culture. On the negative side, I became marginalized—not quite fitting into either cultural setting, not totally belonging to either set of peers.

I lived in an all-white lower-middle-class neighborhood in Omaha, Nebraska, and attended St. Patrick's school—an all-white Catholic primary school nearby. But on Sundays, my family attended Our Lady of Guadalupe church (my mother's family's church where my parents had been married) in South Omaha—a predominantly Chicano part of town. Accordingly, I was able to (and, in fact, needed to) cross cultures frequently—having white friends in my neighborhood and at school and Chicano friends that I met at church or in the South Omaha Boys Club. I learned to embrace both cultures and both groups of friends.

Here is where the conflict and marginalization arose. I played baseball and basketball for my school in a league that included the Chicano church team. There was a continuous and intense rivalry between St. Patrick's and Guadalupe. In the heat of battle, I would hear my coach and teammates make racist remarks about our "Mexican" archrivals that would make me feel very uncomfortable and, frankly, disgusted. Was I Mexican or was I white? I did not know and I kept my uncertainty regarding my self-identity to myself. As a result, I wanted to better understand the complex relationship between self and society and between majority and minority.

This inner struggle continued as I began graduate school in the Department of Sociology at Notre Dame. How would I fit in with all the other Chicano graduate and law students that Julian had assembled and brought to Notre Dame? I did not speak Spanish very well. My language skills were rudimentary at best. Even more important, I did not look Chicano. In fact, I remember vividly that the application required that I attach a photograph of myself. Since I was graduating *magna cum laude* from Bellevue College (now Bellevue University), I was an attractive recruit. However, Notre Dame called Bellevue to inquire whether I was in fact Chicano. When this was confirmed, I was accepted and given a graduate scholarship.

Still the question remained: How would Dr. Samora and the Chicano students react to me. I did not feel Mexican enough. Yet once I arrived, Julian welcomed me with open arms. I was relieved to see that there were other students who were even more Anglo looking than I—even with Anglo or European last names. I learned that ethnic identity is based much more on self-identification than physical appearance. In this open, accepting, and nurturing environment, I flourished at Notre Dame.

I received my PhD in sociology from the University of Notre Dame in 1980. My first position was a joint appointment in the Department of Sociology and as director of Chicano Studies at Colorado State University (CSU) in Fort Collins, Colorado. This position provided yet another link between Dr. Samora and me since many years earlier he had received his MA degree at CSU from the same Department of Sociology in which I began my career in academia.

Julian Samora was an excellent, inspiring teacher and an outstanding scholar in the area of Chicanos Studies, but what I remember most about him was the sense of community that he fostered in his personal relations. When Julian arrived at a party or social gathering, he took the time to introduce himself to everyone.

As a postscript, I wish to close by stating that in 1977, after a series of serious misunderstandings with one of my instructors, I was dismissed from the PhD program in sociology at the University of Notre Dame. I appealed the decision, hired an attorney, and brought him with me to my appeal meeting before the Graduate Program Committee. It became clear that I was being dismissed unfairly and possibly illegally. After my lawyer identified himself, the committee decided to cancel the meeting on the spot before it even began. A vote was taken and Dr. Samora was one of only two faculty members who voted against canceling the meeting. In short, Julian persuaded the committee not to dismiss me from the program. Without his support, I would have never received my PhD or become a professor of sociology and scholar of Chicano Studies. I owe my career to him.

I believe that my record of teaching and publications, participation in professional societies, both national and international, and work on committees of scholarly associations demonstrates a continuation of Julian's legacy of taking intellectual risks and engaging in dialogue across disciplinary and international boundaries. Each year, I teach a seminar, Race, Culture and Social Policy in the Southwest, at the SMU-in-Taos campus in New Mexico. The campus is in rustic Fort Burgwin, a refurbished army fort built in the mid-nineteenth century to protect trappers and travelers from renegade Indians. Fort Burgwin is nestled in the Sangre de Cristo Mountains in Kit Carson National Forest. It is fitting that I am concluding this essay while teaching in New Mexico—the state where Julian Samora lived and died. It is night time. The moon is full. The wind is howling. I feel that his spirit is with me now—and forever.

C. Research and the Integrative Process of Julian Samora

CHAPTER NINETEEN

Translating the Whole Person
Julian Samora as Research Mentor
Alberto López Pulido

The research process modeled by Julian Samora through his scholarship and publications placed value in all scholarly efforts that benefited the community. As early as the 1950s, Samora's style of community-action research focused on using the intellectual imagination to address and move toward resolving dissent within communities. From leadership studies to the impact of migration on communities, Samora's research sought to answer questions that challenged the daily lives of people in a community. His research was consistent in addressing the needs of the whole person defined here as an integrative research process.

All the essays in this section illustrate the philosophy of the integrative research process of Julian Samora. We read about a guide and mentor who served to translate the complex and chaotic world of higher education for his students. Jorge Bustamante, the first Samorista, speaks directly to this issue in his essay as an international student from Mexico studying in the "heartland of America" and trying to decipher a new language and culture within the world of academia. We have Julie Leininger Pycior, who as a young graduate student connects with the stories of struggle of the Chicano experience offered by leading Chicano intellectuals such as Ernesto Galarza and Rudolfo Anaya. This deeply resonates with her life and research interests. Gilbert Cárdenas, also an early Samorista, came from the streets of East Los Angeles and through his connection with Betty and Julian Samora finds a personal and intellectual home. Years later, Paul López, a Chicano Studies major from the mecca of Chicano Studies, California State Northridge, gravitates to the power of the Samora legacy and the important work coming out of the Mexican American Graduate Studies Program on immigration. And Ciro Sepulveda, a principled academic who challenges the legitimacy of the Graduate Record Examination as a measure of academic success, would find a supporting voice and intellectual home emanating from the Mexican American Graduate Studies Program and Julian Samora.

All these essays consistently reveal a mentor who astutely recognizes that the intellectual connection can only be nurtured through a personal connection with his students. Samora's intentions were to both intellectually and personally embrace the whole person by simply recognizing his students as people, with personal stories that if validated would establish the foundation for limitless research opportunities for developing intellectuals. The inherent goal was to instinctively educate the whole person by treating him or her with dignity and respect by honoring his or her history and, through the process, "make history," as Julie Leininger Pycior so aptly identifies in her essay.

In the end, this integrative strategy was extremely successful, as shown by the impressive research careers established by the Samoristas in this section. Julie Leininger Pycior is a well-established researcher in Chicano and Mexican American history. She has uncovered the buried perspectives lost in mainstream history, and her studies of President Lyndon Baines Johnson from the perspective of the Mexican American experience are innovative and important. Jorge Bustamante has become the foremost expert on Mexican and international migration and has had a distinguished career in both Mexico and the United States. He is the Eugene Conley Professor of Sociology at the University of Notre Dame and the special rapporteur on the rights of migrants for the United Nations. Paul López has assembled an innovative research agenda in sociology and Chicano studies. His forthcoming book on the personal lives of Mexican braceros in the history of the United States begins with the assumption that braceros are more than simply "a pair of arms," as the name implies. As his mentor taught, they are people with real struggles who perform as active agents of history shaping and transforming labor relations in both the United States and Mexico. Both Gilbert Cárdenas and Ciro Sepulveda have gone on to distinguished careers in their respective fields. Cárdenas holds the Julian Samora Chair of Latino Studies at the University of Notre Dame, and Sepulveda is chair of the History Department at Oakwood College. Early in their careers they established themselves as creative and groundbreaking scholars by investigating the Mexican American experience in the Midwest. Their work broke new ground and challenged the overarching framework for understanding Chicano history. The Samora integrative process for mentoring students in graduate education is remarkably effective, as illustrated by the personal reflections and narratives that follow. They demonstrate the power of educating the whole person.

CHAPTER TWENTY

Julian Samora

Mentor

Jorge A. Bustamante

To me, Julian Samora was a mentor in the fullest socratean sense of the word. His teachings were beyond the classroom or his office and involved both his past and his present experience. His past is being the first Mexican American/Chicano with a PhD in sociology in the United States. His present included a plethora of role models: as a pioneering scholar in the fields of the sociology of medicine and the sociology of minorities and immigration, as an advocate of civil rights for minorities, as a fundraiser for research projects and scholarships for Chicano graduate students, as a promoter and leader of community development projects, and as a restless backyard farm worker. He was all of this when I first met him as my assigned academic advisor in 1968.

In 1968, Dr. Samora had just been awarded a grant for his U.S.-Mexico Border Studies Project. Who could have told me then that my assignment as a research assistant to the director of that project would provide the foundation for the design of the institution that I founded and headed for sixteen years, that is, El Colegio de la Frontera Norte, a Mexican degree-granting research institute, fully dedicated to U.S.-Mexico border studies?

I used to meet Julian Samora in his office on the eleventh floor of the Hesburgh Library on the Notre Dame campus. It was clear that in those turbulent years on U.S. campuses, Dr. Samora was an actor on more stages than one could think possible for just one man. He would jump from one airplane to another with a perennially hectic schedule, which contrasted with a work style and soft manners that seemed to distill Thoreau's meaning of the word "simplify . . . simplify."

In those years of the late 1960s, there was no other faculty member in the Department of Sociology and Anthropology at the University of Notre Dame more widely known as a national and international scholar than Dr. Julian Samora. Nevertheless, he was gently modest about his personal achievements. In his conversations with me, I always felt he knew when to speak with the wisdom of the ancient cultures his ethnic heritage embodied. He would say with a gentle voice to a green graduate student when I was trying to say or explain or do everything with one stroke: "Jorge, el que mucho abarca . . . poco aprieta" ("Jorge, he who starts a great many things . . . finishes few").

His relationship to me was set not just within the faculty-student framework. He was also sensitive to my cultural preconceptions in a foreign country where I was intent on completing a doctoral degree. He had the ability to reach out to me when I fell deep into a whirl of transcultural confusion. In embarrassing situations or in a crisis, he was the one who sorted out for me the facts and the cultural misunderstandings. There were plenty of both, particularly in my first year as a graduate student. Let me illustrate.

I had been in the United States for no more than two weeks when I was waiting for the elevator in the library on my way to the eleventh floor where I had begun to work as Dr. Samora's research assistant. As I watched the elevator indicator light slowly inch its way down the board, a young lady, one of the first Notre Dame co-ed graduate students, came up by me carrying a huge stack of books in precarious equilibrium. This stack was conspicuously overturned when more persons than the official holding capacity entered the elevator. As I stepped out of the elevator and bent to pick up some of the books lying on the floor, the young lady hit me on the head with one of the books! She furiously scolded me, saying, "you male chauvinist . . . pig." As I was trying to sneak away from the scene, I felt like Adam and Eve after the sinful bite. I could not figure out what I did to cause such a violent reaction from the woman I was trying to help. It took me awhile to again take the elevator and ask somebody to help me understand the incident. I was certain that I had unintentionally overstepped a cultural rule, but I certainly did not know what kind. My inquiry was answered by Dr. Samora with an initial remark followed by a smile: "Welcome to the age of woman's lib."

My own crisis was due to a more serious matter. Dr. John Koval was in charge of a required course on advanced methodology in the fall semester of 1968. He was also in charge of a research project on voting behavior. He thus had a number of objectives built into the graduate course. He was teaching us in the field the research techniques of a conventional survey based on a rigorous sampling design aimed at finding out the electoral preferences of people of Saint Joseph County (where the University of Notre Dame is located), before the election between Richard Nixon and Hubert Humphrey. I mentioned to Dr. Samora the difficulties I encountered in understanding the U.S. electoral process. This knowledge was taken for granted by each graduate student in Dr. Koval's project. Yet for me it was problematic.

The next day John Koval called me to his office and said that Dr. Samora had persuaded him that it was not fair to give a foreign student an assignment that implied knowledge of a significant aspect of U.S. political culture, in addition to the course requirements. Therefore he required me to submit an original research project wherein I could be certified as fulfilling the requirements of the methodology course. My first reaction was one of gratitude for Dr. Samora's thoughtful initiative. However, I was soon confronted, unexpectedly, with the challenge of producing a research design of my own. I felt like I had jumped from the frying pan into the fire!

I again went to Dr. Samora seeking advice. I told him I wanted to do research on a problem that could be directly related to my country. I came away from that conversation in September of 1968 with a research problem for my methodology course and a topic for my dissertation in a field where I have been doing research for the past thirty years: Mexican immigration to the United States.

At the time I was working under him, his involvement in the civil rights movement took him to the Indiana State Civil Rights Commission and to the U.S. Civil Rights Commission. His teachings on the subject of social inequality of ethnic minorities were a combination of a solid grip of the literature and direct personal participation in the struggles for civil rights. There was one occasion in 1970 that Dr. Samora came to our graduate seminar unusually excited. He said to us with a deeper than usual tone of voice that something historical had happened the previous day in California. A court had declared unconstitutional any laws or regulations of that state punishing children for speaking Spanish within school grounds. Dr. Samora explained to us the meaning of that decision by referring to a history of discrimination against children of Mexican origin who attended school speaking Spanish only. He painted with words and emotions the scene of a six-year-old child of Mexican parents, recent immigrants to the United States, who finds herself on the first day of school being told that the language she speaks at home is forbidden in school as something dirty, something deserving of punishment if she is caught speaking it. He took us to his past, which was the history of many generations of Chicanos who at times were muted by the English-only rule on the school grounds. I looked at him as a mentor, teaching and making history at the same time.

Under the guidance of Dr. Samora, I followed the strategy of relating most of my course work for the doctoral program at Notre Dame to some aspect of Mexican immigration. Before I met him, Dr. Samora was interested in the population dynamics of the U.S.-Mexico border, including immigration to the United States. He had developed a broad demographic approach and perspective in his recently funded U.S.-Mexico border project. I persuaded Dr. Samora to concentrate his project on undocumented immigration from Mexico. Thus, under his direction, we designed a research project that involved conducting personal interviews with undocumented immigrants at various U.S. Border Patrol detention centers along the U.S.-Mexico border.

Prior to this project, Dr. Samora had sent me to do field research and interview undocumented immigrants in the Midwest. Through numerous encounters we were able to pilot various versions of questionnaires for personal interviews. His contact with community service personnel in places like Peoria, Illinois; South Chicago or East Chicago; Muskegon, Michigan, and above all South Bend, Indiana, were fruitful avenues for eye-opening fieldwork experiences for me. It was also a way to refine field methodologies to approach the elusive undocumented immigrant. By the summer of 1969 we were ready for the formal study of undocumented immigrants who were detained in U.S. Border Patrol centers along the U.S.-Mexico border.

Dr. Samora had to use his best contacts in Washington to obtain permission from the Immigration and Naturalization Service (INS) for my access to the detention centers in El Centro, California, and El Paso and Port Isabel, Texas. During the summer of 1969 I was to conduct two hundred personal interviews with undocumented Mexican immigrants in each of the three detention centers. I was impressed with Dr. Samora's meticulous care in the design of every methodological step to be followed in the research project. I learned from him the importance of the principle of parsimony in the design of scientific projects. Dr. Samora always tried to simplify procedures. This was particularly important in the design of a questionnaire to be used with undocumented immigrants, who were little or not at all familiar with interviews for scientific purposes.

During the academic year 1968–69, we learned of the difficulties in interviewing documented immigrants from various places in the Midwest. Some of these difficulties forced Dr. Samora to put aside the idea of interviewing undocumented immigrants at large. Instead, he thought of interviewing them at the detention centers. This idea resolved some methodological questions, not just in terms of sampling procedures and interviewing techniques, but also in terms of something of particular importance to Julian Samora: research ethics. He was deeply concerned that our research approach could somehow lead to the identification of the immigrants by the INS and their subsequent expulsion from the United States. That would pose no problem for our research subjects since they were already detained at the detention centers.

The lesson I learned from Dr. Samora's concern was simple yet profound. As lofty as the goals of science can be, they are not so lofty as to justify any personal injury or jeopardizing the mental state or legal status of the individual, documented or not.

My fieldwork at the INS detention centers was preceded by Dr. Samora's visit to the INS facilities in Chula Vista, California. He went there to verify the feasibility of the data collection methods that we later followed in the summer of 1969. His Chula Vista experiences allowed him to plan in detail the procedures I was to later follow at every step of the fieldwork within the INS detention centers. Almost seven hundred individual interviews provided the data that formed the empirical bases for Dr. Samora's book *Los Mojados: The Wetback Story*, published by the University of Notre Dame Press in 1971.

Another personal quality I learned from Dr. Samora, in the context of our academic endeavors, was his generosity. As his research assistant I had the obligation to work for his project. But he saw my work differently. Besides working for his research project, I had to work on my dissertation. His idea was to use the data and research findings that we were producing not just for his project, but also for my doctoral dissertation. Like many other graduate students, I am indebted to Dr. Samora for his generosity. Not only did he provide the financial support that allowed me to finish my PhD at Notre Dame, but also he bestowed an intellectual generosity. His open-mindedness allowed dissent from a graduate student and a research assistant, a personal quality not so frequently encountered in the halls of academia.

Dr. Samora was the director of my doctoral dissertation. We had the opportunity to converse at great length regarding the theoretical frame of reference for my dissertation. I submitted a draft of my dissertation proposal to him, which included a Marxist theoretical perspective as the explanation for Mexican immigration to the United States. After a series of discussions and after listening to me with remarkable patience, he said, "Jorge, I do not agree with your Marxist theoretical perspective. I do not understand Marx's theoretical approach, nor do I want to understand such a thing. Find somebody with the proper credentials in the profession who can tell me that you have done a proper Marxist theoretical analysis, and then you can pursue whatever theoretical analysis you want as long as it is scholarly."

He taught me tolerance toward intellectual, social, and political theories and ideas. I would not have managed the doctoral program had I not received his full support in my right to dissent. One of my professors disagreed with my conceptual approach to the question of undocumented immigration, which resulted in a grade of C on a term paper. That paper was later accepted for presentation at the American Sociological Association meetings in Washington in 1970 and by the International Sociological Association (which selected my paper to be presented to the Seventh World Congress of Sociology in Varna, Bulgaria, in 1970). That paper was later revised and accepted by the American Journal of Sociology for publication in 1971.

Listening to Dr. Samora in our graduate studies seminars, talking to him in his office on the eleventh floor of the library, having a drink with him after a long journey of fieldwork along the U.S.-Mexico border, or traveling with him while crossing the United States from the Midwest to the Southwest, I found Dr. Samora able to point out my mistakes through a masterful and respectful use of common sense.

It was common sense that he used to disagree initially with my proposal to pose as an undocumented immigrant. After two years of fieldwork experience under Dr. Samora's direction, I intended to use the participant observation methodological approach. Dr. Samora's initial disagreement was more an admonition to be careful in the planning of such a project rather than a terminal decision by an authority. Once he was persuaded that I had developed a sensible plan, he gave me his full support and decided to include my research as chapter 7 of *Los Mojados: The Wetback Story.* My participant observation as a Mexican undocumented immigrant "through the eyes of a wetback" opened some professional doors that were crucial in my professional advancement as a sociologist.

Thanks to his generosity and open-mindedness, I had a unique opportunity to profit from his leadership as my academic advisor. In all of this, what was inescapable was his extraordinary sensitivity; he was one of the finest human beings I have ever met. His sensitivity was particularly emphasized in his concern for my family. My adaptation to a foreign society as well as my emotional stability within the family were constant concerns of Dr. Samora. They were no less the concern of his wife, Betty Samora, a lovely human being and a highly sensitive individual who cared for my well-being during stressful times. Many invitations to have dinner with the Samoras were preceded by their mindful sensitivity to a family crisis that was later solved with the tender, respectful, and extremely kind support they extended.

Dr. Julian Samora was to me a mentor in the fullest socratean sense of the word.

CHAPTER TWENTY-ONE

Making History

Julie Leininger Pycior

In many important ways, Julian Samora made history. Although a sociologist by profession, he had an appreciation of history that was bred in his bones as a descendant of people who had settled in Colorado and New Mexico in colonial times. In fact, at the time of his death Samora was investigating the *mestizo* heritage of our nation. He also made history himself, of course, as the first person of Mexican descent in the history of the United States to earn a doctorate in sociology.

Thus it is no surprise that in 1970 his Mexican American Graduate Studies Program would host the very first Midwest Chicano conference, the Midwest Conference of La Raza, or that its keynote speaker would be a pioneering historian, Ernesto Galarza. The first Mexican American to earn a PhD from Columbia University, by the 1950s he had become the chronicler of the farm worker movement.[1]

Sitting there listening to his address, I knew none of this, but one could sense that this intense, dignified historian spoke with wisdom accrued from a lifetime of engaged scholarship. He railed against the historical profession's neglect of the Mexican American role in U.S. history, explaining that a handful of historians had written of the borderlands during the Spanish colonial period, but that once Mexicans became Mexican Americans in the wake of U.S. conquest, they disappeared from the history books. Later, when I learned of the Samora family's presence in Colorado and New Mexico over three centuries, I remembered Galarza's point. At the time, however, all I could think was, "He's so right," and try in vain to recall a single reference to Mexican Americans in any of the history courses I had taken at Michigan State University (from which I was about to graduate.) Oh, historians made fleeting references to Indians, European immigrants—and, less often, to African Americans—amid an overriding preoccupation with politicians and generals, but as for Chicanos, nothing.

The only glimmer came from residents of the local barrio in North Lansing, where I was teaching in a bilingual preschool. Their newspapers, *Sol de Aztlán* and *El Renacimiento,* made reference to the longtime Mexican presence in the United States, even as these periodicals understandably devoted themselves mainly to current events—and what events they were![2] Many of the North Lansing residents hailed from Crystal City, Texas, where La Raza Unida movement was in the process of making history, first by overturning the Anglos that had long held sway over the Chicano majority population, then by sponsoring political candidates from the Southwest to the Midwest. Meanwhile, Chicano students at Lansing's Eastern High School staged a walkout, protesting what they considered biased curricula and guidance policies.[3] A few managed to beat the odds and enroll at Michigan State, where at that time students from Mexico actually outnumbered Mexican Americans from Michigan. In reaction to perceived intransigence on the part of university administrators—and in concert with the Chicano activists on campuses elsewhere—they founded United Mexican American Students at State (UMASS). In fact, UMASS president Juan Marínez would go on to become an administrator of MSU's Julian Samora Research Institute, serving from its founding in 1989 up to this very day.[4]

The UMASS students planned to attend the Midwest Conference of La Raza at Notre Dame, and they invited me to come along. Looking back, I tried in vain to recall whether the conference occurred in the fall of 1969 or the spring of 1970, but now, due to none other than the FBI, we know that the meeting convened in the spring of 1970. It so happened that the conference participants included some government informants, a fact that came to light decades later via FBI documents unearthed thanks to a Freedom of Information Act request by La Raza Unida founder José Angel Gutiérrez.[5]

Sitting at that conference listening to Ernesto Galarza, I thought, "That's what I want to do: help rectify this oversight, mine this rich historical ore." Two years would pass, however, before I would screw up the courage to write him a letter. Back came a prompt reply—personally typed on an old manual machine—recommending that I apply to Julian Samora's program in Mexican American Studies at Notre Dame. I did, was offered a fellowship to be administered by the history department, and the rest is, well, history.

The Mexican American Graduate Studies Program made history by sponsoring several groundbreaking conferences—including the first ones ever held on Chicanas and on Mexican American Catholicism—and by hosting a string of Mexican American trailblazers, from Texas legislator Joe Bernal and folklorist Américo Paredes to demographer Leo Estrada. Then there was the post-performance party with the entire troupe of El Teatro Campesino . . .

My favorite guest speaker was novelist Rudolfo Anaya. Prior to his appearance I dutifully started reading his book *Bless Me, Última*. Not one to seek out fiction—from childhood I was more fascinated with stories about "what really happened"—I nonetheless found myself transported from my library carrel to a remote village in New Mexico and the sacred mysteries revealed to a child in the midst of ordinary life. I finished the book just in time for the luncheon and raced over to the faculty club. Sitting there, the conversation swirling around me, I felt as if I had just emerged from a dark movie theater into broad daylight. Suddenly the author looked straight at me with his deep, wise eyes and said, "What is it that you want to ask me?" I do not recall my question, but I will never forget his somehow knowing that I wanted to ask it.

Yes, we grad students sensed that we were participating in something historic. At our ongoing weekly seminar, we dissected issues ranging from immigration to bilingual education to census policy, eagerly applying to the topic at hand the perspectives of our various academic disciplines— economics, government, literature, sociology, and, yes, history. Sometimes the discussions produced more heat than light, and Dr. Samora presided over the flying words with the equanimity of a proud but long-suffering father, punctuating the occasionally intemperate remark with a wry comment or revealing question, ever conscious that we, too, were driven by a mission to spotlight these neglected topics and analyze them in a way that did them justice.

Those of us in history found that some members of the history faculty— not all, but some—would dismiss research on Mexican Americans as trendy stuff, current events, in a word, unhistorical. In fact, it was our professor of sociology that dipped into his own travel funds to enable us to attend a history meeting, the landmark 1973 International Conference on Mexican History in Santa Monica, California, which drew important historians from both sides of the border. Samora also solicited our suggestions on the two history books he was co-writing in the 1970s: a historical survey of the Mexican American people and a revisionist study of the Texas Rangers.[6] This practice of a sociologist engaging in historical research was taken one step further when sociology grad student Gil Cárdenas landed an Ethnic Heritage Study Grant to document the Mexican American community in South Bend as part of his Centro de Estudios Chicanos e Investigaciones Sociales, Inc. As a result, Barbara Driscoll (another history grad student in Samora's program) wrote a documentary history of the community, while I did an oral history.[7]

Community. It meant so much to both of the Samoras. Betty Archuleta Samora was active in a number of local organizations, and she showed us how to build community, helping us link up with El Campito Day Care

Center, with local activists Olga Villa and Ricardo Parra, with farm worker organizers. She fostered community among us, joyfully giving of herself—her thoughts, her ear, her home, her food, and her love. Her deep, grounded spirituality enriched us, and she and Julian created festive times we will treasure always. When their son Robert died tragically, we instinctively gathered at that modest ranch house we knew so well, with its plants and pottery and colorful weavings, and to this day I can see Gil in the background brewing some soothing cinnamon tea.

Gil Cárdenas and other alumni of Julian Samora's Mexican American Graduate Studies Program made history: the first Chicano professor in a department or the first director of a Mexican American Studies program, often the first to publish on an important Mexican American–related topic. For example, Juan García has written books on the history of Mexicans in the Midwest and on the important if controversial program of the Eisenhower administration, "Operation Wetback." Meanwhile I was the first female to be tenured in the history department at Manhattan College.[8]

The topic that eventually became the book I published while at Manhattan College, *LBJ and Mexican Americans: The Paradox of Power*, first occurred to me while I was still a student in Samora's program. Virginia Espinosa, an undergrad at Indiana University–South Bend, transcribed some of the interviews I conducted for the oral history of Mexican Americans in South Bend, and she happened to mention that her father had been an employee at the LBJ Ranch. "It's not in Johnson City, you know," she confided. "It's actually in Stonewall, Texas, just down the road." I got to thinking about the relationship of this towering political figure to such an important constituency, but one that had been virtually excluded from the inner workings of political power. I recalled that LBJ had taught at a segregated "Mexican" school, had won his U.S. Senate seat with contested Spanish-surname votes, and as president had steered landmark bilingual education and migrant services bills through Congress, only to retire in the face of stiff opposition from presidential rival Robert Kennedy, who drew much of his strength from the Mexican American community. How fascinating it would be, I thought, to look at Lyndon Baines Johnson from the vantage point[9] of a group important to his story—and to America's—but whose activities had been largely overlooked. In the process, LBJ could serve as a kind of hook to get historians to learn something of Mexican American organizational history.

For years I worked at piecing the story together. In the process I interviewed some forty key players, from Texas governor John B. Connally and his nemesis, Texas senator Ralph Yarborough, to veteran Mexican American activists such as Dr. Héctor P. García and, of course, Dr. Julian Samora. Also central to the project were a number of archival collections, particularly in Austin: the Barker Texas History Archives (now the Center for American History), the Benson Latin American Collection, and, most important of all, the LBJ Library, with its thirty-five million documents. There I sat in a windowless room leafing through the contents of innumerable folders, always with an eye to ferreting out those documents that made reference to Mexican Americans. Sure enough, the records revealed a fascinating, paradoxical saga—one with national implications.

Moreover, of the thousands upon thousands of documents I consulted, the most striking one turned out to be a reference to Julian Samora. On a scrap of blue paper stapled to a memorandum, the quote from President Johnson simply read, "Keep this trash out of the White House." To my astonishment, it turned out that the pariahs in question were Julian Samora and his colleague Herman Gallegos.

It all started when, as members of the President's Commission on Rural Poverty, the two men were slated to attend a White House meeting in early 1967. They planned to take advantage of the opportunity; when they met the president, they would remind him of a longstanding demand on the part of Mexican Americans for a White House conference devoted to their concerns. While waiting for the meeting to begin, the commission members were standing around chatting, when "all of a sudden the room was quiet and there were these huge feet standing in front of me," recalled Gallegos. "I looked up and realized that it was the president." Johnson quickly grabbed his elbow, shook his hand, and moved on. Frustrated, Gallegos looked over at Samora, who signaled that he would say something when his turn came. While introducing himself to the president, Samora quickly added that Mexican Americans were looking forward to their White House conference. "I looked Johnson in the eye while I shook his hand," Samora told me, "but he didn't look at me."

Samora and Gallegos then approached White House aide Cliff Alexander, who was standing at the periphery of the gathering. They told him that such a conference would be beneficial to both the Mexican American community and the White House. "You know, we're really struggling with that, and we really need to make a decision," Alexander replied, and he invited them to a meeting the next morning.

After the follow-up meeting, White House special counsel Harry McPherson reported to the president, "I was evasive and non-committal," adding that he tried to convince the two men that a permanent office of Mexican American affairs was preferable to a conference, but that they told me that the Mexican American community wants a conference, expects a conference, will be bitterly disappointed without a conference, and that their bitterness would have serious political consequences. . . . The trouble, they said, is that like everything else ever done for Mexican Americans, *an office would be imposed from above.* . . . When I said I thought a conference would necessarily be angry and vituperative . . . they said it would, indeed, if we planned it and ran it; if the Mexicans were given a large role in developing it, they thought it would be much more coherent and effective.

McPherson characterized the two as "pretty level-headed activists" and noted that "the Mexicans are a major political factor in five states and we should not risk losing them" in the following year's presidential race. He had concluded "that the risk is greater if we deny them the conference . . . than if some hell is raised."

Johnson replied, "Keep this trash out of the White House." Yes, he had appointed them to the commission; yes, they were stalwart supporters of his civil rights and War on Poverty initiatives, but they had the temerity to question the Vietnam War. As bad as such "disloyalty" would have been in Johnson's eyes, I suspected that he considered even more damning their likely support of his political nemesis, Senator Kennedy. RFK and LBJ loathed each other, and Johnson's greatest fear was that he would end up a one-term president sandwiched between the Kennedys. Meanwhile, Bobby Kennedy—who was holding highly publicized Senate investigations into alleged mistreatment of farm workers by growers—was in the process of forging a close alliance with United Farm Workers union president Cesar Chavez. Years later when I posed the RFK theory to Joseph Califano, who had been President Johnson's top domestic advisor at that time, the former White House aide replied, "Bingo—you've got it!"[10]

A Mexican American conference nonetheless did materialize in October of that year thanks in large part to the acumen of Vicente Ximenes, director of the brand-new Interagency Committee on Mexican American Affairs. For the first time in history a president and his cabinet officers listened to proposals and demands on the part of Chicano activists from around the country. The meeting was held not in Washington, however, but in El Paso. This fact, coupled with opposition to the war and rising Chicano militancy, prompted protestors to organize a rump conference at which Ernesto Galarza presided. The dissidents' call for grassroots mobilization received a boost when Samora, Gallegos, and Galarza (among others) established the Southwest Council of La Raza. With the help of seed money from the Ford Foundation, the Southwest Council fostered community organizing in the barrios and paved the way for the National Council of La Raza, to this day the main Washington-based organization championing Latino issues.[11]

Julian Samora's legacy lives on in other ways as well, most visibly through the projects of the Julian Samora Research Institute (at Michigan State), the Julian Samora Scholarship Fund (at the Notre Dame's Institute for Latino Studies), the Julian Samora Collection (at the Benson Latin American Collection at the University of Texas at Austin), and the Julian Samora Legacy Project (in Albuquerque, New Mexico).[12] Meanwhile we, his intellectual progeny, try to follow his example through our research and community involvement, and by encouraging today's young people to make history themselves.

Notes

1. Galarza finished all the course requirements for a doctorate in 1932, but he suspended work on his PhD due to the economic pressures of the Depression, followed by involvement in anti-Fascist activities during the Spanish Civil War and World War II. He received his PhD in history and social science in 1944. Carlos Muñoz, Jr., "Galarza: Scholar on the Ramparts," foreword to "Ernesto Galarza Commemorative Lecture: Inaugural Lecture, 1986" (Stanford Center for Chicano Research), http://ccsre.stanford.edu/pdfs/1st_Annual_Lecture_1986.pdf. Carlos E. Castañeda was the other Mexican American that, against the odds, earned a PhD in history prior to 1950 (in his case at the University of Texas). Félix Almaráz Jr., *Knight without Armor: Carlos Eduardo Castañeda* (College Station: Texas A&M University Press, 1999), 101.

2. Copies of *El Renacimiento* and *Sol de Aztlán* are on deposit at the Michigan Historical Collections of the Bentley Historical Library, University of Michigan, Ann Arbor: http://www.umich.edu/~bhl/bhl/mhchome/news/news1971.htm.

3. Julie Leininger Pycior, *LBJ and Mexican Americans: The Paradox of Power* (Austin: University of Texas Press, 1997), p. 10; Dionicio Nodín Valdés, *Al Norte: Agricultural Workers in the Great Lakes Region, 1917–1970* (Austin: University of Texas Press, 1991), pp. 52, 185. For more on La Raza Unida, see Mario Compeán and José Angel Gutiérrez, *La Raza Unida Party in Texas* (New York: Pathfinder Press, 1970); Ignacio García, *United We Win: The Rise and Fall of the Raza Unida Party* (Tucson: University of Arizona Press, 1989); Armando Navarro, *The Cristal Experiment: Chicano Struggle for Community Control* (Madison: University of Wisconsin Press, 1999); John S. Shockley, *Chicano Revolt in a Texas Town* (Notre Dame, Ind.: University of Notre Dame Press, 1974); Armando Trujillo, *Chicano Empowerment and Bilingual Education: Movimiento Politics in Crystal City, Texas* (New York: Garland Publishing, 1998).

4. http://www.cambiodecolores.org/2004/Speakers/JuanMarinez.html; http://www.jsri.msu.edu/staff/#marinez; Juan Marínez to author, October 1989, East Lansing, Michigan.

5. The papers of the Midwest Council of La Raza are housed at the University of Notre Dame: http://archives.nd.edu/findaids/ead/index/MCL001.htm; Subject Files, "FBI Memos obtained via the Freedom of Information Act, 1961–1983," folder 3, "1970," José Angel Gutiérrez Papers, 1959–1991, MS 24, UTSA Archives, Library, University of Texas at San Antonio.

6. Julian Samora and Patricia Vandel Simon, *A History of the Mexican American People* (Notre Dame, Ind.: University of Notre Dame Press, 1977); Julian Samora, Joe Bernal, and Albert Peña, Jr., *Gunpowder Justice* (Notre Dame, Ind.: University of Notre Dame Press, 1979).

7. The Centro de Estudios Chicanos also sponsored a statistical profile of the South Bend Chicano community by Notre Dame sociology grad student Jim Faught. Barbara Driscoll, *Newspaper Documentary History of the Chicano Community in South Bend* (Notre Dame, Ind.: Centro de Estudios Chicanos e Investigaciones Sociales, Inc., 1978); Julie Leininger, *Chicanos in South Bend: Some Historical Narrative* (Notre Dame, Ind.: Centro de Estudios Chicanos e Investigaciones Sociales, Inc., 1977); Jim D. Faught, "Social and Economic Characteristics of the Spanish-origin Population in South Bend, Indiana," Centro de Estudios Chicanos e Investigaciones Sociales, Inc., 1974, in Box 37, Midwest Council of La Raza Papers, University of Notre Dame Archives.

8. Juan Ramón García, *Mexicans in the Midwest, 1900–1932* (Tucson: University of Arizona Press, 1996); and *Operation Wetback: The Mass Deportation of Mexican Undocumented Workers in 1954* (Westport, Conn.: Greenwood Press, 1980).

9. I would later learn that Lyndon Johnson titled his own memoirs *The Vantage Point* (New York: Holt, Reinhart and Winston, 1971); Pycior, *LBJ and Mexican Americans.*

10. For an insightful book-length treatment of the LBJ-RFK feud, see Jeff Shesol, *Mutual Contempt: Lyndon Johnson, Robert Kennedy, and the Feud that Defined a Decade* (New York: W. W. Norton, 1997); Pycior, *LBJ and Mexican Americans,* pp. 164–65, 187–89; Joseph Califano, telephone interview with Julie Leininger Pycior, August 25, 1992.

11. Recently the National Council of La Raza (NCLR) endorsed Alberto Gonzales for attorney general of the United States despite charges that as White House counsel he authorized the breach of the Geneva Conventions in Bush administration guidelines for interrogating prisoners. The NCLR press release did not address this issue. For its part the Hispanic Congressional Caucus declined to support the Gonzales nomination; my sense is that Dr. Samora also would have differed with NCLR on this issue, and that many of the other Samora alums would as well—though likely not all of them. For a comparison of Alberto Gonzales and Ernesto Galarza, see the web posting by Professor Jorge Mariscal of the University of California, San Diego: http://clah.ucsd.edu/modules.php?op=modload&name=News&file=article&sid=110. http://www.nclr.org/content/news/detail/28109/; http://www.washingtonpost.com/wp-dyn/articles/A42396-2004Nov11.html; http://www.rollcall.com/pub/1_1/breakingnews/7915-1.html; Pycior, *LBJ and Mexican Americans,* pp. 207–14; Matt S. Meier and Feliciano

Rivera, *Dictionary of Mexican American History* (Westport, Conn.: Greenwood Press, 1981), pp. 246–47.

12. http://www.jsri.msu.edu/; http://www.nd.edu/~latino/students/samora_scholarship.htm; http://www.lib.utexas.edu/benson/archives/ma_manuscripts.html;http://www.samoralegacy.unm.edu/pdf/Samora_Container_List.pdf; http://www.samoralegacy.com.

CHAPTER TWENTY-TWO

Reflections on Research Perspectives and Strategies

Paul López

> Well most of the braceros did not speak or understand English so the only way to communicate with the rancheros was through signs. For this reason, most of them treated us like Indians and at times deducted money from our allowances. They took advantage of us most of the time and treated us like animals. The language barrier was a big problem. A percentage of money was also deducted for a savings account that we were supposed to have in a bank. However, we never received that money and this is what braceros are fighting for right now.
> —Bracero testimony

The above testimony is from one of forty former Mexican braceros I have interviewed as part of my forthcoming book.[1] The stories of these former guest workers are important because they detail an important period of Chicano history for which little research exists. This is due directly to the dearth of Chicana/o or Latina/o university professors in higher education today. Just completing high school for some Chicanos is still problematic. Consequently, I recognize the significance of being a university professor where I can bring to life the voices of former Mexican braceros and, with this essay, thank and pay tribute to the person who was influential (and continues to be) in guiding my research perspective and who broke through the barriers that held so many back. I am speaking of my former mentor, Dr. Julian Samora.

Before there was a field of Chicano Studies, the work of Dr. Samora was breaking new ground on research on the Chicano community that non-Chicanos simply ignored or thought unimportant to research. From his early work in the field of medical sociology, community, and leadership studies, Dr. Samora's research was providing sociological insights to the problems associated with being Mexican American in the United States.[2] Very few scholars during the 1950s and 1960s were producing scholarly work on the Chicano community. Among the groundbreaking work besides Dr. Samora's was the work of his friend and colleague Dr. Ernesto Galarza, who provided insight into the effects of Mexican immigration to the United States with his important work on the Bracero Program.[3]

Dr. Samora's work has inspired many to follow his example. It makes me proud to say that I am one of those individuals. I first became interested in Dr. Samora's research on immigration[4] while an undergraduate Chicana/o Studies major. At the time, I did not imagine that I would make the subject of Mexican immigration my lifelong career interest. I have Dr. Samora to thank for providing the intellectual guidance that has driven my research perspective as a scholar and teacher on the topic of Mexican immigration.

I had heard from other Chicano students that Dr. Samora was recruiting Chicana/o students to attend graduate school at Notre Dame. Indeed, one of my friends recalls going to a presentation at UCLA where Dr. Samora and one of his graduate students[5] spoke. They were both there to talk to UCLA students about the graduate program in Mexican American Studies at Notre Dame. That was in 1978 or so. I was still another year away from completing my degree in Chicano Studies at California State University Northridge.

While completing my undergraduate degree I began to determine just what I wanted to do as a career. My decision ultimately was to become a college professor. I had many unanswered research questions and I felt that by pursuing a PhD I would be able to continue working on Mexican immigration. With a Chicana/o Studies undergraduate degree, and with Mexican immigration as one of the issues concerning the discipline, it seemed natural to earn a doctorate in Chicana/o Studies. However, there were no graduate programs that offered PhDs in Chicana/o Studies.[6] As an undergraduate I read about many of the unresolved issues related to the Chicano community and I needed to find a PhD program that would serve my research interests. The issue was highly topical during the late 1970s and early 1980s, as it continues to be today. Few days would go by without a new story covering some issue on Mexican immigration. Indeed, I wanted to examine the complex issue of migration from Mexico because the sociological phenomenon stirred my intellectual curiosity.

I wrote a letter to Dr. Samora and inquired about graduate studies at Notre Dame. Of course, I was surprised that he wrote back, given the prestige of Notre Dame and the unlikelihood that someone such as Professor Samora would have the time to contact me personally. I was overwhelmed when I got a letter back suggesting I apply. Receiving Dr. Samora's personal letter gave me the confidence to apply to graduate school. Dr. Samora's care in recruiting students to Notre Dame was profoundly important to me on that day, and I have no doubt that his letter persuaded me to attend graduate school at Notre Dame.

I recall that when the letter arrived from Notre Dame (I still have it framed on my wall in my home), I let out a loud scream that I had been accepted! My entire family—parents, sister, and brother—supported my move to the Midwest. I was overwhelmed to hear I had been accepted to the one school I had placed all my hopes upon. Now I was on my way to completing some of my academic goals.

Recruiting Chicano students to do graduate schoolwork in the Midwest was a daunting task. Unlike the barrios of the Southwest, the Midwest offered a different climate and cultural atmosphere that Chicano students are sometimes reluctant to experience. My first few days in South Bend reinforced the lack of cultural familiarities from the Southwest. Bonding with other Chicanos already attending graduate school at Notre Dame helped ease the transition. Before arriving in South Bend in the fall of 1982, I had heard from Dr. Samora that there was another Chicano student from San Diego, California, also attending graduate school. To my relief, Alberto L. Pulido became my colleague and friend and helped ease the cultural divide that was part of my cultural shock of attending graduate school at Notre Dame. We both had similar childhoods, which allowed us to connect to one another. It was a relief to find someone who found the Midwest culturally different in comparison to the Southwest. Having a fellow Californian among the cohort of graduate students helped ease the transition.

Dr. Samora was well aware of the cultural divide his students experienced moving from the comfort of the Southwest to the new experiences in the Midwest. The recruitment of Chicano students to the graduate program at Notre Dame did not end with their acceptance and arrival. Dr. Samora would organize social events at his home so all the students could connect with one another. In short, not only was I able to find students with backgrounds like mine, but I also made lifelong friendships with those who went through the program.

I would like to point to one book among the many that Dr. Samora wrote that significantly influenced my view on the topic of Mexican immigration. In 1972, the book *Los Mojados: The Wetback Story*,[7] was published. It was instrumental in placing the topic of undocumented immigration within a sociological perspective. Although I was majoring in Chicano Studies, no classes at California State University Northridge offered a course on Mexican immigration.

I knew little about the subject of undocumented immigration, and Dr. Samora's book provided much-needed direction. The book has proven to be groundbreaking in the study of Mexican immigration. Many of his former students have continued to do research in the area of Mexican immigration and most would suggest that Dr. Samora's work was pivotal in influencing their academic careers. Although *Los Mojados: The Wetback Story* offered insight into the reasons Mexican immigrants migrate to the United States, it more importantly has led others to expand on his work. For example, former students Jorge Bustamante and Barbara Driscoll de Alvarado (just to name two) have continued to work in the area of Mexican immigration. As my career as a professor in the field of Chicana/o Studies has continued, I have remained profoundly interested in the questions regarding migration and the growing phenomenon of Mexican immigration. Without reservation, the experience of studying with Dr. Samora while at Notre Dame was formative in my professional development as a scholar. My current research on the former U.S.-Mexico Bracero Program continues to be influenced by Dr. Samora's prior research.

It was through Dr. Samora's work and mentorship that I turned to what I believe is my most important work to date, studying the effect of migration from Mexico on former guest workers. Dr. Samora's work examined the issue of undocumented immigration from Mexico in his book *Los Mojados*, and it occurred to me to continue investigating Mexican immigration. However, unlike previous investigations, my study would be epistemologically unique. I wanted to interview the actual persons who migrated as former guest workers. The idea became clearer as I learned through my father's stories that he had actually worked with braceros in the 1940s, 1950s, and early 1960s. And, important for my research, he had remained in contact with some of the former braceros with whom he worked. One of my first interviews was with a close friend of his from that era.

Currently I am conducting a study of the former U.S.-Mexico Bracero Program, which was instrumental in bringing to the United States nearly five million Mexican guest workers from 1942 until it ended in 1964. One consequence of the program was the number of former braceros who have for various reasons found themselves living in the United States. Only a few oral histories exist on the experiences of these former guest workers.

I began to consider documenting their oral histories. This project began as a result of my continued interest in understanding my own family's history. After one of many discussions of family history with my father, I discovered that my father had worked alongside braceros as a ranch hand from 1951 to 1961. Since he was bilingual, he was able to translate into Spanish the instructions from the foreman. This was all unknown to me. Since beginning this project, I have found that many colleagues, students, and close friends have relatives who had come to the United States as braceros. Not only does this research allow me to retrace my own family's history of involvement with the program, but it has also allowed me to document the involvement of other Mexican families in the migration experience.

My documentation of the work history of former braceros is a tribute to Dr. Samora's influence. I truly believe that my bracero research is an extension of Dr. Samora's pioneering work on the topic of Mexican immigration. Dr. Samora laid the foundation for future immigration scholars to follow, and I honor his legacy through my research on former Mexican braceros.

The Intellectual Impact of Dr. Julian Samora

Significant breakthroughs have occurred in the examination of immigration from Mexico since Dr. Samora's work was first published. Initial research relied upon push-pull theories, arguing that immigration was a "rational" choice made by immigrants. Overcoming the personal and economic costs, migrants chose to journey across the border at the high risk of being caught. Supporters of the push-pull theory argued a cost-benefits perspective in their explanation for migration by immigrants.[8] Indeed, early studies of migration from Mexico relied upon this theory to explain why immigrants would risk apprehension, injury, or the expense of crossing illegally to the United States. Most supporters of this theory argued that migrating improved the human capital of those who migrated.[9] In the case of Mexican immigration, the lure of higher wages that a country like the United States can offer is too inviting to not take the risks associated with migrating. However, more current research suggests that the push-pull argument is short-sighted.[10] Critics of the push-pull theory argue that if immigrants to the United States decide to migrate due to the lure of higher wages, then most would come from impoverished countries. But previous examinations suggest that most migrants are coming from countries that are in the stage of development known as industrialization. Mexico is one of those countries. The labor surplus in Mexico often uses migration as a means of subsistence.

An alternative theory is that migration is embedded within a structural context. Indeed, international migration involves a series of complex structures that create the opportunity to migrate.[11] Rather than rely upon an individual's decision to migrate, proponents of the structural explanation argue that migration occurs as families, social networks, and the availability of information about the opportunities abroad begin to form. Immigration scholars Massey, Durand, and Malone argue that "international migration becomes a reasonable strategy that poor families can use to accumulate cash in lieu of formal borrowing for consumption or investment. Households simply send one or more workers abroad to take advantage of higher wages to build up savings over a short time horizon."[12]

The last theory is the theory of transnationalism, which argues that migrants begin a series of movements back and forth from the country of origin to the host country. Migrants who migrate back and forth end up living dual lives. Neither the host nor sending countries become their permanent place of settlement. Previous studies of Mexican immigrants found that dual lives become part of their migration experience.

Research Perspective: The Legacy of Julian Samora

I have to give credit to Professor Samora for his academic guidance that continues to shape me in the course of my research. Indeed, I still feel the influence of Professor Samora as I retrace his work from *Los Mojados*. The book and the research I am conducting on braceros covers the same historical period as *Los Mojados,* and my research on the subject of Mexican braceros is following upon the legacy that Professor Samora established long before I arrived at Notre Dame to study under his guidance.

My research on the Bracero Program has led me to interview the workers themselves, and with each interview I gain insight into the complexity of the program. My research is guided by numerous questions, of which I examine only one here. Employing transnational theory, I have sought to examine just how braceros experienced transnationalism through repeated contracting. One former bracero[13] from a little town called Val Paraiso, Zacatecas, described the back-and-forth experience of crossing using the Bracero Program and other times crossing illegally and getting caught:

> We [he came with his father] came in the year '49 and we went back to Mexico in 1950 and I came back by myself in 1951. I was struggling for a while, for

about six months I could not find a job. I would also try to come into California and would get caught and sent back. At night I would come, and they would send me back in the morning. I was friends with a bold guy that was known for getting in and out easily. He had a wife and two kids and he had not sent money for five years. She used to pray for him to get sent back to Mexico. I hanged around with him, I guess that is why God did not help me. As soon as I teamed up with him I was able to cross over. I was here in Goleta after that. I also worked in a chicken farm and then in a pig ranch. I was in the ranch until '55. I was sent a telegram that my dad had died and went to Mexico. I was there for about two months, and then I came back. Then I went to a ranch called El Capitan. In '57 I became legal.

Many of the stories I have documented repeat similar uses of the Bracero Program. Indeed, after coming to the United States by way of the Bracero Program, many of the braceros eventually migrated back and forth before settling permanently. Today, the latest wave of Mexican immigration has stimulated among politicians the feasibility of another guest worker program similar to the former U.S.-Mexico Bracero Program. Should such a program become established, many of the problems that plagued the first program would re-emerge. Indeed, one of the problems associated with the Bracero Program was contracting braceros when there wasn't enough work for them to do, which left them unable to earn any money. Another problem was threatening them with deportation before the contract was completed if they disliked the harsh working conditions. And finally, the lack of adequate housing, particularly in remote areas where housing consisted of former army barracks that lacked suitable protection from wind, rain, or cold weather, was a constant issue.

Conclusion

It has been a rewarding opportunity to write about my former mentor. Dr. Samora's contribution to the research perspective of many scholars remains clear. He was a pioneer when there was a need to provide some clarity on the topic of Mexican immigration. As one of his former students, I am humbled by the fact I was able to study under him. My research on Mexican immigration is influenced by my former advisor, and I will continue to remember just how important it was to study under Dr. Samora as I further my career as an immigration specialist.

One of the enduring memories of attending Notre Dame was being a part of a graduate program headed by Professor Samora. As one of those students who benefited from that program, I have always thought it was my responsibility to help other Chicana and Chicano students complete their degrees, so I do my best to train and advise Chicana and Chicano students to complete their education at Chico State. There have been many success stories of students I have advised and helped to complete their bachelor's degrees, and I have been successful in getting more and more students to enter graduate school and to consider a career in academia. The recruitment and mentoring of students is part of the continued legacy of Dr. Samora. Indeed, I recall how important it was to hear from him personally all those many years ago.

My future research and teaching projects will continue to be guided by Professor Samora's influence. As I train and educate students on the subject of Mexican immigration through my courses in Chicano Studies and sociology, I feel confident that my training from Professor Samora continues to train the next generation of potential immigration scholars.

Notes

The quotation is from a former Mexican bracero whose oral history I have recorded for a book project I am currently completing.

1. The working title of the book is *The Braceros: The Untold Stories of Former U.S-Mexico Braceros and Mexican Immigration.*

2. "Julian Samora," in *Latinos and Latinas in U.S. History and Culture: An Encyclopedia,* ed. Carmen R. Lugo-Lugo and David J. Leonard (Armonk, N.Y.: M. E. Sharpe, Inc., forthcoming).

3. Ernesto Galarza, *Merchants of Labor: The Mexican Bracero Story* (Santa Barbara, Calif.: McNally and Loftin, 1964).

4. I subsequently received my master's degree in sociology from the University of Notre Dame in 1984 and my PhD in sociology from Northeastern University in 1999.

5. A discussion with Dr. Samora's son Geoff suggests that the student that day was most likely Alberto Mata.

6. There are now two doctorate-granting universities that offer a PhD in Chicana/o Studies: The University of California Santa Barbara and Michigan State University.

7. Julian Samora, *Los Mojados: The Wetback Story* (Notre Dame, Ind.: The University of Notre Dame Press, 1971).

8. Gilles Grenier, "The Effects of Language Characteristics on the Wages of Hispanic American Males," *Journal of Human Resources* 19 (1) (1984).

9. George Borjas, *Friends and Strangers: The Impact of Immigrants on the U.S. Economy* (New York: Basic Books, 1991).

10. Alejandro Portes and Ruben Rumbaut, *Immigrant America* (Berkeley: University of California Press, 1996).

11. Douglas Massey, Jorge Durand, and Nolan Malone, *Beyond Smoke and Mirrors: Mexican Immigration in an Era of Economic Integration* (New York: Russell Sage Foundation, 2002).

12. Massey, Durand, and Malone, *Beyond Smoke and Mirrors.*

13. I've conducted more than forty interviews with former Mexican braceros. In order to keep their identities hidden I have not revealed their names. The interviews are part of a larger research project on the former U.S.-Mexico Bracero Program I am currently completing.

CHAPTER TWENTY-THREE

On Respect and Teaching

Ciro Sepulveda

One of the most vivid memories of my time at Notre Dame University took place one Sunday afternoon in the backyard of Dr. Julian Samora's home in South Bend, Indiana. I had been at Notre Dame for about a year and a half doing graduate work in history. During that time my daughter Monica had been born. Dr. Samora invited several of the graduate students in the Chicano Studies Program to his home for brunch. Many of us had become good friends and felt comfortable in the Samora home. His wife became our mom away from home, and we thoroughly enjoyed being with them. Gloria, my wife, and our daughter were also in the backyard. As I sat, talking with one of my friends, I looked up and saw Monica walking toward me with a big smile on her face. To my delight and her overwhelming joy she was taking her first steps. She obviously felt very comfortable.

Not all the experiences in South Bend were as relaxed and contented as those moments in the Samora home. The presence of brown-skinned students with difficult-to-pronounce names caught Notre Dame off guard. In the History Department, several professors looked at us with curiosity, confident that we would not be around for long. In a letter I read from the chair of my department to one of the professors a couple of years after my arrival, he expressed surprise that I was still there. We in turn were not always easy to get along with. The professors were not accustomed to being challenged or having their historical biases questioned by young Latinos. In time both professors and students learned to be civil and tolerate each other.

The tension in the classroom was offset by the presence of Dr. Samora at Notre Dame. Julian Samora was in a league of his own. Most of us had never seen a Latino professor in a university. His presence at Notre Dame transformed the place into a welcoming environment. He made life at Notre Dame bearable. Even though not all the university professors, and certainly not all their white disciples who got most of their attention, were comfortable with our presence, we knew he was, and that made it okay.

When I applied for graduate work, I sent letters to the University of Texas, the University of California, Rochester University, and a couple of others stating that I wanted to do graduate work on their campus but was unwilling to take the GRE exam. I carefully explained that the GRE examination was designed to test the abilities of white males raised in upper-middle-class homes who spoke standard New England English. Since I was not a white male and I grew up in a home in Southern California where Spanish was spoken, I would not be subjected to the ordeal. In my opinion the exam was designed to weed out people of color, and I was not about to give any institution a comfortable excuse to shut their door in my face. I already had an MA and a MDiv, and I felt that if the institution needed evidence of my ability to do graduate work those two degrees from the State University of New York and Rochester Colgate Divinity School should suffice.

All the institutions answered with similar letters stating that if I would not take the GRE they would not review my application. Only Notre Dame accepted my conditions, and I am convinced to this day that the only reason that happened was because Julian Samora intervened.

Since he was a sociologist and I was a historian, the time for professional cooperation was limited. Most of my classes were with the professors in the History Department. Furthermore, sociology, as a discipline, had never impressed me. I had always thought that sociologists kept researching and finding the obvious. However, I did get to know Dr. Samora in informal settings. Whenever he would invite a guest speaker, usually a Chicano scholar from California or Texas, he would be present and would participate in the dialogue. In these settings and especially during the many times he invited us to his home, I developed a profound respect and admiration for him.

Respect, as I have discovered, is not something that one receives but rather something that one gives. Julian Samora modeled this magnificently. He listened and gave you his full attention whenever you sat down with him. His ability to make you feel that the things you were saying were important and worthy of consideration drew most of us to him. At his home and in the informal meetings, we all loved to sit and talk with him. He always listened and participated in our intellectual ruminations. We respected him because we sensed that he had profound respect for our points of view and for us.

I suspect that the whole notion of respect is one of the reasons that many of us had tension with our history professors. Most of them had been schooled in the ideas of Frederick Jackson Turner, a historian who became famous in the first decade of the twentieth century because of his frontier thesis. The frontier thesis basically argued that it was out on the frontier, where the West encountered and confronted the "savages" of America, that the United States forged its culture. Democracy, the Constitution, and all the features of the American republic, according to Turner, were the offspring of this frontier experience.

This metaphor did wonders for the ego of all Anglo Europeans. Historians particularly ate it up like candy. In the light of the frontier thesis the northern Europeans were the enlightened ones of the planet. They supposedly invented science, medicine, and all the important institutions brought to the New World. This Anglo European phalanx, according to Turner and his loyal disciples, many of them teaching at Notre Dame in the early 1970s, brought civilization to the "savages" of the Americas.

Since most of my professors at Notre Dame had embraced and were propagating the greatness of any thing Anglo or European and only tolerated anything Indian, Spanish, or African, it was not at all surprising that they would be uncomfortable with the descendants of the "savages" in their classrooms. If we accepted their perspective, and some of us did, they loved us and thought of us as good natives, but if we questioned it, which I found myself doing quite often, they were uncomfortable at best and hoped for our imminent departure.

In my case the confrontations only reinforced my desire to stay and show my "mentors" that their biases were racist at best. So in most of my classes, the struggle between the Turner thesis and the worldview of a mestizo of the Americas waged on. Since the professors, through grades, final examinations, dissertations, and future professional advancement, etc., had power over our lives, it was always a tense and ongoing battle. They were reluctant to let any of us into their private club, and I was not going to leave because they were uncomfortable.

It was Dr. Samora, not my history "mentors," who suggested I do a history of East Chicago, Indiana, for my dissertation. My area of specialization was Latin America, and although my professors did not see East Chicago, Indiana, as part of Latin America, I did. They saw the Americas in terms of geographical boundaries; everything on one side of the line became United States history and everything on the other side of the line was Latin American history. I have trouble with the arbitrary lines drawn by powerful men. I prefer to see the continent in terms of human beings. East Chicago, Indiana, had one of the largest Mexican communities in the region of the Great Lakes in the 1920s, a fact most Americans, including me, were and are not aware of. I followed Dr. Samora's advice, and my history professors looked the other way.

I had never heard of East Chicago until Dr. Samora suggested the topic. After his suggestion, I drove to East Chicago and loved the place. The city started as a company town in the last decades of the nineteenth century. Inland Steel built its foundry along the edge of Lake Michigan and an immigrant community evolved in the shadows of the smoke stacks. During the great steel strike of 1919 hundreds of Mexicans were bought in boxcars into the foundry as strikebreakers. The five hundred or so strikebreakers who arrived in 1919 gave birth to the Mexican community that is still there today. With each visit to East Chicago my curiosity blossomed, and in time I ended up doing a fourteen-year oral history I called *La Colonia del Harbor from 1919 to 1934.*

Dr. Samora would always ask me about my work and we would sit and talk informally about my findings. Since he himself had completed research on East Chicago, those conversations were always stimulating. He genuinely thought that the work I was doing was important. I would tell him about my oral interviews with the residents of the city and he would make suggestions about further research.

My history professor faked interest. After all, of what earthly importance would a history of a working-class Mexican community in the Midwest be? The important issues, in the opinion of my professors, lay in the large cities, the presidency, the Congress, the economic categories at the bedrock of the real and the meaningful decisions that shaped and formed the history of the nation. The deeds and acts of brown-skinned people were no match for the deeds and acts of white males. Mexican and black strikebreakers who were imported into the foundries of northern Indiana were insignificant or meaningless in the larger scheme of things, so they thought. Ultimately, my history professors did read my dissertation, and they did—reluctantly— give their approval. The chair of the department stated in a letter I read somewhere that Sepulveda found some interesting information.

During my stay at Notre Dame I got an invitation to present a paper at the American Historical Association meeting, which met in Chicago. There I discovered that the hundreds of historians in the nation were not much different than those at Notre Dame. I got the invitation from a graduate student at the University of Illinois who was doing graduate work on Mexicans in Chicago. Her mentor had suggested the session, and the American Historical Association committee approved it. Since I would be presenting in the presence of fellow historians, I took great pains to write what I thought was an excellent paper.

When the meeting started there were six persons present, five of us on the platform and one person in the audience; I think it was my wife. We read our papers to each other, and then listened to the comments. Mexicanos in the Midwest was not the hot topic at the American Historical Association that year. The issue that had most of my fellow historians up in arms was the topic of slavery. It is always much safer to discuss the slaves of the distant past rather than the slaves of the recent past.

A lot of years have passed since my stay at Notre Dame, and in a sense not much has changed. The ghost of Frederick Jackson Turner and his frontier thesis still roams the corridors of the historical profession. Although we no longer call our introductory course for college freshmen Western Civilization, historians in American universities continue to teach of the glories of Anglo European tradition to our young, interspersed with a chapter or two on Africa and Latin America.

Dr. Samora continues to be a refreshing memory in the midst of a parched landscape. When the doors of the academy were closing in the faces of Latinos, he opened them just enough to let a few of us in. When the cold stares of our professors insisted that we had wandered into the wrong hallway, he made us feel that we belonged. When our professors looked at us cross-eyed because our research concerns were not theirs, he assured us that our issues had legitimacy. When our professors would not lift a finger to guide us into the future with letters and phone calls to their friends in other history departments, he did all within his power to find us jobs so we would be assured a presence in the academy.

There are a lot of virtues I can remember in reference to Julian Samora that I try to emulate, but the one that stands out in my mind is his ability to inspire respect. I am sorry he is gone, not only because he was a good friend but also because his presence is still needed in the academy today. The white male historical club, which is still controlling most of the history departments in the nation, continues to hide behind walls they have structured to protect themselves. And although they have permitted a few of the descendants of the "savages" into the country club so that they will not be criticized too harshly, things have not changed dramatically.

The affirmative action initiatives that were pushed by persons like Julian Samora in the 1960s and 1970s have been neutralized. If you look at the faculty rosters of history departments in the United States, you will find that it is mostly white women who have benefited from the intervention of those who fought to integrate the ivory towers of higher education. And even though the statistical information is reported in a way that gives the impression that more and more minorities are getting PhDs, the fact remains that Asians inflate those numbers and Latinos continue to lag behind.

Just out of curiosity, I looked at the list of the faculty members at Notre Dame as I wrote this paper. The university maintains a stable of twenty professors trained in medieval and modern Europe, an insignificant portion of the land mass of the planet compared to the overwhelming territory that is contained in Latin America, Africa, and the Far East. For that two-thirds of the world, Notre Dame hires only six specialists, and apparently none of them are Latino, African, Chinese, or persons of color. Superficially, it would seem that Dr. Samora's efforts had very little effect on the institution he served and enriched.

But if you look a little closer, Dr. Samora's influence was not insignificant. He opened the door that has allowed me to spend my days teaching young African Americans who instinctively know about the biases of historians. They come into my classroom convinced that the discipline of history is mind-numbing, boring, and dull because of large high school classrooms, mindless workbooks, and multiple-choice tests that have fashioned their thinking. There is no greater joy than to watch my students as I ram pins into their ballooned myths. Dr. Samora opened the door for me and I in turn delight in opening doors for my students, who are now in several graduate and law schools.

When my students come over to the house and eat some of my wife's cooking, I sometimes remember Julian Samora, and I smile as we ruminate together.

CHAPTER TWENTY-FOUR

Becoming a Scholar
A Tribute to Julian and Betty Samora
Gilbert Cárdenas

Early Influences

As a sophomore in high school, I was expelled for various infractions of school rules. I had been spending a great deal of time with older students whose commitment to education was weak at best. My mother was a strong proponent of education, and in order to stay in good graces I rededicated myself to purely "college track" courses, in earnest, during my junior year.

During my first year of study at East Los Angeles Community College, I remember being in the parking lot at lunch, a former "vato loco" sitting in what may have been the only low rider on campus at the time. I looked up to see the sign on the building that said East Los Angeles Community College; I concentrated on the word "college" and thought, "My God I'm a college student." This meant a great deal to me, and it signaled a transformation from being a young man adrift to being a man with purpose. I wanted very much to graduate from college.

I first learned of Julian Samora and the University of Notre Dame from Ralph Guzmán. Ralph was a professor at California State University at Los Angeles, where I had transferred to, and he spoke of the pioneering work being done around the country by "Chicano scholars" (an oxymoron in the mind of some in those days) including Samora, Ernesto Galarza, Herman Gallegos, George Schuster Taylor, Charlie Loomis, and others. Ralph sponsored me to assist him in a study of an education project in the San Joaquin Valley of California. This trip took me on an airplane for the first time. On this occasion, after a United Mexican American Students (UMAS) meeting, I remember Ralph looking at me and stating to the group that he expected us to get our PhDs. This was a novel thought for me at the time, but it got me thinking about the possibilities. I had never thought seriously about pursuing a graduate degree. I had not really thought much about what my life's work would be after I graduated from college.

Continuing my studies with Guzman, I attended a youth leadership conference on the coast of Southern California. I was awestruck by the beauty of the setting. My hotel room looked over the ocean. As I watched the sun drop into the water, I experienced an epiphany. The Pacific in its blue vastness made me think of the opportunities available to me, opportunities that were as endless as the ocean. I decided that I would pursue academic studies, but where and with whom would come later.

The single most important decision of my life was to attend Notre Dame and study with Professor Samora. I made my way to Notre Dame after talking with Graciela Olivarez about possibly pursuing law studies. She became the first woman to graduate from the Notre Dame Law School, and her support system at Notre Dame had included Julian Samora. He sent me an application for the doctoral program in sociology with a note about his interest in U.S.-Mexico border studies. I was intrigued because of my interest in immigration. In my first year I was on tuition waiver awaiting funding through Samora's grant funds.

In my second year at Notre Dame I was funded by a Ford Foundation grant Professor Samora had received to recruit and educate students who had an interest in pursuing interdisciplinary graduate studies with a focus on Latinos. I was the first Mexican American graduate student and one of only seven Latino students on the entire campus in August 1969. Jorge Bustamante, a Mexican national, was a year ahead of me as a graduate student in the Sociology Department. Julian and his wife, Betty, took us into their family both in the Notre Dame community and literally into their family home. We socialized, broke bread, talked strategy, drank margaritas, and managed the stress of being far from home in a cold climate and in a new culture.

Samora's Influence

On campus, Julian allowed us to meet with pre-eminent Latino scholars and activists of the day. We interacted with Cesar Chavez, Dolores Huerta, Ernesto Galarza, and Herman Gallegos, among many others. Immigration experts like George Schuster Taylor visited campus or we visited them. We graduate students were actively taken seriously or else we would push the limits of activism on the conservative Catholic campus that Notre Dame was at the time. I was pleased that even though I was an acolyte, I could voice my opinions and move in the direction I chose.

My activism may have struck a nerve with my beloved advisor/mentor. Graduate and undergraduate students, faculty members, staff members, and their wives, including Betty Samora, organized boycotts, picketed the local grocery stores, and twice, in 1970 and 1972, aired our grievances at services at the Sacred Heart Basilica. At that time, Julian was walking a fine line with the administration, which had supported his recruitment of Latino students but balked at our outspoken criticism of their policies and agendas. I remember being in attendance at the Wednesday colloquium when Julian stated, "anyone can be an activist, but only a few can be scholars." This of course referred to some of us, me included, getting sidetracked from our purpose: finishing dissertations and getting tenure-track faculty positions in universities. Julian once introduced me as his "tenured" graduate student, a reference to the amount of time I was taking to finish my PhD. My activism slowed me down, but it prepared me for challenges in the future.

I want to mention once again the important role that Julian's wife, Betty Samora, played in my life. She was a second mom, a stern moral barometer who scolded us if she thought it necessary. She took an interest in the person as a whole, not just the potential scholar whom her husband focused on. Without Betty, many students would have ended their studies prematurely. Many of my classmates' spouses confided in Betty as the stress of graduate school took its toll on their families' lives. She did this while raising her own family of five, teaching Head Start, organizing a day care center for migrant workers' children, and hosting innumerable dinners, luncheons, and picnics for us. I especially enjoyed *las posadas* that Julian and Betty hosted for us at their house. Sociology faculty members, staff members, students, and families gathered for a Christmas celebration Latino style. It was these sorts of gatherings that meant so much to a homesick student from East Los Angeles. Those parties and celebrations recharged my batteries when I was questioning my being at Notre Dame. Doubts about my abilities were washed away when I would socialize with Professor Samora, Betty, and their family.

It was Betty who volunteered to help me raise money for my project. She sponsored a luncheon for potential funders of an organization that would become the Centro de Estudios Chicanos e Investigaciones Sociales under the auspices of the Midwest Council of La Raza. This Notre Dame on-campus organization was unique in that it was started by graduate students, funded from a grant, and intermingled scholarship with activism. Julian was not enamored of the project because it distracted me from completing my work on the dissertation. But the support he gave allowed the fledgling Centro de Estudios Chicanos to exist and prosper. It was the sort of organization that would become commonplace at other universities in later years. Today nearly every university has ethnic studies departments, which include think tanks, writing curriculum, advanced degree offerings, and cultural experiences that link academic communities to the local communities. By the way, Betty served *chilaquiles,* Mexican style, to rave reviews.

Years later at the University of Texas at Austin, while serving on the faculty of the Sociology Department, I became the associate director of the Center for Mexican American Studies (CMAS). My early experiences at Notre Dame as a founding member of the Centro de Estudios Chicanos prepared me well for the challenges at UT Austin.

In 1983, I attended a conference at Stanford University to discuss ways for leading Latino research centers to work together. These centers included the Center for Mexican American Studies at the University of Texas at Austin; The Center for Puerto Rican Studies at Hunter College/City University of New York; the Chicano Studies Research Center, University of California at Los Angeles; and the Stanford Center for Chicano Research, Stanford University. This meeting was the forerunner for what eventually became the Inter-University Program for Latino Research (IUPLR).

In 1992 I began working with the Center for Telecommunication Services in the College of Communications at UT Austin to develop a program for National Public Radio (NPR). In my role as founding executive producer,

I named the program Latino USA. It first aired in 1994 and was ultimately distributed by NPR to more than 110 stations, becoming the first successful Latino radio program in the NPR system. This award-winning program continues to this day, now reaching more than 400,000 listeners weekly.

In 1997 I had a meeting with Father Tim Scully about starting an institute at the University of Notre Dame. I was reluctant to leave UT Austin, but after meeting with students and the director of the Center for Social Concerns, Father Don McNeill, I was reminded of my own experiences as a student at Notre Dame. After my encounter with the Notre Dame students I knew that I had to continue Julian's legacy. In July of 1999, I was awarded the Julian Samora Chair in Latino Studies at Notre Dame. My staff and I moved from UT Austin to South Bend and started the Institute for Latino Studies (ILS). I believe that Julian would be proud to know that the ILS supports a strong research infrastructure, promotes and develops Latino-focused scholarship, nurtures Latino art, actively pursues integration with all academic schools on campus, and is involved with the South Bend community at large.

In the early 1970s, Julian started a Latino book series at the University of Notre Dame Press. At the time it was the only one of its kind and therefore very significant. Because of Julian, I now serve as editor of a new book series at the press, which is inspired by Julian's early work.

To this day, the mentoring that Julian and Betty provided for me influences how I mentor undergraduate students. I try to provide an academically challenging experience that forces students to think about themselves and their places in the community. I try to budge them from the comfort zone of conventional thinking to get them to push and pull as they become adults. I also look at the side of life that Betty taught me was so important. For you cannot be one-dimensional; you must nurture the person as a whole.

I came to Notre Dame an angry, outspoken activist who rattled cages, who threw stones, accused, and indicted. I thought I could effect change with this approach. I thought that change needed to happen quickly and if the powers wouldn't budge, then we needed to push harder.

As I grew to know Julian and Betty, I realized that Julian's seeming stoicism was not a lack of emotion, but a channeling of his anger and frustration toward an effective change of agency. That is, one must be "in" to effect change from within. So Julian's emphasis on finishing the PhD was how he meant to effect change from within. If I had not finished the degree, I would not have the influence that I have today. I finally "got it." I understood Julian's insistence on "being in." In Julian's opinion, activism could wait. But Betty supported my activism, I think, because she knew that without it I would have lost interest and motivation. She helped fuel that part of me that wanted to effect visible change in the community. Our boycotting the A&P grocery store, our "visits" to the Basilica, and our organizing in the community produced quick results that made the community a better place for children and families.

Julian Samora was the well-known scholar and mentor at a Catholic university, Notre Dame. He sponsored a cohort of students in a multidisciplinary program that will likely not be duplicated. Betty Samora was the person behind the scenes who never received nor asked for the public credit she deserved. Each of them had a profound effect on my life, both personally and professionally. It is with love and admiration that I publicly thank them for helping me become who I am today.

CHAPTER TWENTY-FIVE

Personal Visions
"Coming of Age with Samora"
Miguel A. Carranza

The following essays are from students who worked under the leadership, direction, and mentorship of Julian Samora during their education at the University of Notre Dame. They exhibit a personal dimension that is most often missing from the "traditional" student experiences in higher education. These essays reveal that Julian Samora was first and foremost a mentor on numerous levels. They also reflect the deep respect and admiration that each of his students developed for him during their educational careers.

I was also one of those individuals who had the unique opportunity to study and learn under Dr. Samora's leadership as a sociology graduate student from 1971 to 1977. My parents met while working in the sugar beet fields on the Platte River Valley in Nebraska. They married and settled near Kearney, Nebraska, and raised four children—one son and three daughters; I was the oldest. While still an undergraduate student in Nebraska, I had read of Julian Samora's work with Richard Lamanna on Mexican Americans in East Chicago, Indiana. I immediately felt a connection with his work since it focused on Mexican-origin people in the Midwest, people like me and my family. I was awarded a bachelor's degree in education from Kearney State College and was encouraged by a professor to think about pursuing a graduate degree. Hoping to study with Dr. Samora, I applied to the graduate program in sociology at the University of Notre Dame. I was accepted into the program and awarded a graduate assistantship beginning the fall 1971 semester.

Dr. Samora was one of the first researchers to focus on people of Mexican origin in locations other than the Southwest. He was a visionary for preparing his future students to contribute to the field of Mexican American/Chicano/Latino Studies. Faculty members and students today have a broader vision and deeper understanding of the discipline of Chicano/Latino Studies, but it is only because we were able to learn from the wisdom and stand on the shoulders of giants like Julian Samora, and because of the efforts they made to create depth and breadth in the field.

In the first essay, Delfina Landeros talks about the way Julian took into consideration the varied backgrounds of all his students. He could have easily recruited students from only California and other states in the Southwest, yet he recruited from the Midwest and East regions from places like Illinois, Indiana, and Nebraska. Delfina talks about how her father first came across as part of the Bracero Program and then brought the rest of the family to Chicago. This aptly illustrates how Julian enabled us to reflect on our backgrounds and give deeper meaning to our coursework and eventually to our research, teaching, and service. We quickly became part of his extended family, as shown by the Sunday meals he and his wife, Betty, would have for us at their home. He became our father "in absentia" and we became part of his family. Students in the Mexican American Graduate Studies Program were invited over to enjoy New Mexican food on a regular basis. It was the opportunity for us to eat great food, but more importantly we were able to relax and even lament about the rigors of university life. He would always just listen and smile because he had had those same experiences years before.

Julian Samora had an impact on our careers, and he instilled a commitment in us to help other Chicanos/Latinos. Delfina's work in education and her effectiveness in the classroom were given roots in his weekly Chicano seminar. The "Samorista style" was a gentle, yet firm and scholarly approach that impacted our lives long after we left the classroom and the campus.

In the second essay, Frank Castillo discusses the influence Dr. Samora had and continues to have in his life. Dr. Samora allowed a few undergraduate students to register for his graduate-level Chicano Studies seminar, and Frank was one of the fortunate students. It was in this seminar that the seeds of political activism were planted in many students' minds. Castillo's career has been profoundly influenced by Dr. Samora's emphasis on service and giving back to the community. It would have been easy for Julian to rest on his publications and other academic laurels, but he did not. He always reminded us of the struggles and challenges for Latino communities and that we could play an important role in addressing injustice. It was not enough to be an academic, but we also needed to use our skills in outreach to the community.

Today it is seen as the new and emergent field of "outreach scholarship" but this dimension was always present in the work of Dr. Samora in his Mexican American Graduate Studies Program. As Castillo reminds us, we learned what was important in the lives we touched, seeds we planted, and guidance we provided to others during our careers.

The importance of "community" is reflected in the third essay, by Rene Rosenbaum. Dr. Samora worked aggressively to recruit students into his program, but he quickly impressed upon us that we were part of a community and that this community extended beyond the campus. We were encouraged to better understand the plight of the United Farm Workers (UFW), the Farm Labor Organizing Committee (FLOC), and other organizations that dealt with social injustices. These were not just academic issues to read about in textbooks, but real issues we should comprehend. This was the beginning of a "consciousness" which we acquired in Dr. Samora's program. This consciousness and community service went hand in hand. It was in this area that Julian was the master teacher in getting us to understand how essential this consciousness was in striving for social change.

Many of us were drawn to the Golden Dome because of the Samora legacy. Amelia Muñoz, an undergraduate, went to Notre Dame because of that same legacy and reputation. Her essay relates to the tremendous persistence she demonstrated in getting into the university, as well as the good fortune to attend Julian's seminar as an undergraduate.

One of the attributes of the "Samorista style" was his ability to reach out and make you feel part of his world. Dr. Samora could have easily placed himself on an academic pedestal and created a distance between himself and his students. He related to his own experiences and did his utmost to give us opportunities to succeed, but we still had to do the work. Muñoz talks about the numerous efforts made on behalf of students by Dr. Samora; he indeed was a trailblazer for us. Although Dr. Samora did not talk about the day-to-day obstacles he faced in running the Mexican American Graduate Studies Program, many of us recognized the institutional challenges he encountered. His determination to persevere only deepened our resolve and commitment to work even harder to improve the lives of Chicanos/Latinos who need an advocate and mentor.

The essay by Alberto Pulido highlights the seemingly "invisible" visionary role that Dr. Samora represented in our lives. He wanted us to not only be scholars but to also have the much-needed compassion necessary for social change. Samora recognized that there were boundaries and barriers in higher education, and he walked the delicate balance of being a professor, an administrator, and an activist.

As discussed in Pulido's writing, Dr. Samora displayed a tremendous amount of patience in working with universities, administrations, and foundations. His "bend but do not break" approach opened many doors, not only for himself but also for his students. In this way we learned the value of patience in making progress. This also highlights a second attribute of Dr. Samora—his multiplication factor. He was able to touch many lives through his students; in fact, he measured his success not by personal accomplishments, but by the number of individuals touched by his students. Even in his role as trickster, he was subtle yet effective. He demonstrated to us as students that we could accomplish great things as long as we were patient, dedicated, and committed to our values.

It is difficult to summarize the impact of an individual like Julian Samora. I know when my parents first visited Notre Dame and met him they were in awe of his gentle yet humble persona. They held him in high esteem and were proud I was privileged and lucky enough to study under his guidance. There was a *presence* about him that touched the lives of all who interacted with him. The essays that follow reveal and connect common themes that naturally arise when talking about Dr. Samora—activist, father figure, leader, mentor, sower, teacher, trickster, visionary, and more. These personal essays are indeed the reflections of being mentored by and coming of age with Don Julian Samora.

CHAPTER TWENTY-SIX

Reflections on the Impact of Dr. Julian Samora

Delfina Landeros

> The wise man is he who loves and reveres God. A man's merit lies in his knowledge and in his deeds, not in his color, faith, race or descent. . . . Knowledge is your true patent of nobility, no matter who your father or what your race may be.
> —K. Gibran

Dr. Julian Samora was a very knowledgeable person with deep understanding, indeed a noble person. I will elaborate on some of my accomplishments in the field of education and in the community and how Dr. Julian Samora influenced both my work and my life.

Family Background

I was born in Guanajuato, Mexico, the second child of a family of eight children. I met my husband, Ricardo Chapa, at the University of Notre Dame, and we have been married thirty-one years. Together we have three lovely children. Xavier, the eldest, studied filmmaking with Luis Valdez at Cal-State University and is now teaching English in Germany. Emilio majored in aerospace engineering, but in his senior year he decided to study for the priesthood. Our fourteen-year-old, Adelita, is a budding actress.

I am the second child of Selerina Torres and Dionicio Landeros. Both my parents were born in villages near Leon, Guanajuato, Mexico. At the age of twenty, Dionicio persuaded Selerina, then fifteen years old, to elope with him. On the morning of their wedding, my parents and twelve other people rode on saddled horses ten miles to the church where they were blessed as husband and wife. On their return, a band of eight musicians joined them before they entered Jalapa, my father's village. Jalapa is my birthplace. At that time, its population was about one hundred people and its houses curled up a hill. During the rainy season, Jalapa dressed in green. I remember flowers growing everywhere. In the early evening, my little girl cousins and I picked bouquets of flowers to take to "La Virgen," who was in the chapel in the middle of the village where the villagers gathered to pray the rosary. Jalapa, amidst the flowers, is where I played as a child and dreamed as a child.

My father was a *campesino*, a farmer, and my mother was a homemaker. They both had no more than a month of formal education. Long droughts made life miserable for my father, who depended on the harvest for his livelihood. So in 1943 my father applied to and was accepted into the Bracero Program, a program established by the United States government to provide cheap labor to agriculture, railroads, and other industries. He made two trips to the United States under the Bracero Program. Some of his bosses treated him decently, but others did not respect his dignity as a worker. During the second year, he left the Bracero Program to go live with an aunt in Chicago, Illinois. Why did my father make sacrifices to come to the United States? This is a familiar question that was well-researched in one of my favorite books written by Dr. Samora called *Los Mojados: The Wetback Story.* Later we will see how my father responded to the same question.

I was nine years old when my mother received a letter from my father informing her that all the arrangements were made for us to come and live with him in Chicago. We traveled to Nuevo Laredo, Mexico, and in the evening we were smuggled into the United States by walking on the international bridge that joins Nuevo Laredo to Laredo, Texas. We pretended to be the children of a family who lived on the U.S. side of the border. After what seemed to be a never-ending trip, we finally arrived at our destination—Chicago. As we drove into the city and saw the tall skyscrapers, I was completely mesmerized. I remember leaning out of the car in a failed effort to see the tops of them. Our whole way of life was about to change dramatically from rural to urban.

As newly arrived immigrant children, school was rough. My siblings and I were teased and made fun of by some of the students for not knowing English. Some of the teachers were compassionate. For example, my third grade teacher kept me after school on a regular basis to teach me English with flash cards. Soon I was "flying" in school. My teachers told me to read and read a lot, which I did. It didn't take me long to receive two double promotions, based not on social promotion but on the results of standardized tests I took. In high school, I was proud of myself because I was placed in an honors English class and an honors French class. Reading helps a student in amazing ways even when parents can't help with the homework. Because of the language barrier for my mother and the many overtime hours that my father worked, my beloved parents never could help us, but they made sure of two important things: (1) that we always did our homework and (2) that we never once thought of dropping out of school.

After graduating from high school I went to work as a secretary for Mr. Edward Custer, project engineer for Kaiser Engineers, Inc. I worked full-time and attended evening classes at a community college for several years. When he learned that I did not want to be a secretary for the rest of my life and that I really wanted to be a social worker, Mr. Custer insisted that I enroll at Northern Illinois University (NIU) and finish college and also be his daughter's roommate. At twenty-seven years of age, I argued with him that I was too old to do this, but in the end I took his advice.

A Research Experience before Meeting Dr. Julian Samora

In my last year at NIU, I launched a student-run teacher evaluation project, funded by the Student Union. I had no previous knowledge about how to do this, but I read a lot and spoke to experts. The results of the study, two thick paperback books titled *Query I* and *Query II,* were placed in the school library and served the students well in later semesters. Little did I know it then, but a giant in the field of research, Dr. Julian Samora, would someday teach me scientific methods for investigating social issues. In June of 1969, I earned my bachelor's degree.

After graduation, my sister Melin and I went to California and traveled all over the state, spending a week or two in each of several cities, working as temporary secretaries. A temporary work agency in Chicago had prepared our work itinerary by contacting offices in California in advance.

At the end of June 1969, Melin went back to Chicago, but I stayed in California for most of a year working as a bilingual secretary with Dr. Rudolfo Acuña, who at that time was department chair of Chicano Studies at the University of California Northridge. While in California, I discovered and immersed myself in the Chicano movement. I was actively involved in it, and I learned a lot about the various causes such as the Chicano or Mexican American Studies programs that sprouted in various California universities; the migrants' plight headed by Cesar Chavez; the political cause under the umbrella organization of the Mexican American Political Association or MAPA; and the student cause out of which MEChA, Movimiento Estudiantil Chicano de Aztlán came to be. When Melin wrote to me that she was getting married and that I was to be her maid of honor, I decided to resign my job with Dr. Acuña and return to Chicago. He, not being satisfied with my having only a bachelor's degree, insisted that I go see Dr. Julian Samora at the University of Notre Dame to see if I qualified for the doctoral program in sociology. I applied at the end of June 1970, and in August I received a letter of acceptance.

The California experience, particularly my involvement in the Chicano movement, was a highlight in my life. This experience literally remolded me into quite a different person. Gone was that shy, not very confident young lady. In came the self-confident, assertive young woman of the 1970s. In August of 1970, I walked onto the beautiful grounds of the University of Notre Dame as a brand-new student in the graduate school of sociology. I was extremely happy to be there. I had made the right decision.

How Dr. Samora Personally Influenced Me

In California, during my involvement in the Chicano movement, my eyes were opened to the injustices done to *Mexicanos* and other people of color, and there grew in me a certain anger I had never felt before. I learned from a few leaders in the Chicano movement, through their modeled behavior, that it was okay to express this anger when we addressed the problems of our community. Dr. Samora was different. He was a very gentle and soft-spoken person. He affected people like me in a quiet way, in a way that we didn't even notice. He taught me to fight the system not with anger but with serenity and hard facts. I cannot say when his influence became a part of my being, but it did, and I began to fight differently. I began to fight using what I term the "Samorista style." He quietly pursued his goals and objectives. They were data-driven objectives. I learned the power of this combination of facts and patience. His quiet demeanor impressed me; I could sense his quiet strength. His influence on me was such that when I left Notre Dame in August of 1973 and went to work for the Bureau of the Census in Suitland, Maryland, I no longer felt like being contemptuous or being a "rabble rouser." As usual, I encountered discrimination and other forms of injustices on the job and elsewhere, but instead of expressing myself irately, I confronted those in power in a scholarly manner, always fortifying myself with good solid data before meeting with them.

Applying the Quiet and Scholarly Approach— "The Samorista Style"

Upon receiving my master's, I was hired as a trainee statistician at the Bureau of the Census along with a young man who also had just obtained his master's degree. Our boss spent many hours every day training this young man as a statistician. With me, it was different; I was assigned mostly secretarial work. I talked to the boss several times about his unequal treatment, but nothing changed. Then, to add insult to injury, at the end of six months when I received my evaluation, I was stunned! All the points he gave me were extremely low and did not represent my efforts. So I gathered all the information I could find to prove that I had done an excellent job for him and set up a meeting with him. The end result was that he denied that there was any problem at all. So I informed him that I would next meet with his superior. Before I left that meeting room, however, I told my boss's superior that I didn't accept the way my boss had treated me and that I was considering contacting the Equal Employment Opportunity Commission to present my case. In the end, I requested that I be transferred to a different department and be re-evaluated. After my reassignment and re-evaluation, my new boss turned out to be quite the opposite of the "old" boss. He was a respectful and polite gentleman from whom I learned much. I quietly savored the joy of justice. I had been brave to stand up for my rights, and I had used the "Samorista" style to address a problem—the quiet, scholarly approach. It worked!

> A little knowledge that acts is worth infinitely
> more than much knowledge that is idle.
> —K. Gibran

Dr. Samora in the Area of Student Mentoring

Caring, mentoring, and encouraging students to achieve great heights in education was what Dr. Julian Samora did. So as an educator, I have been imitating him ever since. A case in point is this: In the past four years principals from both a public and a private school have shared with me information about competitions for students for scholarships and other awards in a variety of fields. I wonder why in my other twenty-two years of teaching this information had not been shared with me. Even recently, some of the students I had in middle school who are now in high school have not been informed by their teachers or counselors of these available competitions. How many talented students, especially Mexican American students, have lost opportunities to compete for scholarships because they weren't informed or not encouraged and assisted to apply? It occurs to me that this might be a critical area for research.

Students who are mentored well "rise to the occasion." For fourteen years I have taught in several middle schools in Tucson, one of them a particularly memorable school. Wakefield Middle School is designated as a neighborhood school, meaning it is not part of the Tucson Unified School District's desegregation program. About 99 percent of Wakefield students are Mexican Americans from the neighborhood. In meetings with language arts teachers I learned that the school had a bad reputation with people outside the neighborhood, so I suggested that we develop a strategy to change the label and the perception. Not one teacher or administrator burst out with great enthusiasm for this idea. In fact, one of the school's top Mexican American teachers plainly said, "It can't be done." With that statement, I decided to work alone.

In 2000, I received information from the National Association for Bilingual Educators (NABE) regarding a bilingual essay contest. At the time, I was teaching Chicano Studies, reading, English, and Spanish classes. I invited students in all my classes to "jump in" and participate in this contest. Out of approximately 135 students, four students volunteered to enter the contest. This small number completely devastated me! But, "*ni modo*," what can one do? At least I had four to work with. On the other hand, there was excitement in the air. The director of the bilingual program in our school district was highly enthusiastic about NABE's contest and began to advertise his own local bilingual essay contest and a plan to honor the winners. The local winning essays would then be forwarded to NABE's national bilingual essay competition. One of my students, Jennifer, was awarded third place in this local contest, and she, her parents, and I were invited to a dinner where

Rigoberta Menchu Tum, Nobel Peace Prize winner from Guatemala, spoke on the importance of language maintenance and language use. Ms. Menchu Tum "*con mucho corazón*" warmly honored our winning students.

My other gem student, Oscar Zepeda, won first place in NABE's national contest at the middle school level, besting all other eighth grade middle school contestants from bilingual communities all over the country. He earned a $5,000 scholarship plus a trip to San Antonio, Texas, accompanied by his parents and his teacher to participate in NABE's Annual National Conference. There he received a standing ovation from about nine hundred people for the superb presentation of his essay in perfect English and perfect Spanish. Congressman Ed Pastor later read his essay on the floor of the House of Representatives and entered it into the Congressional Record. Long after we returned from San Antonio, Wakefield Middle School finally received the publicity it deserves. Several language arts teachers, including the teacher who said it couldn't be done, now encourage and assist students in applying to scholarship competitions.

Currently, I work with an alternative educational program at Tucson Youth Development and Ace Charter High School. Our students are at-risk students, about 99 percent Hispanic, who have been falling behind in the regular public schools. My students have competed for and won many training competitions and poetry contests. I've learned from Dr. Samora to give them sound guidance. Most of them do not have parents who graduated from high school, let alone college. So who will teach them how to edit their essays? I MUST help them experience success if they are to believe "Sí se puede!" "Yes, it can be done."

In Dr. Samora's Classroom

Dr. Samora's classes were interesting because he was a knowledgeable person with deep understanding. He had the chutzpah or moral fiber to come down from the ivory tower and work and learn from all kinds of communities, then bring this experience, the history of his community involvement, to the classroom. In his course "Mexican Americans in the U.S.," Dr. Samora told us of the hidden agendas of powerful figures. To make us think, he would ask analytical questions to challenge us. And just as important was the humor. Once he got us started with the jokes he got our full cooperation. Learning, trust, respect, and an overall joyful experience is what I got from his classes. When the hour was over, a few would get up and leave, but most of us milled around asking him further questions.

As I end my journey in this paper, I ask again: Why did my father, Dionicio, sacrifice to come to the United States? His response was no different than most immigrants' response. He said, "I want a better life for my wife and my children." Well, lo and behold, he and his family became United States citizens and his first child, Victor, graduated valedictorian of his high school, a school that was Anglo dominant. All of the other children, Delfina, Melin, Michael, and the four children who were born in the United States, Maria, Rosa Elvira, Jaime, and Carlos, have earned degrees in the fields of teaching, law, accounting, engineering, urban planning, and administration. This is the way the Landeros became contributing members of this great society, through their talents and hard work. We are grateful to our father, Dionicio Landeros, and our mother, Selerina, for believing in us, for their great heart, their hard work, and their bravery in risking all to come to this country and start anew. We are also grateful to this country for the opportunities it made available to us.

Two Noble Men

One of the most beautiful acts in this life is to believe in someone. Mr. Custer, Dr. Rudy Acuña, and Dr. Julian Samora, not to mention many women in my life, all believed in me. Dr. Samora also taught me to appreciate the importance of researching problems, devising solutions reinforced with reliable data, encouraging students to reach higher education goals, and promoting social justice in the community.

Jesus "Chuy" Negrete summarizes Dr. Samora's story succinctly in one of the verses of his inspirational ballad "El Corrido de Julian Samora" (1996). I have taken the liberty of translating this verse below:

> It's a story of a struggle and permanent accomplishments
> He struggled all of his life for his community and his people
> for his students as he molded their minds.

In a way, Dr. Samora reminds me of my father. My father helped many Mexican immigrants, relatives, friends, and acquaintances to adjust to living in Chicago by feeding them, sheltering them, helping them find jobs, etc. Dr. Samora helped Mexican Americans and other ethnic "immigrant" students from all parts of the country, especially the Southwest, to adjust to higher education at Notre Dame by finding them jobs, counseling them, and feeding them dinner at his home. They both gave immigrants the gift of believing in them, of befriending them, and of loving them. My father and Dr. Samora were both quiet, unassuming, knowledgeable, and very wise men. I believe that Kahlil Gibran would say, "The richness of their spirit beautified their face and gave birth to our honor and respect for them. They had the true patent of nobility." I am very proud to be a part of "Samoristas @ 57."

CHAPTER TWENTY-SEVEN

The Seeds We Plant

Frank M. Castillo

I was introduced to Professor Samora during a time in my life when I was searching for answers and direction. I had recently had my late adolescent life turned on its head by two close brushes with death and one intimate encounter with it. As a direct consequence, in 1978, I transferred from the University of Chicago to the University of Notre Dame on a transcendent spiritual search for a deeper understanding of my faith and my purpose in life. It was during this particularly impressionable time that I met Professor Samora.

It was while choosing courses for my sociology major that I read about an undergraduate course titled Chicanos in the U.S., described as an introduction to the Mexican American experience in the United States. I was enthralled to imagine an academic study and analysis of the experiences of families like my own and individuals like myself. In fact, I later learned that one of Professor Samora's early research efforts had been focused on studying the population of Indiana Harbor, the urban Mexican barrio of East Chicago, Indiana, where I was born. Through his teachings and his book *A History of the Mexican American People,* a whole new world with familiar details was revealed to me by looking at the struggles of my parents and all my family through the academic lens of social research.

As an undergraduate student, I was impressed by Professor Samora's gentleness. His was a personable and approachable teaching style. His humility, sharp wit, and willingness to offer encouragement and assistance to students stand out in my mind. Outside of the classroom, he served as the faculty sponsor for a fledgling chapter of MEChA there at Notre Dame. He encouraged me, along with a small number of other interested students, to join. There were few Latino undergraduate students on campus in 1980, but he encouraged us and challenged us to be more socially conscious and politically aware, always with an eye toward serving the larger community.

Through his words and his teachings, Professor Samora captured my interest and my imagination. I petitioned him to allow me into his graduate colloquium on the Chicano movement during my fourth year as an undergraduate. I wanted to learn more about my heritage and the larger epic and struggle of *La Raza*. He graciously allowed me into the weekly colloquium, which profoundly affected my understanding of where and how I was to fit into the dynamic story about which I was learning.

It was while under the direct tutelage of Professor Samora that I learned about political activism and the power of organizing thoughts and ideas into statements and actions. My maiden activist effort was around 1980 and was a direct result of what I had just learned from Professor Samora. As part of a small group of Notre Dame students, I traveled to Dayton, Ohio, to lend support to a group of migrant farm workers protesting unfair labor practices through a farm labor organization action. There were no arrests. It did not get much press, and I do not even remember if it was effective. But it was an experiential introduction to the role of activist and the tool of political protest.

The words of two other men on campus also greatly influenced my thinking at that time. Fr. Bill Toohey, the director of campus ministry, had written an essay in his book *Life After Birth* about the threat of nuclear war and the horror wrought by nuclear destruction. That impression was galvanized by Fr. Ted Hesburgh's comments during my last year as an undergraduate that the threat of nuclear war was the single most apocalyptic danger to our world then in 1981. So, as I was wrestling with the choices for a career path in my life, the words and inspirational examples of Professor Samora, Fr. Toohey, and Fr. Hesburgh were all working together to shape the direction of things to come.

In 1983, I enrolled in medical school at the University of Wisconsin–Madison. Professor Samora's teachings to be socially conscious and politically aware manifested themselves there, and I became involved with issues of civil rights and minority affairs. That activism led to my membership on the University of Wisconsin's Center for Health Sciences Minority Affairs Committee and to my spearheading the reorganization of the minority medical student group on campus into the Medical Students for Minority Concerns. This heightened awareness of social justice issues led to my involvement with a medical student group at the University of Arizona called Commitment to Underserved Persons (CUP) and served as the impetus for my involvement with Physicians for Social Responsibility (PSR), the U.S. affiliate of the International Physicians for the Prevention of Nuclear War (IPPNW)—a recipient of the 1985 Nobel Peace Prize.

The bridge between these two areas of my burgeoning activist energy—minority affairs and the prevention of global thermonuclear warfare—was the theme "Destruction before Detonation," first introduced to me by Dr. Victor Sidel at the 1986 PSR national convention in Chicago. The message behind the thematic phrase was that our tax dollars were being used to build and maintain a multibillion-dollar military establishment and nuclear weapons arsenal at the expense of educational, developmental, and health care programs for the poor and disadvantaged—this economic and social destruction all occurring within our own borders without the weapons of mass destruction ever being detonated.

With Professor Samora's words of encouragement etched in my mind, and those of Fr. Toohey, Fr. Hesburgh, and Dr. Sidel spurring me on, I unexpectedly became a player in the international peace movement as a medical student and physician activist. That role in pursuit of peace took me on romantically intoxicating journeys to the Soviet Union, Canada, France, the United Kingdom, the Federal Republic of Germany, Japan, the Kazakhstan Republic, Sweden, Cuba, Mexico, and El Salvador.

Just before starting my postgraduate medical training, however, the lessons I had learned in Professor Samora's graduate colloquium were projected into a much larger arena than my first protest participation in Dayton, Ohio. As part of a small group of antinuclear peace activists from the IPPNW, I traveled to the Kazakhstan Republic, which was still a part of the Soviet Union at that time. This journey took me to Alma Ata and Semipalatinsk to participate in the International Citizens Congress for a Nuclear Test Ban.

We were there to give support to the "downwinders" protesting nuclear testing at the site in the Soviet Union that was the equivalent of the Nevada desert test site where U.S. nuclear weapon test explosions had been conducted. The "downwinders" are the indigenous peoples who are suffering from higher than epidemiologically predictable rates of leukemia, various cancers, and birth defects after exposure to the radioactive winds and fallout from the nuclear test explosions in Kazakhstan.

Soon after our international citizens protest, President Mikhail Gorbachev closed the nuclear test zone in Semipalatinsk and gave credit to the International Citizens Congress and to the IPPNW for focusing the educational spotlight to help bring this about. The message that Professor Samora had planted in me about political activism and the power of organizing thoughts and ideas into actions had grown to tangible fruition and become part of a larger global movement that truly made a difference.

My involvement with the medico-political lobbying arm of preventive/social medicine revealed my lack of background in international relations and hegemony. Therefore, soon after finishing medical school, I accepted a minority fellowship to earn a master's degree at the Kroc Institute for International Peace Studies at the University of Notre Dame. The focus of my studies and research was Latin America and the use and, at times, misappropriation of foreign aid funds for an inappropriate military buildup in developing countries.

My time at the Institute for International Peace Studies also allowed me to study with Professor Samora's first graduate student, Jorge A. Bustamante, PhD, whose work and expertise on Mexico-U.S. border issues secured him a role as a teaching fellow with the institute and later earned him a nomination for the 2006 Nobel Peace Prize. My work with Professor Bustamante harkens back to my time with Professor Samora as an example of the living legacy he left through the many former students carrying on his scholarly work and activism.

In 1990, I returned to postgraduate clinical medical training at the University of Wisconsin in family and community medicine. Throughout my residency training, Latin America seemed to be the arena calling to me. I continued my peace activism with my travels to Cuba, Mexico, and El Salvador. And in 1993 my review of a book titled "A New Dawn in Guatemala: Toward a Worldwide Health Vision" was published in the *Journal of Health Care for the Poor and Underserved.*

As I began to focus more and more on the care of individual lives in my practice of medicine, however, the international/global perspective of preventive medicine that had so attracted me as a student began to become more domestic in focus.

At the end of my residency training, I traveled to El Salvador to investigate a possible position with Doctors of the World. It was while I was climbing the lush jungle pathways of the mountains of El Salvador that the "scales fell from my eyes" and an obvious but profound realization occurred to me. The role of a physician in a Spanish-speaking community for which I was searching was readily attainable and equally needed back within the borders of the United States.

My journey was brought full-circle back to the dynamic microcosm of the Latino community about which Professor Samora had taught me so much. I returned to the United States to pursue my career as a community family physician. My first position out of residency was with the Health Centers of Northern New Mexico, working with the poor and largely Spanish-speaking population of northeast New Mexico. After a year, my family drew me back to Indiana, where I set up practice in South Bend.

Soon after my arrival in South Bend, through my work at St. Joseph Medical Center, I became a regular volunteer staff physician at St. Joseph Health Center (the Chapin Street Clinic). Once there, I recognized an unfilled need of the underserved Latino population of South Bend, Indiana, and the surrounding St. Joseph County. Professor Samora's encouragement of community service echoed in my mind and the inspiration of my newly acquired friend Sr. Maura Brannick, the founding visionary of the Chapin Street Clinic, gave me direction. Subsequently, I successfully spearheaded a Spanish-speaking evening clinic at the Chapin Street Clinic. Soon after, I became the medical director for the Hispanic Health Task Force of St. Joseph Medical Center. I used that role to reach out and develop working partnerships and trusted relationships within the local Latino business and educational communities.

Since I was working only one mile from campus, I became involved with the Hispanic Alumni of Notre Dame. My memories of the support and assistance that Professor Samora offered to students when I was an undergraduate encouraged me to become active with students on campus while I was on the Board of Directors from 1995 until 1998.

One of the initiatives of the board was to try to establish at Notre Dame the presence of an institute dedicated to the study of the Latino culture, in posthumous honor of Professor Samora. Because of the tireless efforts of the Board of Directors of the Hispanic Alumni of Notre Dame and the support of Fr. Tim Sculley, C.S.C., the Institute for Latino Studies was established on campus in October 1999. Under the leadership of Dr. Gilberto Cárdenas— another former student of Professor Samora—and Allert Brown-Gort, the institute has flourished and grown on campus, with multiple grant awards and research initiatives. The institute's library/reading room was named and dedicated in honor of Professor Samora in March of 2000.

Although I had thought that I was going to grow old and retire in South Bend, an opportunity to expand my service to the larger Latino community presented itself in Chicago. Alivio Medical Center, a community health center in the large immigrant Mexican community of Pilsen on the lower west side of the city, was in need of a medical director. It seemed to be a role for which I had been preparing all my adult life. In June of 1998, filled with a spirit of zeal and mission, my bride of less than a year and I moved to the city.

In late 2001, an opportunity became available to refocus my career on my original interest in family and community medicine. I left Alivio Medical

Center and became the director of the Department of Family Practice at Erie Family Health Center in Chicago, where I have been since December 2001. There I am the primary clinical preceptor in family practice for the training of medical students who rotate at the Humboldt Park Site of Erie Family Health Center, which serves a 90 percent Spanish-speaking population. In that role I believe I have been a positive model. Many Latino medical students have shared with me their excitement of seeing and working with a Latino doctor who is serving the Latino community in ways they hope to be able to do some day. In this role, I feel one of the legacies of Professor Samora continues, that is, his willingness to offer himself as a model as well as to provide encouragement and assistance to students.

My career as a physician trying to care for the unmet needs of the most marginalized of *La Raza* and my historic role as an antinuclear activist were profoundly influenced by my time at Notre Dame. The most important driving force for the direction of those roles was my time learning about my heritage from Professor Samora. As I stated at the planning session for the Institute for Latino Studies at the University of Notre Dame in February 1998, "no matter what major I had chosen or career path I had sought, the passion instilled in me by Professor Samora from the scholarly understanding of my roots would have permeated my efforts."

Professor Samora taught me that community service, first and foremost, was to be directed back into the community from which I came. His gentleness and humility modeled for me the way to try to do that. My brief time with him also showed me that who we are is not so much measured by our achievements, but by the individual lives we touch, the seeds we plant, and the encouragement and guidance we give along the way.

CHAPTER TWENTY-EIGHT

The Legacy of Latino Consciousness

Rene Rosenbaum

I went to Notre Dame at the age of twenty-two, and I graduated with a PhD at the age of twenty-eight. I was a graduate student in economics, rather than in sociology, which was Dr. Samora's area of study, but there were plenty of opportunities to be around him and to be influenced by his thinking. Because of Dr. Samora and the Mexican American Graduate Studies Program he created and administered, the years I spent at Nuestra Dama remain the most influential and memorable of my life. The values I currently hold, and the work I currently do, clearly are linked to my intellectual development that occurred during that time. Indeed, it's difficult to reflect on my life without thinking of Dr. Samora and the Notre Dame experience he made possible; he touched my life in so many ways.

The Opportunity Created

My whole life was changed by what happened to me in the summer of 1976. I remember it as if it were only yesterday. I had graduated from St. Edwards University in Austin, Texas, and had taken a job in the state of New York at a summer camp for the blind. Earlier in the year, I had given up hope of going to graduate school. At the urging of my department chair at St. Edwards, James Koch, I had applied to the Notre Dame Economics Department to do graduate work and had been accepted. However, I had applied late and financial assistance was no longer available.

Two weeks into my New York summer job, I learned that my sister, Viola, who earlier had been diagnosed with cancer, would need surgery. I was full of guilt for having left home knowing that she had been ill and now needed surgery. So I quit my summer job and returned to my hometown of Brownsville, Texas, to be by my sister and family.

I was determined to help my family in whatever way I could, and for as long as was necessary. With the help of my older brother, I got an hourly job at the local shipyard, where I worked separating the iron from the stainless steel in old World War II battleships. While my sister was recovering from surgery, I also tended to the family flower shop, where I was the weekend sales clerk.

One weekend in July, while sweeping the flower shop patio, I got a surprise call from Roger Skurski, then faculty member and graduate student advisor in the Department of Economics at the University of Notre Dame. He was calling to tell me that a graduate assistantship had become available and I could have it if I wanted it. Apparently, another student who had received the assistantship had changed his mind about attending Notre Dame.

I discussed the phone call and opportunity with my parents, who spoke only Spanish and had been migrant workers most of their lives. My parents did not know a thing about Notre Dame or graduate school. I remember looking up Notre Dame on the map and showing them its location. Nor did they know a thing about what economics was about or what it would do for me. All my parents knew was that someone was giving me money to go to school, and that was good. So, despite my family situation, they let me go. My mom gave me her blessing and my dad gave me $300. He also lent me his car that first semester so I could make the trip to South Bend.

One thing I will always remember from the summer of 1976 was the conversation I had with Roger when I called him back to tell him I would accept the graduate assistantship. I remember in particular asking him how I had been chosen for the assistantship. It was then that I heard about Dr. Samora for the first time. Dr. Skurski told me that Dr. Julian Samora had been working with them to get more Hispanics into the Economics Department. It had been Dr. Samora who had urged them to consider me for the assistantship, and it was because of his efforts that I was being given the opportunity to attend Notre Dame. Later that summer I got a letter from Dr. Samora welcoming me to the university.

The graduate assistantship I received from the graduate school only lasted one year. Luckily, I had Dr. Samora on my side. At his urging and with his support, I applied for the Ford Foundation fellowship in year two of the program, which I also received. I know that Dr. Samora's support was instrumental in my getting the fellowship. I probably would not have received it without his endorsement. I also know that without the fellowship, it would have been impossible for me to continue my studies.

The Notre Dame/Mexican American Graduate Studies Experience

The financial support I received to go to graduate school, and eventually to get my PhD, is only one of the many ways Dr. Samora changed my life. Perhaps more important is the Latino group conscience and sense of Latino community he instilled in me and in the many other students in the Mexican American Graduate Studies Program. Dr. Samora and his family helped me and others find community. His weekly colloquium and other discussions instilled in me a sense of Chicano/Latino community that I hold dear to this day.

As one who grew up embedded in the migrant stream, I did not always have the sense of the Chicano/Latino community I hold today. The mid- and late 1970s were turbulent times for Latinos, and the search for identity, as is the case for many young Latinos today, was urgent and real. When I joined Notre Dame I had been three years removed from my experience as a migrant farm worker. Although I had a strong sense of identity and knew who I was, I did not have the Chicano group conscience that prevailed at the time among some of my classmates. Concerns for *La Raza* were still too much of a luxury for me. My family and I were poor, and my main motivation for going to Notre Dame and majoring in economics was to earn money. Although I had experienced discrimination, either I did not know it or I just preferred to give people who had discriminated against me the benefit of the doubt. That way of thinking changed for me, however, after Dr. Samora and others at Notre Dame exposed me to the systemic patterns of disparities and discrimination experienced by the Chicano community. Dr. Samora's teachings helped me see the broader picture. He made me recognize the injustices that were occurring to a group of people. He gave intellectual legitimacy to La Causa.

In graduate school you can lose your direction and sense of community very easily. In my case, I was challenged by different theoretical economic perspectives, which led me to question the value of focusing on the Mexican American community as the unit of analysis and study. Marxist theory emphasizes, for example, the concept of class rather than race or ethnicity as the unit of analysis and the cause of poverty. In writing this essay and reflecting on my good fortune to have shared my life with Dr. Samora, I recognize that it is he who deserves the credit for creating in me the Latino group conscience I now carry. It was exciting for me, as a student at Notre Dame, to be part of an active community seeking to bring attention and legitimacy to the condition of Latinos in the United States for the first time. If Dr. Samora had not been there to support and legitimize the Mexican American perspective, I could have easily adopted another frame to analyze today's contemporary problems. More importantly, Dr. Samora and his program brought meaning and relevance to my life as a student, which sustained and motivated me to complete my program.

In my mind, Dr. Samora was above all about the production of Mexican American/Chicano scholars and scholarship. Although his focus was on Mexican Americans and Chicanos, he was open to all students irrespective of their race or nationality, so long as their scholarship and interest was in the field of Mexican American/Chicano Studies. Dr. Samora also recognized the importance of recruiting students from across all the disciplines to better study the Mexican American population. His hope was that as researchers we would bring our disciplinary training to bear on Latino issues and problems. If we don't do it, who will? In that regard, Dr. Samora was an example to us all.

Community Service

I think about Dr. Samora's scholarly work as a community service for the Latino community, because his work contributed to the nascent understanding of the Latino community. Dr. Samora's work was not just about Latino scholarship and its contribution to the Latino community; it was also about being engaged in community service. He was an activist, deeply engaged in issues of public policy and the provision of service for the betterment of the Latino community. From a founding leadership role with the National Council of La Raza to his involvement with the Ford Foundation, he gave us many examples of his commitment to the Latino community and of his support for numerous causes. His commitment was so great that many times he gave of himself at the expense of his own family.

Dr. Samora's Mexican American Graduate Studies program was not just about Latino scholarship. He was mindful of the need to expose students to the important links between scholarship and community issues and service. His program exposed us to many prominent national leaders, such as Cesar Chavez, Baldemar Velasquez, and Arturo Madrid, who shared with us the problems of the day from a Latino perspective. He also introduced us to, and got us involved with, local activists such as Ricardo Parra and Olga Villa, both leaders of the Mexican American community in South Bend.

Dr. Samora did both the big and the small things to help La Causa. I vividly remember once when we were selling tamales to support the activities of the Farm Labor Organizing Community (FLOC). Unannounced, one cold and rainy Friday night, he came into a volunteer's house and purchased his order of tamales to support the cause. He did not say much and stayed only long enough to get his tamales. This deed, as minor as it was, is very memorable to me, not because it was a surprise to see Dr. Samora supporting the cause, but because it was raining and cold and he had gone out of his way to support our local efforts, even in this small way.

Dr. Samora once told me that being a professor would not make me financially rich, but it would make my life rewarding. Today, I am proud to say, I follow in Dr. Samora's footsteps. I take great pride and feel a great reward in being an associate professor at Michigan State University, where I have been the past fourteen years and where I am able to bring attention to the problems and issues of the Latino community. In addition to teaching community economics in the Department of Community, Agriculture, Recreation, and Resource Studies, I am also affiliated with the Julian Samora Research Institute, where I conduct research with and about Latinos. The position

I currently hold also allows me to do extensive outreach and community service with Latinos and poor people across the state and to continue Dr. Samora's work.

Certainly, the focus of my work on the Latino community would not have been what it is today without Dr. Samora's influence. I, for one, feel I learned the Latino group conscience lesson very well. Much of my work has focused on using my training in economics to address Latino issues. My dissertation, for example, focused on the problem of collective bargaining power among farm workers. My current work remains very much focused on Latino issues, be it education, jobs, or poverty. I am also extensively engaged in outreach and community work with Latinos.

I find it quite inspiring that many of the students Dr. Samora brought to the Notre Dame/Mexican American Graduate Studies Program, like me, acquired a Latino group conscience. Much of their work also addresses the Latino condition in the United States. To me, nurturing that Latino group conscience is the greatest community service Dr. Samora, with the wonderful support from the Samora family, ever performed. In so doing, the seeds he planted are now grown, perpetuating anew seeds of Latino group conscience and scholarship and service to the Latino community. It is no wonder Dr. Samora considered his students his greatest contribution, if not his greatest community service.

Conclusion

Inasmuch as Dr. Samora is recognized as the father of Chicano Studies, his commitment to community service cannot be discounted. Indeed, his scholarship was intended to inform public policy and to enhance community service. He had a strong sense of the land grant philosophy of education and taught us the importance of linking research to community outreach and service.

The Julian Samora Research Institute (JSRI) at Michigan State University was created in 1989 to continue Dr. Samora's legacy and work. Like Dr. Samora, the institute is committed to the production of Latino scholars, Latino scholarship, and community service. I am very proud of the fact that when the institute was created, Dr. Samora recommended me for the institute's first postdoctoral fellow position. It is because of that invitation, extended to me by the former director of the institute, Richard Navarro, that I am currently at Michigan State University.

When the institute was in its formative years in the late 1980s and early 1990s, we had the distinct pleasure of having Dr. Samora visit Michigan

State University. My family and I were able to spend time with him again. He was working on a book on *mestizaje,* which he was not able to complete due to illness. Until his death in 1996, Dr. Samora remained committed to Latino Studies and community service. His legacy survives through such institutions as JSRI, which serve to remind us that Latino scholarship and community service remain unfinished business. The need for Latino scholars and Latino scholarship, and for service to the Latino community, is greater than ever. He has passed the torch on to us, and I for one will proudly carry his work forward.

Let me conclude by saying that the task of writing this essay has made me realize more than ever the importance of Dr. Samora's work and his influence on my own life. In all honesty, I do not know who I would be today if I had not had the good fortune to have Dr. Samora as a mentor in my life. I am certain I would not have the Latino group conscience I have today, and who knows what I would be doing professionally. Dr. Samora instilled in me a true purpose in life, one that I continue to instill in my children and my students. He influenced me to be not just a teacher, but a teacher who recognizes the importance of nurturing Latino scholars and doing research to elucidate Latino problems. In these ways I try to continue Dr. Samora's practice of service to the Latino community through scholarship, community involvement, and the production of Latino scholars.

CHAPTER TWENTY-NINE

Julian Samora and His Lesson of Revelation

Alberto López Pulido

If I could name a school in honor of Julian Samora, it would strive to master the art of *teaching revelation.* If I could design an area of study after Julian Samora's contributions, it would concentrate on how he taught us to *understand revelation.* Julian Samora was a scholar whose deep stillness was commonly misunderstood. Several of us took his stillness as evidence that he was a conformist and accommodationist. We thought he was isolated from the most current intellectual challenges to mainstream scholarship posited by the "new" and "progressive" voices coming out of Ethnic and Chicano

Studies. Our youth, idealism, and impatience blinded us and kept us from seeing and appreciating the gifts of his teaching, of his scholarship, and of his mentoring that was the essence of his person. As I now write nearly twenty-five years after my first encounter with my mentor, I have come to learn and can now articulate the single most important lesson left to us by his deliberate expressions of silence and stillness: the lesson of *revelation* that represents the core of Julian Samora's mentoring.

Revelation was an expression of humanity years ahead of its time. Professor Samora actively sought to galvanize and energize the compassion common to all of us in an attempt to generate collective and effective social change for the oppressed. As a quiet and thoughtful scholar and academic, Julian Samora was an individual of little fanfare who did not draw attention to himself. Instead, he lived and taught by his *ejemplo* or example through accumulated stories from his long and distinguished career. He taught us about racism, university politics, and social justice through the metaphorical stories drawn from his life experiences. If one was not continually vigilant and quick to decipher his subtle words and actions, then one missed the lesson. His advanced approach and philosophy was outside the normative frames of reference familiar to us. Our inability or unwillingness to be open to his teachings and perspectives was a common occurrence. Consequently, time has been the best agent to unveil Samora's pearls of wisdom that were previously hidden from our purview and understanding. Herein lies the important lesson of revelation by Julian Samora.

As a pioneer of Mexican American and Chicano Studies, he worked incessantly to bestow decency upon the disenfranchised. The revelations provided to us by Professor Samora were too powerful for the world to fully comprehend, and in response, Samora was forced to endure many painful obstacles and challenges wrought by the insensitivity and ignorance of individuals and institutions that were closed to his intellectual work and vision. As a result, Dr. Samora learned early on that he would have to truly know himself to survive the numerous personal and intellectual assaults that accompanied his persistent and pioneering efforts to be a productive scholar and contributor in an academy that was not receptive to his message. He had to live with both feet firmly planted on the ground, aware of where he stood in relationship to the dominant culture. This resulted in an academic and administrator who became skilled at clever subtleties that served as a two-sided shield; one side he used to protect himself from the powers that be, and the other side he used as a tool of resistance to bring changes to the existing system. Two key examples of these subtle strategies were the virtues of patience and multiplication.

Julian Samora had a great deal of patience. In my memory of talking and strategizing with him about Chicano politics and higher education, Dr. Samora always spoke from a confident place of patience and with an optimistic view of the struggles and sacrifices that had been made by those who came before us. He persistently advanced his intellectual agenda, then patiently waited for institutions to respond to his vision. On more than one occasion, he would get institutions, administrations, and foundations to eventually see things his way, and they would grant his requests. At another level, Professor Samora recognized that his goals were long-term and that he might not witness the full impact of his work during his lifetime. Yet he patiently challenged closed systems with an eye toward opening doors for others regardless of the obstacles or the time frame.

He also lived by the virtue of multiplication and realized that touching the life of just one of his students meant touching the lives of hundreds. Dr. Samora knew that his students would continue the transformative work he had begun in their lives by touching the lives of their own students who came after. His former colleague, Dr. Rudy Sandoval, captured the essence of Dr. Julian Samora's collective vision by stating, "Samora measured his success through the success of others." He fully realized what he was doing through this multiplication strategy.

His most powerful yet least understood strategy of subtlety and resistance was his humor about the academy and life in general. As someone who witnessed and experienced extreme poverty and marginality throughout his childhood, Dr. Samora was keenly aware of the power differentials between individuals. He found that people in power who took that power too seriously were a wonderful source of amusement. Such life experiences taught him to navigate the borderlands between the calculated and emotionless academic world and his community that, by contrast, was alive with rituals, symbols, and humor. His encounters within the academic world were filled with humorous irony and deliberately unorthodox actions that continually challenged the limits of so-called civility as defined by the academic world.

As a result, he took on the role of a masterful trickster for all his students to observe and learn from. His trickster strategy in the academy was a way to keep his strategies or trump card concealed from those in positions of power and authority. It represented a subtle yet strategic form of resistance that reminded us all that these gringos didn't control our lives. Yes, we had to jump through their hoops and follow their program, but in the end we would set the agenda for our work and scholarship.

Dr. Samora never allowed his fame to go to his head, as seen in his dry sense of humor. These were important lessons and revelations for us young graduate students. We learned a great deal about surviving graduate school and the academy, and his unique style and approach helped relieve the stress and pressure of being the first in one's community to venture into the treacherous world of post-baccalaureate studies. This was an extremely important survival skill he taught his students!

Julian Samora's trickster style required that he be extremely subtle in all his actions and deliberations. These subtleties even extended to his students. I vividly recall a meeting I had in Dr. Samora's office one hour before my scheduled oral examinations to become a doctoral candidate. He sat me down and proceeded to ask me a set of questions regarding Chicanos and the Catholic Church, which was the topic of my dissertation. I naively proceeded to enter into an impatient and cavalier dialogue with him about my work, unclear as to why we were having this conversation. Little did I know that Professor Samora was preparing me for my oral exam by peppering me with questions that he would proceed to ask in a formal setting in the presence of my committee. It goes without saying that I performed brilliantly and made all the members of my committee proud of me. I left that meeting extremely humbled and impressed by the deep, subtle wisdom of Julian Samora.

A more humorous and unorthodox story occurred at the same oral examination meeting. At this gathering were the members of my committee and a professor of psychology who served as the outside observer to regulate the quality and integrity of the oral examination process. How I remember this distinguished and accomplished middle-aged professor of psychology's look of shock when Professor Samora introduced him by telling me this professor was an outside observer. "Don't worry about him," he said openly. "His vote doesn't count." There was a real moment of disbelief from all of us except for Professor Samora, followed by feelings of affirmation within me that Don Julian was in charge and everything would be okay. This is how he took care of his students.

Even up to the last time I met with my esteemed mentor in Albuquerque, New Mexico, he never ceased to share with me his vast knowledge and resource base. As we sat in his daughter's living room, the signs of illness were apparent as he was losing control of his most basic motor skills. His determination was as strong as ever, and he asked if there was anything further he could do to support me. He wanted to affirm that I knew that he was available for anything I might need.

In retrospect, my relationship with Dr. Julian Samora was part of a legacy that spans the centuries with the encounters in the Americas between Indians and Spanish and between Mexicans and Anglos. This mestizo reality was embodied in the life and studies of Julian Samora. It culminated with his expansive career at the University of Notre Dame, from whence a beacon of justice emanated that attracted so many of us from all over the land. Many of us chose to follow this lighted path and embark on the journey that led us to his doorstep and into a relationship with a person who would leave us with the lesson of revelation that would transform our lives forever.

It is powerful to reflect that this lesson is at the core of Ethnic and Chicano Studies, since so much of the work in these emerging fields of study is challenging people to broaden their perspective to include the historical narratives of people and communities of color. The pedagogy of Ethnic and Chicano Studies is directly dependent on revelation, because it forces us to discover, through teaching and research, something that was previously unknown or hidden from us, a process that inevitably brings forth a new awareness and understanding.

This paradigm describes the true impact of Professor Julian Samora's mentoring. On behalf of every life you touched, Professor, I thank you for your example of courage, wisdom, and vision.

CHAPTER THIRTY

"Pues aquí me tienen"

Amelia M. Muñoz

"Pues aquí me tienen."[1] This was Dr. Samora's response when I asked him what he was doing sitting in the crowded office.[2] It was late August 1986 and I had just returned from volunteering with the Farm Labor Organizing Committee (FLOC)[3] in Toledo, Ohio. I spent the summer convincing farm workers to join the union and was excited to share the experience with my mentor, Dr. Samora. To my surprise I found him in a small library basement office, sitting on a stool and surrounded by unpacked boxes. Instead of rehashing the summer experience, I found myself unpacking boxes and hanging pictures. How could this be? Is this how we treat someone who helped numerous Latinos obtain doctorate degrees and in my case a bachelor's degree, the key to my future?

In September 1984, I knew my education at Notre Dame was underway only after a very uncertain start. My journey began in 1983 after I read Dr. Samora's book *The History of the Mexican American People*. It helped me realize that Mexican Americans were making history and if I could just study under Dr. Samora maybe I could help move our history forward. I was surprised when I learned that Notre Dame had accepted me. My surprise was not based on the fact that Notre Dame had a great football history or because of its Irish roots; I would learn of this reality only after I began my course of study. My surprise grew from knowing that I was going to be able to study under Dr. Samora! My only other concern was how to pay the tuition.

I was raised in a single-parent household in California, the eighth child of nine, in a family that worked in the fields as farm workers and followed seasonal work in the canneries. These facts helped me know that my family could not help finance my education. Fortunately, my employment at the U.S. Catholic Conference[4] afforded me the opportunity to meet a lifetime friend, Olga Villa Parra, the director of the Spanish-Speaking Catholic Commission. In our first conversation she asked me what I was going to do after my one-year employment contract was up at the conference. I had just finished reading Dr. Samora's book so I said, "I'm going to college to get my bachelor's degree." Her response was, "If you get into Notre Dame you can live with us." I did not think about our conversation until my acceptance letter arrived. Notre Dame accepted me with advanced standing as a transfer student into the College of Arts and Letters as a junior![5] How exciting. I was going to study under Dr. Samora, but how would I pay my tuition?

I applied for financial aid, but unfortunately I missed the deadline and as a transfer student the university decided they would not provide me with any assistance. My luggage was packed and I had a one-way ticket to South Bend when I received the notice that Notre Dame was not going to help me. My first reaction was panic, then disbelief, and then I noticed a phone number for financial aid. I thought if I explained my situation to them they would help me resolve my predicament. The receptionist transferred me to a priest who said, "If you don't have the money, don't come." With those words I saw my future disappearing. I did not have the courage to tell my family, so I first decided to call Olga to let her know I was not going. This was a blessing because as I read the letter to Olga, she said to me, "You can work, take out a loan, start at IUSB.[6] Don't worry we will figure it out. *Vente.*"[7]

One week later I arrived in South Bend, Indiana, with the belief that I was going to study under Dr. Samora, although I was not sure how. The next day I headed to the financial aid office and they refused to see me. I was told that the director was out of town and there was no one else who could see me. I felt the door slam in my face. What should I do? What next? They could not stop me from my future. I thought of Dr. Samora and went to see him, but unfortunately, he was not in his office. As I walked away from his door, I thought of other people I should talk to. My only concern was that since they didn't know me, why would they talk to me? I couldn't bear another negative experience, so I told people that I knew Dr. Samora and just as I had suspected they were very open and listened to my predicament.

Although I had not met Dr. Samora, I knew I had to see him, so after meeting with various people I headed back to his office. This time he was in. I quickly introduced myself and apologized profusely for having told others that I knew him and for using his name to get into the door. I explained what I had been through, and before I could finish Dr. Samora had pulled a slip out of his desk and offered to hire me as his receptionist. Furthermore, he called the financial aid office and asked if the director had any appointments available, and the next thing I knew Dr. Samora had scheduled me to see the financial aid director at 3 p.m. that very day. He also asked me to return to his office after the meeting to check on my progress. Just as I had suspected, I had an advocate in Dr. Samora.

Dr. Samora wanted to help me, but the Financial Aid office wanted nothing to do with me. They asked why I had come. The director told me he could not help me, but I refused to leave. As I sat there asking for help, he reluctantly put a hold on my account and said I could register while I continued to look for resources. The director stated, "If this is not resolved and if you don't come up with the money, you'll have to leave." At least I had hope. I could now register for classes. I joyfully headed back to Dr. Samora's office to update him on the situation. To add to my delight, Dr. Samora allowed me to register into his colloquium. I had no idea that the course was only for graduate students, but I was grateful because it was the only course he was teaching that semester. I was pleased that my reason for entering Notre Dame had finally come to fruition.

Dr. Samora hired me as his receptionist through the work-study program, but now I needed to come up with the rest of my tuition. Since I had worked at the U.S. Catholic Conference, I decided to write to every bishop I knew requesting their assistance. What could I lose? I needed to come up with approximately ten thousand dollars. Fortunately, donations began to come in, with twenty-five to five hundred dollar checks in each letter. I deposited those checks at the bursar's office, but I had a long way to go to reach my goal.

In addition to my letter-writing campaign, I continued to meet and talk with anyone who would listen to my plight. The associate director of the Center for Social Concerns, Mary Ann Roemer, listened to my troubles and advised me to write a letter to Father Hesburgh. I was not sure how this letter would help resolve the situation, but what did I have to lose? I wrote the letter and delivered it within the hour. Three days later I had an appointment with the vice president of the university, Fr. Beauchamp, who was kind and asked me what I was doing to raise the money. I showed him copies of the checks from various bishops across the United States. I think he was surprised to see that I was chipping away at my goal and that numerous bishops had responded to my plea. Father gave me hope. He asked me to continue in my money-raising campaign and promised to do what he could to help me. Once again there were no absolute promises, but I had permission to start classes, and if in thirty days we had not come up with the money I would have to withdraw from the university.

I entered my first class, which was held in the La Fortune Center's little theater. I chose a seat three rows back so I could absorb the full experience. Students began to arrive and then the professor entered. I was ecstatic. Did these students realize how blessed they were to be studying at this university? I furiously took notes on everything said so I would not miss a word. Would I be here in thirty days? It didn't matter because I was here now.

Checks for my tuition continued to arrive, and on day twenty-nine of my thirty-day deadline, I received a financial aid award letter. In addition to the donations I had received, work-study, loans, grants, and scholarships completed my tuition. I was officially a student, but most importantly I was a student in Dr. Samora's class and enjoying the opportunity to work even closer with him as his receptionist. At the time, I could not know how fortunate I was. In January 1985, at the end of the semester, Dr. Samora suffered a heart attack and never taught another class.

My job as the Mexican American Graduate Studies receptionist continued until my graduation in 1986 and kept me going because I could talk and continue to learn from Dr. Samora. Mostly I answered the phone, took messages for Dr. Samora, and discussed my classes with him. However, I did help process his notes from a research trip he took in the summer of 1985 to the *Archivo General de las Indias* in Spain as part of a project to research the history of the Archuletas, his deceased wife's family.

I thoroughly enjoyed my experience as Dr. Samora's receptionist, although it made me a witness to the dismantling of the Mexican American Graduate Studies Program. I recall the day in the spring of 1986 that I found Dr. Samora posting notes on the various shelves of books located in his office. These, he stated, were tagged to be donated to the University of Texas at Austin. When I asked him why there, he simply said, "Notre Dame does not want them." I knew by his response that he was not happy with the situation, but this was the best offer he had. On the day scheduled for the books to be picked up, Dr. Samora asked me to wait for the movers and then he left. It was a sad day as I watched them take away years of history and information about Mexican Americans. Would they cherish them as much as we did? Most important, who would be here to help future students navigate the cold halls of Notre Dame?

This last question was answered in the coming months when, upon my graduation from Notre Dame in May 1986, I left to volunteer with the Farm Labor Organizing Committee. FLOC had won a major victory when they signed a three-way contract with Campbell Soup and growers in Ohio and Michigan. The contract gave the workers the right to be represented by FLOC; all they needed was a majority of the workers to sign on with the union. Notre Dame students had supported a campus-wide boycott of Campbell products and FLOC was now asking for help from those same students to organize farm workers. This was my chance to begin giving back to my personal community: people who had believed in me, people who sent me financial resources, and people who, like me, were seeking a better way of life.

The summer of 1986 was long, hot, challenging, and fruitful. We managed to sign enough workers to have the union represent workers throughout Toledo and its surrounding counties. I had taken enough money with me to purchase a ticket home to California, but before the summer was over every last dime was used to purchase medicine, school supplies, and from time to time shoes for migrant children. Thus my plan to head home to California meant hitching a ride back to South Bend, where I had friends who could help me earn money to get home.

Coincidentally, my time in South Bend also gave me the opportunity to check in with my professor, mentor, and friend, Dr. Samora. To my dismay his office had been moved from the upper floors of the University Library to the basement, allegedly part of a library building renovation. It was a maze, but I found Dr. Samora . . . a resigned person. As I reflect on the experience, I wonder if Dr. Samora had encountered the same unwelcome messages and discouragement from the university that I had found. "Pues aquí me tienen." Whether he had been subjected to Notre Dame's ambivalence early in his tenure at Notre Dame or not, he certainly was experiencing it in his retirement.

I had planned a short stay in South Bend, Indiana, that summer with just enough time to earn the resources to purchase a ticket home. Fortunately, I found another way to serve my community while at the same time continuing my conversations with Dr. Samora.

Unexpectedly, I was offered a job with the South Bend Community School Corporation's Bilingual Education Department. The director, Maritza Robles, made me an offer that I could not refuse. The reality was that I had no other offer, so I agreed to work through the end of December. My new employment opened a path that allowed me to affect the lives of many young Mexican American students positively. I began advising and assisting bilingual high school students about the college admissions and financial aid process. When December 1986 arrived, I could not leave because these students were only beginning the process of admission to higher education. Who would be there to help them complete their financial aid forms? Who would be there to assist the next generation of Mexican American students?

In fact, returning to South Bend was a blessing in disguise for me; my living there provided the opportunity to spend time with Dr. Samora. He was no longer active at the university. My relationship with Dr. Samora, of course, changed during this time. As his illness weakened him, I became more of a friend and care provider and he relied on me for social outings. As he grew progressively sicker, I visited with him at his home on Cowles Avenue, a wonderful home with many framed awards and honors that I would not have known about had I not visited with him there.

Dr. Samora still grew those sour grapes,[8] which he insisted that I take in full bags each time I visited, although I threw them away without his knowledge. I was just lucky that I could spend time talking with him! We often went to the movies. I drove and a couple of times on our return to the house Geoff, his son, was there worried, concerned about where his father was. I think Dr. Samora was supposed to let him know where he was going, but he purposely would not. I suppose it was difficult for Dr. Samora to surrender his independence. On another occasion, I invited Dr. Samora to my annual Christmas Eve open house in 1992, and Geoff was delayed in picking him up. Dr. Samora called us and asked that we pick him up and of course we did. Geoff called us, very upset, because he could not find his father.

Dr. Samora blazed a trail for countless students to earn undergraduate and graduate degrees. It is now time for those of us who have benefited from his advocacy to hear the call and follow in his footsteps. So as Dr. Samora stated in that tiny basement office, "Pues aquí me tienen," here I am doing my part to improve the lives of Mexican Americans, Chicanos/as, women, and other minorities who need an advocate and mentor. . . . Pues aquí me tienen.

Notes

1. Editors' translation: "Well, here they have me."

2. The university relegated some retired faculty members to these small offices in the basement of the Hesburgh Library. Dr. Samora had occupied rather sumptuous quarters on the eleventh floor of the library.

3. FLOC was founded in 1967 by Baldemar Velasquez in Toledo, Ohio, as an advocacy organization representing farm labor in the East. It is a social movement as well as a labor organization.

4. Ms. Muñoz worked for the U.S. Catholic Conference on a one-year contract as the national Hispanic youth and young adult coordinator in Washington, D.C.

5. Ms. Muñoz received an associate's degree in 1971 from Chabot Community College in Hayward, California, with the career goal of becoming a dentist.

6. Indiana University at South Bend.

7. Just come.

8. Samora's property included a large grape arbor where he grew Concord grapes, a juice grape not well-suited to eating out of hand.

Appendix:
Seventh Annual Ernesto Galarza
Commemorative Lecture 1992
Mestizaje: The Formation of Chicanos

Ernesto Galarza In Memoriam 1905–1984

Presented by Julian Samora, Professor Emeritus,
University of Notre Dame

This lecture was named in honor of Dr. Ernesto Galarza, a Stanford alumnus, intellectual, visionary, and activist scholar who galvanized national attention on the plight of farm workers in the 1940s and 1950s and later focused on urban institutions that impeded the health, educational, and socio-economic development of Chicana/os in the United States. The legacy of his contributions to civil rights include the founding of the Mexican American Legal Defense and Educational Fund (MALDEF) and the National Council of La Raza (NCLR). A few years before his death, Dr. Galarza donated all of his files to Stanford. Several renowned scholars conduct research based on his materials in the special collections archives at Stanford University's Green Library.

Mestizaje: The Formation of Chicanos

Julian Samora

Let me begin by stating that I am very happy that the Stanford Center for Chicano Research established the Galarza Lectures and I am particularly happy to have been chosen to present the lecture this year.

Dr. Ernesto Galarza was a great person. I first met him and his wife Mae in 1964. I had known about him before and had read about his work with the Bracero Program, which was instituted as an emergency war program by our government. The war ended in 1945 yet the Bracero Program continued until 1964! Dr. Galarza was quite instrumental in ending the program. When Ernie and I were working together in the late 1960s and early 1970s he told me two things that have stayed with me. The first thing is that I should never pursue power and the second thing was that it is important to organize people, two very important principles that I assume guided his life. At one time we were writing a book on the reassessment of the role of the Texas Rangers in today's society and I couldn't come up with an appropriate title for the work. I asked Ernie for a suggestion and two weeks later he sent me a title. It was *Gunpowder Justice*, the title by which the book is known today.

The topic for this lecture is intermarriage or intermating. Let me tell you something that everyone knows: Chicanos are mestizos, and the arrival of the European male who mated (legally or illegally) with the indigenous females became the basis for the formation of the Chicano in this country. Our ancestry is mostly European and Native American. Very few scholars have dealt with this phenomenon in the United States. Only three come to mind. Dr. Forbes—a professor at the University of California, Davis is one of them. He wrote a book in 1973 called *Aztecas Del Norte: The Chicanos of Aztlán*. In this book Forbes discusses *mestizaje* and describes this phenomenon, claiming that in order to be mestizo the group must be an outcast.

According to Forbes, "*Mestizo* and such comparable terms imply outcast (i.e. belonging to no ethnic group or *casta*). *People who possess a national or ethnic identity, no matter how much they have mixed historically with other peoples, can never be mestizo*" (Forbes 1973, 185). Thus the Spanish and the Irish, although thoroughly mixed, are not mestizos. In his more recent writings, Dr. Forbes hasn't really changed his definition of mestizo too much. On pages eight and nine of his new work he says, "*Individuos que poseen una identidad nacional o étnica, no importa tan mesclados estén históricamente con otras gentes, nunca podrán ser mestizos.*" (Forbes' italics) Another person who has written about *mestizaje* is James Diego Vigil in his book *From Indians to Chicanos: The Dynamics of Mexican American Culture* (1984).

For many years I have been interested in the formation of the Chicano people. It has been noted that the Chicano, while closely resembling the Native American, is Spanish or Mexican in culture, speaks Spanish generally, is nominally Catholic in religion, and does not wish to be identified as Indian, nor does he wish to discuss his obvious "Indian-ness." The Native American of New Mexico, who may have been baptized in the Catholic religion and may bear a Spanish surname, does not emphasize his "Spanish-ness" or "Mexican-ness." Although related genetically it appears that both prefer not to acknowledge the relationship.

This is an issue of identity. In truth, the Chicano people should identify with the Mexican culture rather than the Spanish culture. Yet this has not always proven the case since in our society the dominant group has usually abhorred Mexican things (Robinson 1969, passim; North 1948: foreword and chapter 1; Rios-Bustamante and P. Castillo 1985, 51). For example, when I was a child, growing up in Colorado, in Spanish we called ourselves "*nosotros los Mejicanos.*" In English we were "Spanish Americans" because if we labeled ourselves "Mexican" it would be like Negroes calling themselves "niggers."

Fray Virgilio Elizondo, a Catholic priest who has written extensively on the Chicano community, recounts personal experiences while growing up in a segregated Texas: "I remember very well one of the old grandmothers whose ancestors had always lived in the San Antonio, Texas area telling us: 'When the Spaniards arrived hundreds of years ago, we welcomed them and taught them how to survive in these hostile lands, and pretty soon they dispossessed us. Then came the Anglo immigrants from the United States, and the same thing happened. We don't know what country will be coming through here next, but we will still be here!'"

In another instance illustrating the prejudice against those of Mexican heritage he says: "When the Mexican soccer team came to San Antonio and beat the American team, there was great joy, pride and jubilation, as if Mexico had conquered the United States. But walking around the downtown area of San Antonio every day brought some new experiences. I started to discover blacks. Before, I had never even known about their existence. Those were still the days of segregation when blacks had to sit in special 'colored' balconies in theatres, attend black churches, sit in the back of public buses, and use separate toilets in public places.

"Indeed many of my school friends had darker skin than myself and I remember well the problems we experienced just trying to go to the toilet. If we went into one marked 'colored' we were chased out by the blacks because we were not technically black. Yet, we were often chased out from the ones marked 'white' because we had dark skin. So we didn't even have toilets to which we could go. Our being was actually our 'non-being.' This consciousness of 'non-being' would deepen and broaden as I gradually moved from a very secure experience of being to one of non-being, to one of new being" (Elizondo 1988, 18).

The following must be said several times because it is not understood: In many towns in Colorado, Mexicanos had to sit on the right or left side in movies and churches and in many schools we had to go to the "Mexican" room because ours was a Spanish surname. The idea was that by separating Spanish-speaking children, they would thereby learn English sooner and better! Yet some children with Spanish surnames did not know Spanish, only English!

The research for my lecture was undertaken generally as a genealogy trying to trace four families from the 1500s to the present time. The families were: Samora, Archuleta, Trujillo, and Medina. After considerable research and using the *Catalogo de Pasajeros a Indias en los Siglos XVI, XVII, y XVIII* [a catalog of passengers to the Indies in the sixteenth, seventeenth, and eighteenth century], it was discovered that many of the surnames did not correspond to alleged established ways of naming a person. According to scholars (Peter Boyd-Bowman, Modern Languages & Literatures, University of Buffalo/SUNY and David Ringrose, History, University of California, San Diego), during the sixteenth and seventeenth centuries parents were free to chose any surname for their child—their own surname, that of a relative, or that of an unrelated person. Because of this practice, genealogical records in Spain tend to be chaotic, and social historians have not attempted family reconstruction studies in that country.

Having spent several years doing genealogical research, I turned to another topic that has been of great interest to me, namely, the racial intermixture between the population from Spain and the indigenous population of the New World in the United States.

The term *casta,* meaning "caste," will be used since it was used by the Spaniards between the sixteenth and nineteenth centuries to denote ethnic categories throughout the New World. The term caste is more formal and connotes a more traditional social system and a categorization of class. Although in colonial New Mexico the caste system was supposed to be rigid, as it was in Spain, the system broke down because of acculturation and other mitigating circumstances (Bustamante 1991, 144). While the New World government and church attempted to implement a system to keep elements of a polyethnic society identified and stratified so that the mixed offspring of the Spanish, Indians, and blacks could be kept in socially subordinate positions, such a system did not work most of the time because Spain also required that individuals speak Spanish, become Catholic, obey the law, etc. (ibid.). The ultimate category was Spanish or white. The range was from white (top) to black (bottom). The laws of biological mixing being what they are, many persons became lighter and were able to pass for white since appearance was what counted. Thus the *casta*-categorizing nomenclature became muddled and useless (not unlike the Census Bureau's term "race" in the United States at the present time). Table 1, Ethnic Mixture of Castas, adapted from Dr. Adrian Bustamante's latest article, is self-explanatory (Bustamante 1991, 44).

In New Mexico, the term *coyote* became a generalized term meaning a mixture of white with Indian or mestizo. In Colorado, during my lifetime, the term *coyote* usually referred to a mixture of white or American with Chicano or Mexican.

Table 1. *Ethnic Mixture of Castas*

1. Español × India = Mestizo (NM)
2. Español × Mestiza = Castiza (NM)
3. Español × Castiza = Torna a Espanol
4. Español × Negra = Mulato (NM)
5. Español × Mulata = Morisco
6. Morisco × Española = Albino
7. Albino × Española = Tornaatras
8. Mulato × India = Calpamulato
9. Calpamulato × India = Jívaro
10. Negro × India = Lobo (NM)
11. Lobo × India = Cambuja
12. Indio × Cambuja = Sambahija
13. Mulato × Mestiza = Cuateron
14. Cuaterón × Mestiza = Coyote (According to Census report, in New Mexico the term "coyote" included the mixture of Mestizo and Indian and that of Spanish and Indian).
15. Coyote × Morisca = Albarazado
16. Albarazado × Saltaatras = Tente en el aire
17. Mestizo × India = Cholo
18. Mulato × India = Chino
19. Español × China = Cuaterón de Chino
20. Negro × India = Sambo de Indio
21. Negro × Mulata = Zambo
22. Cambujo × China = Genízaro (in New Mexico, the Genízaro had a somewhat different meaning -/Swadish detribalized Indian/.)

Note: Composite List from Nicolás de León, *Las Castas del Mexico Colonial o Nuevo España* (Mexico: Talleres Gráficos del Museo Nacional de Arqueología, Historia, y Etnografía. 1924).

Geographical Area

The geographical area to be covered will be New Spain of the seventeenth, eighteenth, and nineteenth centuries, which will include primarily Mexico and the area north of El Paso del Norte. We will be concerned with Mexico and its conquests only briefly since the main emphasis will be colonial New Mexico and the territorial New Mexico after the conquest of the area by the United States of America in 1846. The territorial area actually included most of present-day Arizona, all of present-day New Mexico, and parts of present-day Texas, Colorado, and California.

In his writings of New Mexico, Fray Angélico Chávez says that neither Spain nor Mexico had ever drawn definite boundary lines away from the settled parts. For two and a half centuries, New Mexico had consisted of the undefined populated in the north Rio Grande watershed consisting of Hispanic and Pueblo Indian people. He divides the geography into different periods. During the first century, 1598–1680, the area was sparsely settled and El Reino de la Nueva Mexico had only one town, her capital, Santa Fe, with a barrio, Analco, for some Indian servants. North of Santa Fe were a small cluster of Spanish homesteads, La Cañada, or present-day Santa Cruz. South there were other homesteads of Los Cerrillos and along the Camino Real [royal road] near present-day La Cienega. Further south in what became El Rio Abajo, other clusters of homestead were in Angostura, Bernalillo, present-day Albuquerque, Tomé, La Joya, Alamillo, and Socorro. Besides these regular homesteads, then called *estancias,* there were far-flung Pueblo Indian missions. At the major ones there would be soldiers with their families, helping to protect the missionaries and their charges.

When the Pueblo Revolt of 1680 broke out, these Spaniards and twenty-one Franciscan priests were massacred. Some young females were kept as captives. Thirteen years later, they, along with their mestizo children, were rescued when Don Diego de Vargas brought back most of the original colonists from El Paso del Norte, where they had fled during the Pueblo Revolt of 1680. A new colony of *Españoles-Mexicanos* (Spaniards from the city and valley of Mexico) arrived in Santa Fe in the spring of 1694 and Governor Vargas founded the Villa of Santa Cruz in 1696. The following year brought another sizeable colony from Zacatecas (Spaniards again but with several mestizo families among them). (Chávez 1982, xvi–xviii).

In 1706 New Mexico's third Spanish villa, Albuquerque, was founded. Colonists settled along the Rio Grande as far south as Tomé but were stopped here by Apaches and some Navajos who ruled the land as far south as El Paso del Norte. North of Santa Fe, colonists spread from Santa Cruz, northeast into Chimayó and up the Rio Grande as far as Velarde. In the meantime the Franciscan priests had restarted their missions in all the major Indian pueblos. Following the Vargas resettlement (1693), the Spanish starting buying (or ransoming) women and children captives from the Comanche and Plains Indians. Others were captured by the Spanish militia.

The offspring of these mixed nomadic tribes were then designated as *genízaro.* They had Spanish names and a Spanish upbringing. Some of these offspring remained as servants, but the majority remained homeless and landless and settled in Abiquiú near Tomé and in Los Jarales near Belen. Those in Santa Fe inhabited the barrio of Analco.

Before the mid-1700s Spanish people from the Santa Cruz–Santa Clara valley had begun settling Abiquiu as well as Ojo Caliente and the Taos valley. But these later settlements were wiped out by the northern Utes and Apaches. New Mexico, a "kingdom" since 1610 then later demoted to one of New Spain's "internal provinces" in the 1760s, was still confined to the settled Latino and Pueblo Indian area of the upper Rio Grande Basin. Its inhabited area was somewhat smaller than in the previous century, but the population itself had become more concentrated, although new towns had sprung up. Other settlers ventured westward into the Jemez region and present-day Cuba (Chavez 1982, xx–xxiii).

In the third century a number of changes took place after 1800. A major expansion started with the establishment of a Spanish fort and *genízaro* settlements at San Miguel del Vado on the upper Pecos River east of the great sierra. The *genízaros* came from the Santa Fe barrio of Analco.

The landless Latinos began many towns along the Pecos River, from Pecos itself downriver to Antonchico, with a southeast thrust to present-day Las Vegas. Up in the Taos valley a new town of Don Fernando de Taos was born, followed by a number of villages in the area. The Mora valley east of the great sierra was settled as well as Socorro to the south of Tome-Belen and Cebolleta and San Rafael.

Thus when the United States conquered the territory in 1846, New Mexico did not have sharply mapped borders. Some New Mexico families unwilling to live under United States jurisdiction founded the town of Mesilla and the neighboring towns of Las Cruces and Doña Ana, all in the fertile area north of El Paso, Texas. Soon, however, the Gadsden Purchase put them all back in the United States! (Chavez 1982, xxiii–xxv).

In order to explain the phenomenon of how the conquered people really absorbed the conquerors, one needs to understand a few historical occurrences. The papal bull of 1537, *Sublimas Deus,* declared that the Indians were human beings capable of salvation. This meant that the Spaniards had, most importantly, to save souls. As badly as the indigenous population was treated and exploited, their souls still had to be saved. This was in contrast to the Protestant colonizers, who exterminated the Indian or pushed him off onto a reservation. The Spanish baptized the native, permitted him to enter his households as servant or slave, and allowed intermarriage. One must remember that in the Europe of that time slavery was common, and we cannot judge them by today's standards.

The Spanish society in the New World was not as rigid and absolute as it was in the Old World. It was more open. A number of factors contributed to this: (1) few Spanish females came in the early period of conquest; (2) Indian women were given to the conquerors by the Indian *caciques* in Mexico; (3) land was available; (4) slaves and servants were available; (5) the openness of the class structure permitted Indians and persons of mixed parentage to "pass" for Spanish; and (6) the institution of marriage enabled Indians and persons of mixed parentage to marry into the dominant class.

Although the institution of slavery was prohibited by the New Laws of 1542, the Crown expected tribute from the indigenous population as well as from whatever wealth the conqueror came upon. Thus, in collecting tributes, the Crown tacitly encouraged slavery since about the only way to pay tribute was by having slaves and working them hard. A market for selling Indian captives to the Spanish was thus created. An owner of a ransomed Indian had the obligation of Hispanicizing and Christianizing him. If the Spanish refused to buy him from other Indians offering tribute, the captive might possibly be beheaded or threatened with death, and some Spaniards usually bought him. The concept of a "just war" against non-Christian Indians or against Indians who had taken up arms against Spain produced many captives (Tyler 1988, 214–17).

Weber says: "Scholars in United States history have been writing on immigrant groups for more than a century. . . . Ironically the oldest immigrant people, the descendants of Spaniards and Indians, received almost no scholarly attention until the 1960s. Up to that time, no historian had written a book about the Mexicans and their descendants, and just a handful of sociologists had taken note of them. Yet the six million Mexican Americans comprise the second largest ethnic minority in the United States today: in the Southwest, no minority group surpasses them in numbers" (Weber 1987, vii).

He reiterates: "If there was little love lost between Indians and Mexicans in the Southwest in general, there was, nevertheless, a good deal of intermixture between individuals of both groups. This continuing process of racial mixture produced a racial and cultural blending in Mexico and the Southwest. . . . Racial mixture is also one of the salient features of Chicano ethnicity, for most Mexican Americans remain highly visible. Once a source of shame, even in Mexico, Indian ancestry and dark skin color have become a source of pride for Chicanos who identify themselves as belonging to La Raza de Bronce—the Bronze race" (Weber 1987, 5).

Weber continues with this theme: "Chicanos reject the necessity for Americanization and argue that a unique culture already exists in the Southwest which is neither totally American nor totally Mexican. The culture requires its own name if it is to find its identity. Chicano, judging from its widespread popularity, serves that purpose well. Much energy has been expended in the search for the etymology of Chicano, while the real meaning of the word has been often overlooked. (Ruben Salazar, a talented reporter for the *Los Angeles Times,* put it best a few months before his tragic death in August 1970: "'A Chicano,'" he wrote, "'is a Mexican-American with a non-Anglo image of himself'" (Weber 1987, 9).

Regarding the Spanish and Mexican character Weber writes: "Some Spaniards were cruel, indolent, treasure-hungry adventurers. So, too, were some Englishmen" (Weber 1987, 69). An historian of the Texas Rangers says about Mexicans: "Without disparagement it may be said there is a cruel streak in the Mexican nature, or so the history of Texas would lead one to believe. This cruelty may be a heritage from the Spanish Inquisition; it may, and doubtless should be, attributed partly to the Indian blood" (Webb 1965, 114).

Weber continues: "The new wave of Mexican immigration, then, resulted in a schism in the Spanish-speaking community in the Southwest which was evident by 1910 and remains to the present day. By the 1920s if not earlier, older residents of New Mexico began to refer to themselves as "Spanish Americans or *Spanish Colonials,* in order to disassociate themselves with the opprobrious term *Mexican.* The same process occurred in California, Arizona, and in Texas, where older residents came to prefer the term *Latin American.* Frequently accompanying this change in name was the self-delusion that the older Mexican residents of the Southwest were of 'pure' Spanish blood and racially superior to Mexicans. This attitude of superiority antagonized Mexican immigrants, of course, occasionally leading to friction between the two groups" (Weber 1987, 224).

"The Anglo newcomers also frequently married women of Mexican descent, thus lessening the social distance between ethnic groups. Contrary to popular stereotypes about Mexican docility and cowardice, Mexican American fighters served with distinction, as Anglo and *Hispano* fought together against the common enemy" (Weber 1987, 241).

Again he says: "The recognition of the role that colonial Mexicans—that is, the role that persons of mixed-blood—played in settling Borderlands and especially California does not reject the essential part that Spaniards performed in the exploration, colonization, and missionization of the Southwest. Spanish *peninsulares* overwhelmingly were the *adelantados,* the officials, and the priests who explored, governed, and served settlers" (Weber 1979, 119).

Weber proceeds: "Most of those baptized were registered as *Spaniards,* followed in order of importance by the *Mestizo;* but a scholar has to be gullible to accept such racial classifications without reservations. In many cases it was possible to verify that children of the same parents were registered as belonging to different, and sometimes surprisingly clashing, racial groups. These errors were partly due to the ignorance of the local parish priests or to the absence of rules for such classification, but mainly the responsibility for such 'mistakes' is the outcome of *racial prejudice,* whose pressure to attain the 'whitening of the skin' was so strong that it sensitized the parish registrars or misled them, as when they recorded as *Mestizo* the offspring of Spaniard and mulatto interracial marriages" (Weber 1979, 153).

Again: "Many of the so-called Spaniards who arrived in Alta, California, beginning in 1769, were of mixed ethnic and racial backgrounds. But as *gente de razón,* or people of reason, they considered themselves distinct from and superior to both the unconverted and Christian Indians" (Weber 1979, 262).

Weber continues: "White people, that is European or American Spaniards, were the most numerous in Texas, followed in importance by the Indians, the castes known as *color quebrado* (brittle or frail color), which included the *mestizos, coyotes, mulattoes,* and *lobos,* and finally the Negroes. . . . It is known, however, that many of these soldiers of the Spanish garrisons were *mestizos,* and some were even *mulattoes,* a fact rejected by the census report, which enrolled all military personnel as 'Spaniards'" (Weber 1979, 157).

As a result of the European conquest of the New World, one can say then that an interracial mixture had taken place to such an extent that the Spanish conquerors, in a real sense, became the conquered[1] and in many instances—the two populations shared the same genetic pool.

Given my interest in our shared history, a few years ago I wrote an introduction to a work by E. Galarza, H. Gallegos, and myself in which I say about the Spanish *conquistadores:* "Racism was not one of their contributions to this land" (Galarza, Gallegos, and Samora 1969, viii). After further research, I wish to retract that statement, because racism did begin with the Europeans and it spread wherever they went.

When the Spaniards set out to conquer and colonize the "New World" in the early 1500s, they brought few women with them, and time after time Indian chiefs in Mexico presented the Spanish *conquistadores* with Indian maidens in order to bring the two populations together legitimately through a process of intermating called *mestizaje.* This process produced mestizo or mixed-blood offspring throughout Mexico and Central and South America.

Bernal Díaz del Castillo, one of the conquistadors who accompanied Hernán Cortéz, who wrote *La Verdadera Historia de la Conquista de Nueva España,* because he thought the official chroniclers and historians had not done justice to the conquest, documents a number of instances in which Indian females and Spanish males marry or where the Spaniards are given Indian females by the Indian chiefs, etc. This began the gradual process of *mestizaje* in the Western Hemisphere (Díaz del Castillo 1956, 59, 69, 73, 76–77, 95–96, 101, 145, 147, 232, 238). "*Mestizaje*" is a perfectly good word in Spanish, but in English it unfortunately comes out as "mixed blood" or "half-breed" with a moral and pejorative twist, which gives it a bad connotation.

In what became New Spain, colonial New Mexico, or the present-day American Southwest, the situation was complicated somewhat because many of the colonizers were not Spanish, some were Indians and some were mestizo from Mexico. The first colonists into present-day New Mexico came with a very rich miner, Don Juan de Oñate, in 1598, from Zacatecas, Mexico. Oñate himself was married to a mestiza. Upon reaching the Española Valley (north of present-day Santa Fe) he occupied the Indian pueblo of Okeh which he renamed San Juan de los Caballeros to honor his troops. Soon the Spaniards settled in the pueblo of Yuquequnque and renamed the pueblo San Gabriel.

"Oñate brought with him 130 soldiers, many of whom traveled from Mexico with their wives and Indian servants. It is likely that Mexican Americans, both servants and soldiers, outnumbered the Spaniards. In 1610, when the capital villa of Santa Fe was built as the main population nucleus of the colony, a special barrio (district) was set aside for these Indian colonists, who were referred to as Tlaxcalan" (Swadesh 1974, 12).

It is not too difficult to document the intermixture that has taken place throughout this period: "Finding thirty Spaniards at Culeacan living with Indian women, Coronado, seconded by Fray Marcos, required them to be married in *facie ecclesia* and thus legitimized a goodly infusion of Indian blood into the pioneer stock of that frontier" (Bolton 1949, 3).

Again Bolton says, "Their (Indians') daughters were pleasing, so there were many thousands of 'Pocahonteses' in America long before the days of John Smith of Jamestown" (Bolton 1949, 3).

Elizondo's definition of *mestizaje* is more acceptable to me than many of the others because to him it is a process of the blending of the biological and the cultural aspects. To Rios-Bustamante and Castillo it is a fact. To Forbes it is something else.

The myth of the Spanish origin and settlement was quickly acceptable to most United States citizens since the writing about and the criticism of things Mexican was so widespread. Knowledge about things Spanish, Mexican, and Hispanic is just now beginning to spread. To be sure, the settlement of the U.S. early on was Spanish in a governmental sense. But the people were not Spanish.

The settlers of Santa Fe and Los Angeles were mostly Mexican, Indian, or mestizos. But they worked under the Spanish government. I believe this is where the confusion lies. Also, the U.S. *Mexicano* needed to be accepted as an individual. Since most U.S. citizens thought that being *Spanish* rather than *Mexican* was okay, the Chicanos in various parts of the country took up the less offensive label of *Spanish* for identity purposes while speaking English. Just as when the U.S. Census Bureau categorized him a Caucasian or white, the Chicano took such a label to heart because of the consequences relating to discrimination in education, employment, public accommodations, jury service, etc.

Most Chicanos that I know prefer the label *Latino* to *Hispanic* when such a broad term has to be used, but we will see what happens over the years. The myths of the use of the term *Spanish* developed by McWilliams and later presented by Weber, are very significant due to the widespread discrimination that occurred in all fields. It is difficult for a people to identify with something considered undesirable.

Now, let me give you a little history of myself to help illustrate the process of *mestizaje*. When I retired at the University of Notre Dame at age sixty-five, my graduate students gave me a surprise by holding a symposium in which they presented papers in my honor, etc. The president of the university, Reverend Theodore M. Hesburgh, who spoke at one of the lunches, said that he had never seen anything like this before in his years as a faculty member and administrator. I had not either in my forty-some years of teaching.

The symposium lasted about three days. The wire service picked it up and a person unknown to me wrote from Kansas City to ask if I was the Julian Samora who was born in Pagosa Springs, Colorado, some time back. She had been married to a Navajo and had two sons by him before he died.

Elise Harris also wrote that her maiden name was *Sánchez Espinosa* and perhaps we were related. Elise was now married to Lloyd B. Harris who left Pagosa in 1920 to go to law school in Kansas. His brother, Fred Harris, was my father. Therefore, her husband Lloyd and she were my uncle and aunt. She had read about my retirement in the *Kansas City Star*.

We started a lively correspondence, which goes on today. My uncle Lloyd passed away in January 1990 at age eighty-nine. My father died in Boulder, Colorado, at age sixty-five. My mother passed away in Pagosa Springs of breast cancer at about the age of forty-one.

My mother and father were never married. Why not? I do not know! I never asked! My paternal grandfather, Charles E. Harris, and his wife or my grandmother, Deluvina Gallegos Harris, used to come visit us in the winter on a sled pulled by a team of workhorses. They would stay a week or more and bring meat and vegetables. He spoke English and Spanish; she, as I remember, spoke only Spanish. They were both born and baptized in Saguache, Colorado, and were also married there by Reverend A. Brucker, S.J. in the Catholic Church on February 8, 1890. They moved to Pagosa Springs later.

My great-grandfather, Edward Russell Harris, was born in Massachusetts about 1830. His wife was Juana Jaquez from New Mexico. He was a carpenter according to the 1880 U.S. Census. His father and grandfather were also born in Massachusetts. Thus on my father's side we are of Irish, French, and Mexican heritage, but there must also be some kind of American Indian and some black heritage. Thus the Harris name seems to be legitimate. When my wife and I were in Sevilla, Spain, I looked in the *Passengers to the Indies in the 16th, 17th, and 18th Centuries* under *Jerez* as so often happens in the U.S., but to no avail. Thus *mestizaje* has occurred to a great extent in my own background and I suspect in the backgrounds of all peoples throughout the world.

Elise's son at SUNY in Buffalo has done some genealogical research on his own and has found that his father, Fred Woodson, was a Navajo Indian who was bought at age ten by James Woodson. His father was Navajo and Spanish on the maternal side. He traced his mother's (Elise's) genealogy to her great-grandfather, José Ramon Sánchez in *El Rito* of Rio Arriba County in New Mexico. Some of the records were lost at about this time.

I have mentioned that persons of certain ethnic groups tended to marry each other. However, there was also a certain amount of exogamy as Fray Angelico Chavez indicates in his eleven-volume work on the prenuptial investigations, which the Catholic Church conducts for every couple wanting to marry.

Fray Angelico speaks of the nature of the population in New Mexico in the first, second, and third centuries of colonization and ends his general introduction with the following paragraph:

"In substance, Hispanic New Mexico, along with her *genizaros* now having some Spanish Blood together with their likewise acquired Spanish customs, preserved her own identity both in blood and culture for three full generations. The story is different in her Fourth One (our own 20th century), what with the admixtures of race and culture which keep increasing all along" (Chávez 1982, vol. I, xxv).

I have attempted to show that the *mestizaje* that took place in colonial New Mexico was the beginning of the Chicano people or the Mexican

Americans. In addition, it is my belief that because of the early and continuing process of intermating, the identity of the people should be more with Mexico than with Spain.

It is difficult to prove any of this given the definitions of what a Spaniard was, or an Indian, or a mestizo. But it is clear to me that the formation of the Mexican and Chicano people was a direct result of the admixture of the whole (in this case the Spanish European), and the Indian peoples, in Mexico and what became the United States Southwest.

Notes

1. This does not mean that the Spanish were conquered politically; rather it means that the indigenous groups, through their women, absorbed the conquerors in many instances. Thus began the Chicano people or the Mexican Americans in the United States and the Mexicans in Mexico, who more often than not are a mixture of Indian or black and European people.

References

Boyd-Bowman, Peter. *Indice Geobiográfico de Cuarenta mil Pobladores Espanoles de América en el Siglo XVI, 1493–1539.* Mexico City: Editorial Jus. Academia Mexicana de Genealogia y Heráldica, a.c. 1968.

Bustamante, Adrian H. "The Matter Was Never Resolved: The *Casta* System in Colonial New Mexico, 1693–1823." *New Mexico Historical Review,* April 1991.

———. "*Los Hispanos:* Ethnicity and Social Change in New Mexico." Albuquerque, NM. Ph.D. Dissertation, University of New Mexico. 1982.

Bustamante, Charles J., and Patricia L. Bustamante. *The Mexican-American and the United States.* Mountain View, CA. PATTY LAR Publications. 1969.

Carlinsky, Dan. "Christopher Confusion: Much of What We Know about the Legendary Explorer Isn't True," *Modern Maturity.* Volume 35, Number 1, February-March, 1992.

Carver, Rebecca McDowell. *The Impact of Intimacy: Mexican-Anglo Intermarriage in New Mexico, 1821–1846.* Monograph Number 66. El Paso: The Texas Western Press. 1982.

Chavez, Fray Angelico. *New Mexico Roots.* L.T.D. Santa Fe, NM. 1982. 11 volumes.

Díaz del Castillo, Bernal. *Historia Verdadera de la Conquista de Nueva España.* Mexico: La Libreria de Manuel Porrue, S.A. 1956.

de la Garza, Rudolf, Z. Anthony Kruszewski, and Tomás A. Arciniega. "*Chicanos* and Native Americans: The Territorial Minorities." Englewood Cliffs, NJ. Prentice-Hall. 1973.

Elizondo, Virgilio. *Mestizaje: The Dialectic of Cultural Birth and the Gospel.* Volumes III. A Ph.D. Dissertation in Theology presented in Paris in June 1978 under the title: *Metissage, violence culturelle, annonce de l'evangile.* San Antonio: Mexican-American Cultural Center. 1978.

———. *Galilean Journey: The Mexican-American Promise.* Maryknoll: Orbis Books. 1983.

———. *The Future Is Mestizo.* Bloomington: Meyer-Stone Books. 1988.

Ellis, Richard N. *New Mexico Past and Present: A Historical Reader.* Albuquerque: University of New Mexico Press. 1971.

Foote, Timothy. "Columbus and the World He Left Behind." *Smithsonian,* Volume 22, Number 9. 1991.

Forbes, Jack D. *Apache, Navaho, and Spaniard.* Norman: University of Oklahoma Press. 1960.

———. *Warriors of the Colorado: The Yumas of the Quechan Nation and Their Neighbors.* Norman: University of Oklahoma Press. 1965.

———. *Mexican-Americans: A Handbook for Educators.* Berkeley: Far West Laboratory for Educational Research and Development. 1970.

———. *Aztecas Del Norte: The Chicanos of Aztlán.* Greenwich, CT: Fawcett Publications, Inc. 1973.

———. "El Concepto de Mestizo-Metis." Publication 81. *Novedades de Baja, California* (no date, about 1982).

Galarza, Ernesto, Herman Gallegos, and Julian Samora. *Mexican-Americans in the Southwest.* Santa Barbara: McNally and Loftin. 1969.

Galeano, Eduardo. *Memoria del Fuego: El Siglo del Viento.* Vol III. Mexico City: Siglo Vientiuno Editores, S.A. 1986.

———. *Memoria del Fuego: Las Casas y Las Mascaras.* Vol. II. Mexico City: Siglo Vientiuno Editores, S.A. 1984.

———. *Memoria del Fuego: Los Nacimientos.* Vol. 1. Mexico City: Siglo Vientiuno Editores, S.A. 1982.

Gates, Zethyl. *Mariano Medina: Colorado Mountain Man.* Boulder, CO: Johnson Publishing Company. 1981.

Griffith, Stephanie. "Area's Black Hispanics Torn Between 2 Cultures, Many Feel Peer Pressure, Tug of History." Washington, D.C. *Washington Post,* October 8 (no year).

Gutiérrez, Ramón A. *When Jesus Came, The Corn Women Went Away: Marriage, Sexuality and Power in New Mexico, 1500–1846.* Stanford, CA: Stanford University Press. 1991.

———. "Honor Ideology, Marriage Negotiation and Class-Gender Domination in New Mexico, 1690–1846," *Latin American Perspectives* 12 (1985): 81–104.

Horvath, Steven Michael, Jr. "The Social and Political Organization of the Genizaros of Plaza de Nuestra Senora de Los Dolores de Belen, New Mexico, 1740–1812." Ph.D. Dissertation, Brown University. 1979.

Jackson, Donald Dale. "The Countdown Begins for Columbus-Bashing," *Smithsonian,* Volume 22, Number 6. 1991.

Jones, Oakah L., Jr. *Los Paisanos: Spanish Settlers on the Northern Frontier of New Spain.* Norman: University of Oklahoma Press. 1979.

Las Casas, B. de. "Historia de las Indias." Mexico: Fondo de Cultura Economica. (c. 1951). 1559.

León, Nicolas. *Las Castas del Mexico Colonial o Nueva Espana.* Mexico: Talleres Gráficos del Museo Nacional de Arqueología, Historia, y Etnografía. 1924.

MacLeish, William H. "1492 America: The Land Columbus Never Saw," *Smithsonian,* Volume 22, Number 8. 1991.

McWilliams, Carey. *North from Mexico: The Spanish-Speaking People of the United States.* New York: J. B. Lippincott. 1949.

O'Cauley, Sr. Dn. Pedro Alonso. *A Description of the Kingdom of New Spain 1774.* Translated and edited by Sean Galvin. John Howell-Books. 1972.

Ríos-Bustamante, Antonio, and Pedro Castillo. *An Illustrated History of Mexican Los Angeles: 1781–1985.* Los Angeles: University of California Chicano Studies Research Center. Monograph No. 12.

Robinson, Cecil. *With the Ears of Strangers: The Mexican in American Literature.* Tucson: University of Arizona Press. 1969.

Rodríguez, Roberto. "The Columbus 1492–1992 Quincentennial Debate. Part I. African-American Scholars Respond." *Black Issues in Higher Education.* September 26, 1991. Fairfax, VA: Cox, Matthews & Associates, Inc. 1991.

———, "Part II. Quincentennial Debate. How Columbus' Voyages Changed the World." *Black Issues in Higher Education.* October 10, 1991. Fairfax, VA: Cox, Matthews & Associates, Inc. 1991.

Rosenbaum, Robert J. *Mexicano Resistance in the Southwest.* Austin: University of Texas Press. 1981.

Sanderlin, George (editor and translator). *Bartolomé de Las Casas: A Selection of His Writings.* New York: Alfred A. Knopf. 1971.

Senate Documents. Vol. 36,1 Nos. 426–452. Miscellaneous. 56th Congress. 1st Session. #3878. Document No. 426. 1899–1900. "Insurrection in New Mexico and California."

Servín, Manuel P. *The Mexican-Americans: An Awakening Minority.* Beverly Hills, CA: Glencoe Press. 1970.

Spicer, Edward H. *People of Pascua.* Edited by Kathleen M. Sands and Rosmand B. Spicer. Tucson: University of Arizona Press. 1988.

Stephens, Thomas M. *Dictionary of Latin American Racial and Ethnic Terminology.* Gainesville: University Press of Florida. 1990.

Swadesh, Frances Leon. *Los Primeros Pobladores: Hispanic Americans of the Ute Frontier.* Notre Dame, IN: University of Notre Dame Press. 1974.

Tyier, Lyman S. *Two Worlds: The Indian Encounter with the European, 1492–1509.* Salt Lake City: University of Utah Press. 1988.

Valdés, Dennis Nodín. "The Decline of the Sociedad de Castas in Mexico City." A

Dissertation submitted in partial fulfillment of the requirement for the degree of Doctor of Philosophy (History) at the University of Michigan. 1978.

Vigil, James Diego. *From Indians to Chicanos: The Dynamics of Mexican American Culture.* Prospect Heights, IL: Waveland Press. 1984. 5th printing.

Viola, Hernan J. *After Columbus: The Smithsonian Chronicle of the North American Indians.* Colchester, VT: Smithsonian Books. 1990.

Warner, Lloyd W. *Social Class in America.* Chicago: Science Research Associates. 1949.

Webb, Walter Prescott. *The Texas Rangers.* New York: Houghton Mifflin. 1965.

Weber, David J. (ed.). *Foreigners in Their Native Land: Historical Roots of the Mexican Americans.* Albuquerque: University of New Mexico Press. 1973.

———. *New Spain's Far Northern Frontier: Essays on Spain in the American West, 1540–1821.* Albuquerque: University of New Mexico Press. 1979.

———. *Myth and the History of the Hispanic Southwest.* Albuquerque: University of New Mexico Press. 1990.

Stanford Center for Chicano Research

The Stanford Center for Chicano Research (SCCR) was established in 1980 to promote cross-disciplinary research on Mexican American and Latino communities in the United States. Under its current director Luis R. Fraga, associate professor of political science, the center continues to promote interdisciplinary study and focuses on major issues of public policy through projects that examine implications of the presence of Latinos in California and the United States generally, as well as the implications of increased diversity among Latinos themselves.

One important goal of the SCCR is to enhance dialogue between the research community and the public. As concerned citizens as well as researchers in academia, faculty members want to contribute to the local, state, and national discourse of public policy and promote effective long-term problem solving through their work at the center.

In 1992–93 projects at the SCCR included: *Environmental Poverty: Assessing the Risk of Pesticides to Farm Labor Children; Latinos, Voting Rights and the Public Interest; The Public Outreach Project; Pediatric AIDS and Infectious Diseases; Cultural Citizenship; Civic Capacity & Urban Education; Bay Area Latino Community Studies Project; The Uses of Languages Other than English in the Courts;* and *International Childhood Immunization Strategies.*

The SCCR holds public forums, coordinates research seminars, and presents the Annual Ernesto Galarza Lecture each spring. Research activities are published through the center's newsletter, *La Nueva Visión,* and the SCCR Working Paper Series. In tandem with the Chicana/o Fellows program and the Chicano Graduate Student Association, SCCR sponsors colloquia that highlight the research of faculty, visiting scholars, and graduate students.

SCCR sponsors programs that focus on students, a central part of our academic mission. Beginning in the fall of 1993, the center implemented the SCCR Student Research Fellows Program to link targeted minority undergraduate students with faculty members conducting interdisciplinary research projects at the center. Currently this program receives funds from the James Irvine Foundation.

Each spring, we call for summer research project proposals from the Stanford graduate and undergraduate student community. Funded by the Escobedo Commemorative Fund, students may create an original research project or may join an ongoing project at the SCCR. The center also hosts the Latino Leadership Opportunity Program (LLOP), a one-year national program of study and practicum designed for undergraduate Latina/o students interested in public policy and governance.

INDEX

TERESITA E. AGUILAR graduated from Belton High School and received her undergraduate degree from the University of Mary-Hardin Baylor. Her master's and doctoral degrees were granted from the University of North Texas. Prior to her academic career, she worked as a recreation director in a youth club and as a mental health caseworker. Her twenty-plus years of service in higher education include academic program coordination and progressive administrative responsibilities with strong emphasis on diversity, global education, and inclusiveness. She is currently dean of the School of Professional Studies at Our Lady of the Lake University, and is the former dean of graduate studies at UNM-Albuquerque and associate dean at Cal Poly Pomona. She was a participant in the 2002 Bryn Mawr Summer Institute for Women in Higher Education Administration, was faculty associate to the chancellor, vice chair in curriculum and instruction, and chair of the Graduate Program in Curriculum and Instruction at the University of Nebraska-Lincoln. She has held faculty positions in the University of New Mexico, the University of Nebraska-Lincoln, and Arizona State University. She has mentored bachelor's, master's, and doctoral degree students, coauthoring publications and copresenting at national and international meetings with her advisees. She has reviewed grant proposals for the NSF, NASA, and U.S. Department of Education and has presented at international meetings in Brazil, Cuba, Mexico, and Canada, and at national meetings for the American Educational Research Association, the National Association of Multicultural Education, the Council of Graduate Schools, the American Association for Colleges of Teacher Education, and the National Recreation and Park Association. She has led several cultural immersion study groups of university faculty and staff members and students to Cuernavaca, Mexico.

JORGE A. BUSTAMANTE has held an endowed chair (Eugene Conley Professor of Sociology) at the University of Notre Dame since 1986. He was also president of El Colegio de la Frontera Norte, a research and degree-granting institute in Tijuana, Mexico, from its creation in 1982 until January of 1998. He has more than two hundred publications in scholarly journals in the United States, France, Germany, Italy, Japan, Venezuela, Spain, and Mexico. The majority of these publications are research reports on Mexican immigration to the United States, U.S.-Mexico border phenomena, and U.S.-Mexico relations. He was the winner of the National Award on Demography on October 20, 1994, for his research on the Mexican migration to the United States. In 1995 he was a member of a binational group of researchers, appointed respectively by the governments of Mexico and the United States, to conduct research on various aspects of the Mexican migration to the United States. On January 3, 2005, the Permanent Committee (Comisión Permanente) of the Legislative Power of México unanimously adopted a resolution to nominate Dr. Jorge A. Bustamante for the Nobel Peace Price. On January 14, Dr. Bustamante was notified by the president of the American Sociological Association that he was selected as the 2007 recipient of the Cox-Johnson-Frazier Award, one of the two highest granted to a sociologist in the United States.

GILBERTO CÁRDENAS earned his master's and doctoral degrees from the University of Notre Dame. A sociologist by training, Cárdenas specializes in immigration, race and ethnic relations, historical and comparative sociology, and visual sociology. He has written or edited numerous books and monographs and more than two dozen articles and book chapters. He has been named by *Hispanic Business* magazine three times as one of the one hundred most influential Latinos in the United States. Cárdenas joined the Notre Dame faculty in 1999 as an assistant provost and director of the university's Institute for Latino Studies. He is also executive director of the Inter-University Program for Latino Research, which relocated with him from the University of Texas at Austin to Notre Dame. Cárdenas was appointed to the Advisory Council of the Bill and Melinda Gates Foundation, the Gates Millennium Scholars Program, the Smithsonian Institution's National Board for Latino Initiative, and the Board of Directors of the Mexican Fine Arts Museum in Chicago. He continues to serve on the Board of Directors for the Mexican American Legal Defense Educational Fund.

MIGUEL A. CARRANZA is professor of sociology and Ethnic Studies and holds a joint appointment with the Department of Sociology and the Institute for Ethnic Studies at the University of Nebraska-Lincoln (UNL). Dr. Carranza has been teaching at the University of Nebraska-Lincoln since 1975. He was awarded the Chancellor's "Fulfilling the Dream" Award for Exemplary Service to the University Community (1999) and the Chancellor's Commission on the Status of People of Color Award for Distinguished Service (1998). Dr. Carranza attended Kearney State College (now the University of Nebraska at Kearney) where he received a BA degree in education in 1971. He then attended the University of Notre Dame and completed a master's degree (1974) and a doctorate

(1977) in sociology, where he studied under Dr. Julian Samora. His areas of interest/specialization are Chicano/Latino Studies, Minority/Majority Relations, Minorities in Higher Education, Sociolinguistics, and the Sociology of Health. Dr. Carranza is coauthor of *Ethnic Studies in the United States: A Guide to Research,* published by Garland Publishing, and author and coauthor of numerous articles and book chapters. He is presently is involved in several collaborative research projects, including his role as principal investigator of a HUD Community Outreach Partnership Center New Directions grant and project manager of the Latino Achievement Mentoring Program. As cofounder of the Latino Research Initiative, he is conducting research on the integration of Latino immigrants into the northern Great Plains/Midwest.

FRANK M. CASTILLO, MD, MA, FAAFP, is a 1981 graduate of the University of Notre Dame with a BA in sociology and, in 1990, with an MA in International Peace Studies. In between those two degrees from Notre Dame, he attended medical school at the University of Wisconsin–Madison and received his MD in 1988. His specialty training in family and community medicine also occurred through the Medical School of the University of Wisconsin–Madison, which he completed in 1993. In pursuit of his mission, he has practiced with the underserved Latino populations of northeastern New Mexico, South Bend, Indiana, and the Pilsen community of Chicago, and he currently serves as the head of the Department of Family Medicine at a busy community health center, taking care of a predominantly Latino population in the near northwest side of Chicago. At the time of this writing, he is a clinical assistant professor of family medicine at the University of Illinois at Chicago. His clinical interest is diabetes mellitus, which is one of the most prevalent diseases affecting the Latino population. For all of the efforts and achievements in his career, Castillo was recognized in 2005 with the distinction of becoming a Fellow of the American Academy of Family Physicians.

ANTHONY J. CORTESE is professor of sociology at Southern Methodist University (SMU) in Dallas, Texas. His major areas of research and teaching are ethnic and race relations, media and gender, social problems, social policy, and social theory. He is the author of more than forty scholarly articles and essays and of *Ethnic Ethics: The Restructuring of Moral Theory* (1990), *Walls and Bridges: Social Justice and Public Policy* (2004), *Opposing Hate Speech* (2006), and *Provocateur: Images of Women and Minorities in Advertising* (3rd ed., 2007). He is currently writing another book, *Contentious Social Issues,* which examines Mexican immigration, racial profiling, capital punishment, affirmative action, and environmental racism. He received his PhD from the University of Notre Dame in 1980 at the age of twenty-five. As a Fulbright Fellow in Japan in 1990 and 1991, he taught courses on ethnic diversity in the United States. He has also taught maximum security inmates at Illinois's Pontiac Correctional Center. He has served as director of Ethnic Studies and director of Mexican American Studies at SMU and has served on the American Sociological Association's Committee on Professional Ethics. He has recently been appointed to the Advisory Board of the Perkins School of Theology's newly established Center for Latina/o Christianity and Religion.

LYDIA ESPINOSA CRAFTON received a master's degree in sociology at the University of Notre Dame through her enrollment in the Mexican American Graduate Studies Program. More recently, she has accrued extensive experience working with the Latino community in Maryland and holds a master's degree in Conflict Resolution from Antioch McGregor University in Yellow Springs, Ohio. In February of 2008, she was appointed to the Governor's Maryland Hispanic Affairs Commission.

BARBARA DRISCOLL DE ALVARADO received a BA with Honors from Boston State College, and a master's and PhD in history from the University of Notre Dame. She has worked at Texas A&M University, El Colegio de la Frontera Norte, Universidad de las Américas, Universidad Nacional Autónoma de México, and other institutions of higher learning in Mexico. More recently, she was the Antonio Madero Fellow at Harvard University, and Visiting Professor at Tufts University. She is assistant professor of humanities and Latin American studies at Anna Maria College. She published *The Tracks North: The Railroad Bracero Program of World War II* (Austin: CMAS Books-University of Texas, 1999) and several volumes in Mexico. Her research interests include world migration (particularly from Mexico to the United States), temporary contract labor programs, ethnicity in the United States and Latin America, and U.S. and Latin American women's history.

HERMAN GALLEGOS for more than fifty years has successfully undertaken important and challenging work seeking the betterment of Hispanics and other minorities, from community-based organizing in the Mexican American barrios of the Southwest to pioneering work with non-profits, philanthropy, and the boardrooms of corporate America. As a civil rights activist in the early 1950s with Cesar Chavez, Gallegos was active in the formation of the Community Service Organization (CSO), a self-help group organized to promote citizenship and naturalization classes, non-partisan voter registration campaigns, programs aimed at improving neighborhoods, and advocacy to end unwarranted actions by police and immigration officials. Since 1974, Gallegos has been among the first Hispanics elected to serve on various corporate and philanthropic boards, including Pacific Bell, Pacific Telesis Group, SBC Communications Inc., UnionBanCal Corporation, Transmetrics Inc., and, by presidential appointment, the Student Loan Marketing Association. Past philanthropic boards he has served on include the Rockefeller Foundation, the Rosenberg Foundation, the California Endowment, the San Francisco Foundation, the Hogg Foundation, the Poverello Fund, and the National Campaign for Human Development. Gallegos is a trustee emeritus of the University of San Francisco; emeritus, Board of Overseers, the University of California, San Francisco; Hispanics in Philanthropy, and co-founder of the National Council of La Raza. Gallegos is a graduate of San Jose State University and the University of California, Berkeley.

PHILLIP GALLEGOS was born and raised in Pueblo, Colorado, the son of Phillip Gallegos Sr. and Antonia Santos. Phillip attended high school in Pueblo, the University of Notre Dame, the University of Colorado, and the University of Hawai'i Manoa, where he earned a Doctorate of Architecture. He is a licensed architect in Colorado and New Mexico and has practiced architecture, urban design, and construction. He established a certificate program in design-build education at the University of Colorado, where he was also chair of the department of architecture and held the rank of associate professor of architecture with tenure. He is currently the director of the Design Planning Assistance Center at the University of New Mexico and is an associate professor of research. His company, located in Pueblo, designs and builds child care centers, drug detoxification facilities, schools, and churches throughout the western United States.

JOSÉ R. HINOJOSA, emeritus professor, Masters of Public Administration Program, University of Texas-Pam American, Edinburg, Texas, received his BA and MA in government and history at Texas A & I University, Kingsville, Texas, and his PhD in government and International Studies at the University of Notre Dame in Indiana. Dr. Hinojosa has had extensive teaching experience in various universities. He has taught at the University of Texas–Pan American (UTPA), Edinburg, Texas, since 1978. He was visiting professor of government at the University of Texas at Austin in 1982–1983, and visiting Hispanic scholar, Department of Political Science, Ohio State University, Columbus, Ohio, for the 1995 summer session. He taught at Southwest Texas State University, San Marcos, Texas, from 1968 to 1970. He served as lecturer in the Department of Government at Saint Mary's College, University of Notre Dame, Notre Dame, Indiana, where he was also research assistant to Professor Julian Samora in the Mexican American Graduate Studies Program and in the Institute for International Studies. His research experience has been in American immigration policy toward Mexico, United States-Mexico border relations, South Texas politics, and Texas minority politics. He has presented numerous papers relevant to immigration policy, U.S.-Mexico border problems, South Texas politics, and the questions of justice toward Mexican Americans. Presently he is working on research on environmental and hazardous waste management issues along the U.S.-Mexico border and on the problems of *"colonias."* He has served as a member of the UTPA Faculty Senate, was chairperson of the Presidential Search Advisory Committee, and was the chair of the Vice President of Academic Affairs Search Committee. He was appointed by education secretary Shirley Hufstedler to the National Advisory Council for Ethnic Heritage Studies during President Carter's administration and was appointed by Texas governor Mark White to serve as special consultant to the Job Injury Interagency Council and Advisory Committee. He currently serves as adjunct lecturer to the Mexican American Cultural Center, as associate researcher for the Tomas Rivera Center on Public Policy, Trinity University, San Antonio, Texas, and as adjunct special faculty at the Lyndon B. Johnson School of Public Affairs, the University of Texas at Austin. Dr. Hinojosa is a native of Jim Wells County and the son of the late Mr. and Mrs. Teodulo Hinojosa of Palito Blanco, Texas. He is married to Irene Vallejo Hinojosa, a native of Brownsville, Texas, who taught business education courses at McAllen High School, McAllen, Texas. They have two sons, José II, who graduated from the University of Iowa College of Medicine and practices family medicine in Corpus Christi, Texas, and Javier, who is a graduate from the University of Texas–Pan American in Edinburg, Texas, majoring in psychology and biology and presently is a graduate student in speech pathology and clinical psychology at the University of Texas–Pan American.

DELFINA LANDEROS was born in the beautiful state of Guanajuato, Mexico, and migrated with her parents to Chicago, Illinois, at the age of nine. She earned her bachelor's degree in Spanish at Northern Illinois University and her master's degree in sociology at the University of Notre Dame. She has been a teacher for thirty years and has taught at all grade levels from college to kindergarten, including teaching adults in an alternative college setting accredited by Antioch University. She loves being a teacher, and when asked she gladly provides academic advice to current and former students. She is currently an instructor at Pima Community College in Tucson, Arizona. As a teacher, she believes in doing her work with dedication, professionalism, and integrity. Ms. Landeros is also active in her church, teaching young women about their faith and culture. She is active in her community, dealing with issues affecting youth and immigration. She enjoys spending time with her family, reading, writing poetry, traveling, and cooking traditional Mexican dishes such as tamales, enchiladas, and chiles rellenos. Lastly, to nurture her soul with nature's beauty, she hikes in the nearby mountains, canyons, and other beautiful local spots.

PAUL LÓPEZ was born and raised in Santa Barbara, California, and is currently an associate professor of Chicano Studies and sociology at California State University, Chico. Prior to joining the faculty at Chico, he taught at Boise State University, the University of California, Santa Barbara, the University of San Francisco, and numerous other colleges and universities. He has taught courses in Chicano Studies, sociology, and Ethnic Studies. Dr. López first earned his BA in Chicano Studies at California State University, Northridge, in 1981. He earned his MA in sociology at the University of Notre Dame in 1984 and his PhD in sociology at Northeastern University in 1999. Dr. López's teaching and research interests are Chicano and Latino Studies, racial inequality, labor markets, and Mexican immigration. Dr. López is currently completing a book manuscript on the former U.S.-Mexico Bracero Program that employs oral histories to examine the settlement process of former Mexican braceros.

SERGIO X. MADRIGAL, a native Texan, received his BA in mathematics in 1972 from the University of Texas at Austin. He received his MA in economics in 1982 and doctorate in economics in 1983 from the University of Notre Dame. Madrigal has diverse professional experience from working from 1983 to 1984 as an economist for the U.S. Department of the Treasury, Washington, D.C, and from 1985 to 1993 as an economist in the private sector in Washington, D.C. Since 1993, he has worked for the state of Texas as an economist for the State Legislature in Austin.

KEN MARTÍNEZ is the New Mexico House of Representatives majority leader from District 69, which includes Cibola, McKinley, and San Juan Counties. Mr. Martínez graduated from Notre Dame Law School in 1984 and was a 1980 graduate in political science from the University of New Mexico. Mr. Martínez serves on the following committees: Advisory, Courts, Corrections, and Justice Committee (Interim); Advisory, Election Reform Task Force; Member, Interim Legislative Ethics Committee (Interim); Member, Judiciary; Member, Legislative Council (Interim); Vice Chair, Lottery Tuition Scholarship Study Subcommittee (Interim); Member, Printing and Supplies; Vice Chair, Rules and Order of Business; Member, Voters and Elections. He lives in Grants, New Mexico.

VILMA MARTÍNEZ joined Munger, Tolles & Olson LLP as a partner in 1982. Her practice focuses on federal and state court litigation and employment counseling. Ms. Martínez has spent the last twenty-five years advising and defending corporate employers in labor and employment matters. She honed her understanding of employment issues in the areas of diversity, discrimination, EEO compliance, and Title VII compliance prior to joining the firm. Ms. Martínez served as president and general counsel of the Mexican American Legal Defense and Education Fund (MALDEF) for nine years. Prior to that, she was a litigation associate at New York's Cahill, Gordon & Reindel, specializing in employment discrimination matters. She started her career as a staff attorney with the NAACP Legal Defense Fund in 1967, where she worked on a number of early Title VII cases.

ALBERTO MATA JR. is a professor in the Department of Human Relations, University of Oklahoma. Born in El Paso, Mata has been a resident of Lawton since 1965. Upon graduating in 1967 from Lawton High School, he attended Cameron Junior College and the following year transferred to OU. He graduated from OU with a BA in 1970 and master's degree in 1971. He was awarded a fellowship to complete doctoral work at Notre Dame. He taught at the University of Northern Illinois in Chicago, the University of California Berkeley, the University of Wisconsin-Milwaukee, and the University of Texas at Austin before returning to the University of Oklahoma in 1991. Also, he has held postdoctoral fellowships at the University of Michigan's Institute of Social Research; UCLA's Community Mental Health Evaluation program; and the University of Texas Health

Science Center-Houston's Center for Health Promotion and Prevention. His original research began exploring and describing Mexican American youth involvements with "street life—gang and drug use patterns in a midwestern blue collar community." Later field studies involved Oakland, California; East Los Angeles, California; Austin, Texas, and the rural South Texas communities of Dilley and Pearsall. His more recent efforts have been concerned with national and state policies concerning health and human services. With colleagues at the University of Texas San Antonio, he is completing a major three-year study of gangs, drugs, and violence among high-risk delinquent youth in South Texas.

AMELIA M. MUÑOZ is an experienced community organizer and advocate for emergent and vulnerable populations. Born and raised in northern California, Amelia learned firsthand about the challenges many Latinos face in the United States. Amelia received an associate arts degree from Chabot College and a Pastoral Education Certificate from the Mexican American Cultural Center. She worked for the U.S. Catholic Conference to involve Latino youth in the *encuentro* process. In 1984, she returned to school to study sociology under Dr. Julian Samora at the University of Notre Dame, graduating with honors in 1986. Afterwards she volunteered with the Farm Labor Organizing Committee to educate workers about their rights. For the next twelve years, Amelia provided supportive services and taught Mexican American literature in the South Bend schools. In 1998 she received her master's degree in social work with highest honors from Indiana University. She moved to Tucson, Arizona, to assist Latino families to gain access to school and community resources. In 2002, Amelia returned to Indiana to direct programs and projects that positively impact Latino families' health and education across the state. Amelia founded AMM and Associates, specializing in cultural diversity consulting and organizational development for educational, health, and non-profit organizations.

RICHARD A. NAVARRO is professor of education, California State Polytechnic University, Pomona. He holds a doctorate in international development education and a master's degree in anthropology from Stanford University, as well as a master's in education from Harvard University. He has diverse administrative experience, including as the founding director of the Julian Samora Research Institute at Michigan State University, manager of the Teacher Education Program (TEP) for the Ministry of Education of Afghanistan from January 2005 to January 2006, Senior

Project Office for UNICEF in Kabul, Afghanistan, from February 2003 to August 2004, and dean of the College of Education and Integrative Studies, California State Polytechnic University, Pomona, from September 1997 to January 2003. Navarro has extensive experience in education advocacy, policy development, and teaching in the international arena, from Latin America, particularly Mexico, to Afghanistan and China. He has also published referred articles, books, and monographs in education and international education.

JESUS "CHUY" NEGRETE, with guitar in hand, performs traditional "*corridos*," the folk music of his native Mexico. The son of migrant farm workers who later settled in Chicago, Negrete went on to become one of the nation's foremost musicologists and interpreters of Mexican and Chicano music. He is the founder and director of the Mexican Cultural Institute in Chicago and has performed at universities nationwide. Through concerts and workshops, Negrete takes you on a musical journey from Aztlán to the fields of Cesar Chavez, instilling in audiences an understanding and respect for the culture of his people.

OLGA VILLA PARRA was born in San Antonio and grew up in Michigan. She attended Muskegon Catholic Central High School, graduated from Northeastern Illinois University with a BA in sociology and received an MA in Religious Studies with a concentration on Hispanic Ministry from Loyola University. Olga has worked in administration and as a project director for Midwest Council of La Raza, Institute for Urban Studies, University of Notre Dame, and later executive director of the Midwest Hispanic Catholic Commission based at Notre Dame, serving the National Catholic Conference of Bishops of Regions VI and VII, which includes Ohio, Michigan, Indiana, Wisconsin, and Illinois. Olga also served as a member of the South Bend Community School Corporation Board of School Trustees and South Bend Library Corporation. More recently, in a past relationship with the Lilly Endowment, she played an unprecedented strategic role in the development of creative programs for Latino religion in the United States and in the fundraising that made the programs possible. Her counsel in the area of philanthropy has benefited both existing institutions and new initiatives. In 1996, the National Catholic Council on Hispanic Ministry conferred upon her an honorary lifetime membership for her extraordinary service to the Hispanic Catholic communities of the United States. In 1995, she received the Archbishop Patricio Flores' Medal for outstanding contributions to the past fifty years of Hispanic ministry. The state of Indiana awarded Olga the prestigious Governor's Sagamore Award in 1989.

RICARDO PARRA is a Midwest writer residing in Indianapolis. In 2004, he collaborated with a group of scholars on a book published by Arte Público Press titled *La Causa: Civil Rights, Social Justice, and the Struggle for Equality in the Midwest,* and wrote the lead chapter, "Latinos in the Midwest: Civil Rights and Community Organization." A long-time activist in civil rights, he is the past executive director of the Midwest Council of La Raza based at the Institute for Urban Studies at the University of Notre Dame, a ten-state organization serving the Midwest during the 1970s. He is a past member of the Indiana Advisory Committee to the U.S. Commission on Civil Rights. Ricardo is an avid writer and community volunteer, has written numerous articles ranging from essays, histories, memoirs, news stories, editorials, poems, book reviews, and other kinds of articles. His articles and writings on topics such as civil rights, economics, immigration, labor, farm labor, health, education, demographics, globalization, community studies, language and culture have appeared in various publications. As a journalist and writer, he is a member of the National Association of Hispanic Journalists and a past member of the Writers' Center of Indiana. Ricardo is a co-founder of the Poetry Alliance of Indy. He has a BA from Northeastern Illinois University, Chicago, Illinois, and has done graduate work in public management at Indiana University. Ricardo is married to Olga Villa Parra.

ALBERTO LÓPEZ PULIDO is the son of Velia and the late Alberto Pulido Velasquez. He was born in East Los Angeles and grew up along the U.S.-Mexico border. He completed his undergraduate studies at the University of California San Diego in sociology and Chicano Studies and continued his graduate studies at the University of Notre Dame as a proud member of the Mexican American Graduate Studies Program in sociology. Alberto was one of the first research fellows of the Julian Samora Research Institute at Michigan State University and has taught at the University of Utah, Arizona State University, the University of California Santa Barbara, and Brown University. He currently holds the title of chair and professor of the Ethnic Studies program at the University of San Diego. His areas of specialization include research that examines the intersection of race, religion, community, and social justice issues. He is the author of *Sacred World of the Penitentes,* published by the Smithsonian Institution. His current research includes a history on the sacrality of maize in Mexican culture on both sides of the border and a study on the creation and recreation of jazz as a musical art form of resistance for marginalized communities. He is proud to be called a Samorista.

JULIE LEININGER PYCIOR is professor of history at Manhattan College. Leininger Pycior received a BA with Honors from Michigan State University, as well as an MA and a PhD from the University of Notre Dame. In 1997 she published *LBJ and Mexican Americans: The Paradox of Power* (University of Texas Press), for which she was awarded the T. R. Fehrenbach Prize by the Texas Historical Commission. In 1978, she published *Chicanos in South Bend: Some Historical Narratives* (Centro de Estudios Chicanos e Investigaciones Sociales). Currently, she has a contract with Texas A & M Press for the book *Mexican American Community Organization in Texas, 1900–1930*. She is also editor for *Moyers on America: A Journalist and His Times,* by Bill Moyers (New Press, 2004).

VICTOR RIOS is professor of sociology at College of the Desert in Palm Desert, California, where he teaches Introduction to Sociology, Sociological Analysis & Critical Thinking, Minority Groups in America, and Mexican American Culture and Society. Victor is a native of South Texas, where he received his BA degree in psychology and sociology at Texas A&I University, Kingsville. He received his MA and PhD degrees in sociology from the University of Notre Dame. His PhD dissertation was titled "International Capitalism and Mexican Labor Migration to the United States." In addition to teaching at College of the Desert, Rios taught at the University of Redlands in Redlands, California, and Macalester College in St. Paul, Minnesota, and he spent a year as a postdoctoral fellow at the University of Texas at Austin as the first researcher of the Julian Samora Papers. His recent publications include "The Legacy of Julian Samora: Development of Theory for the Study of Undocumented Immigration," in *Diverse Histories Of American Sociology,* ed. Anthony J. Blasi (Leiden: Brill, 2005); and "Julian Samora," in *Encyclopedia of Race, Ethnicity, and Society,* ed. Richard T. Schaefer (Newbury Park, Calif.: Sage, 2007).

MARCOS RONQUILLO is the president, chief operating officer, and managing partner of Godwin Pappas Ronquillo and is the chair of the firm's public law section. Marcos Ronquillo represents governmental agencies and Fortune 500 companies in high-profile litigation where politics, media, and social concerns collide in the courtroom. Marcos is a past recipient of the State Bar of Texas Presidents' Special Citation Award and Out-standing Lawyer of the Year Award from the Texas Mexican American Bar Association. He is the former president of DHBA (formerly known as Dallas Mexican American Bar Association) and former chairman of the Dallas Hispanic Chamber of Commerce. *Texas Monthly* and *Law and Politics* magazines have consistently honored him as a Texas "Super Lawyer" from 2003 to 2006. Marcos has served on numerous boards and commissions including DART, United Way of Metropolitan Dallas, JPMorgan Chase, Children's Medical Center, and KERA, to name a few. Marcos received a JD from The George Washington University Law School in 1979 and a BA from the University of Notre Dame in 1975.

RENE ROSENBAUM received his PhD in economics from the University of Notre Dame and is currently an associate professor in the Department of Community Agriculture, Recreation and Resource Studies (CARRS) and senior scholar with the Julian Samora Research Institute (JSRI) at Michigan State University. He has also taught at the University of Wisconsin-Whitewater and Radford University. Since 1992, he has served as faculty in CARRS, where he has taught environmental and natural resource economic issues and community economic development. He currently teaches The Theory and Practice of Community and Economic Development. Dr. Rosenbaum's research interests are in the fields of community economic development, community-based studies, farm worker studies, and Latino issues. He is lead faculty for the farm worker research and outreach initiative at JSRI and currently serves as principal investigator on two research grants funded by the U.S. Department of Health and Human Services that deal with access to health care issues for migrant farm workers, college credentialization barriers for migrant Head Start teachers, and labor needs in the Michigan green industry.

CARMEN SAMORA was born in Denver, Colorado, raised in South Bend, Indiana, and has lived in Albuquerque, New Mexico, since 1982. Samora earned a BFA from St. Mary's College and an MFA from Notre Dame. She has worked as a professional artist creating fabric, clay, and paper collages. Samora worked for the state of New Mexico for twelve years at the Commission for the Blind teaching blind adults how to sew, conceiving of and marketing blind-made tote bags for convention use. In 2000, Samora developed the Samora Legacy Project, a project designed to mine Julian Samora's archive and produce materials for teachers about his work and legacy of leadership development. More currently, Samora earned a master's degree in education and an ABD in American Studies, both from the University of New Mexico. When time permits, she enjoys sewing, finding it a stress reliever from the rigors of graduate school. Samora plans to continue writing about her family and has begun a book about her mother.

RUDY SANDOVAL is an associate professor of business law and former associate vice president for administration at the University of Texas at San Antonio. He founded and directed the international program and has served as the international coordinator for the College of Business at UTSA. He has also taught at the University of Notre Dame School of Law and the University of San Diego School of Law. Professor Sandoval has served as a visiting professor of law at a number of Mexican institutions, including El Instituto Tecnologico de Estudios Superiores Occidental de Guadalajara, La Universidad de Las Americas, and La Universidad Nacional Autonoma de Mexico in Mexico City. He has served as president and executive director of the San Antonio Mexican Chamber of Commerce in San Antonio and has worked with United States federal agencies and American embassies abroad. He has written extensively in law review journals on issues related to international law, NAFTA, civil rights, and Hispanic issues. His articles have appeared in the *International Journal of Legal Information,* the *University of Miami Inter-American Law Review,* the *International Trade Law Journal,* and the *Maryland Journal of International Law and Trade,* among others. His latest book publication is *Moments in Contract.* He has served with distinction in the academic arena at the state, national, and international levels. Dr. Sandoval is listed in Who's Who among Hispanics. A graduate of Texas A&I University, Dr. Sandoval has an MA in Economics from Notre Dame University and law degrees from both the Thurgood Marshall School of law and the Harvard Law School.

ALFREDO RODRIGUEZ SANTOS c/s, a high school dropout and former migrant farm worker, was an active participant in the Chicano movement and a member of the Mexican American Youth Organization in Uvalde, Texas. In the early 1970s he made the switch from the agricultural fields to the academic fields when he decided going to Vietnam was not an option. After extensive retooling and many hours spent with tutors at San Joaquin Delta College in Stockton, California, Santos c/s managed to sneak into the University of California Berkeley where he graduated in 1974, with a bachelor's degree in economics. After a two-year stint as a labor organizer with Cesar Chavez's United Farm Workers of America in Watsonville,

California, he went on to do graduate work at the University of California at Los Angeles, the University of Notre Dame, Texas Southern University, Sul Ross State University–Rio Grande College, and the University of Delaware. His varied work experiences as a labor organizer, locksmith, school teacher, waiter, program administrator, Houston taxicab driver, journalist, college instructor, and community activist have helped him over the years to become a better storyteller. For the past eighteen years he has worked as the editor in chief at various newspapers including *La Voz de Brazoria County, La Voz de Uvalde County, La Voz de Zavala County, La Voz de Austin,* and *La Politiquera.* When he is not too busy, Santos c/s finds time to practice the accordion and paint minimurals on plywood. *También le gusta bailar.*

CIRO SEPULVEDA graduated from Notre Dame in 1976 with a PhD in history. Prior to that, Sepulveda obtained a BA from Loma Linda University, a Master of Divinity from Rochester Colgate Divinity School, and a master's degree in urban history from State University of New York at Brockport, New York. He has always been interested in the history of oppressed communities and how they shape and give form to society. His dissertation was an oral history of a Mexican community that emerged in the shadows of the steel mills in East Chicago, Indiana. Most of his publications deal with this theme. He believes power comes not from the barrel of a gun or a fat bank account but rather from serving the poor. After his training at Notre Dame, Sepulveda taught at Wayne State University and directed their Chicano Boriqua Studies Program from 1976 to 1978. From there he traveled to Montemorelos, Nuevo Leon, in Mexico and taught at the University of Montemorelos for five years. Since then he has taught in California (Cal State L.A. and Cal State Northridge) and Massachusetts (Atlantic Union College), and he is currently teaching and the chair of the History Department at Oakwood College in Huntsville, Alabama.

LATINOS IN CHICAGO AND THE MIDWEST

Pots of Promise: Mexicans and Pottery at Hull-House, 1920-40
    Edited by Cheryl R. Ganz and Margaret Strobel
Moving Beyond Borders: Julian Samora and the Establishment of Latino
    Studies   *Edited by Alberto López Pulido, Barbara Driscoll de Alvarado,
    and Carmen Samora*

The University of Illinois Press
is a founding member of the
Association of American University Presses.

Composed in 10/13 Sabon
with Sabon display
by Celia Shapland
at the University of Illinois Press
Designed by Dennis Roberts
Manufactured by Cushing-Malloy, Inc.

University of Illinois Press
1325 South Oak Street
Champaign, IL 61820-6903
www.press.uillinois.edu